Sport and the Law

Deborah Healey is a senior lecturer in the Faculty of
Law at the University of New South Wales, where she
teaches competition law, tort and the commercial
aspects of sport and law. As a solicitor for many years
in two of Sydney's largest law firms, she represented
sports clients and organisations, drafted competition
rules and set up sporting tribunals. She has chaired and
sat on selection, disciplinary and doping tribunals.

Deborah was a foundation member of the Australian and New Zealand Sports Law Association. She
incorporated the NSW Sport Federation, is on the
board of the Australian Baseball Federation and
povides advice to clients in the area of sport. Her other
publications include several on the *Trade Practices* Act,
and misleading or deceptive conduct.

SPORT
AND THE LAW

Third edition

Deborah Healey

A UNSW Press book

Published by
University of New South Wales Press Ltd
University of New South Wales
Sydney NSW 2052
AUSTRALIA
www.unswpress.com.au

© Deborah Healey 1989, 1996, 2005
First UNSW Press edition published 1989
Second edition 1996. Reprinted 1998, 2000, 2003.
Third edition 2005. Reprinted 2006.

National Library of Australia
Cataloguing-in-Publication entry
        Healey, Deborah, 1955– .
        Sport and the law.

        3rd ed.
        Includes index.
        ISBN 0 86840 643 0.

        1. Sports - Law and legislation - Australia. I. Title.

        344.94099

Cover Di Quick
Printer Ligare

Contents

Foreword ix
Acknowledgments xi
Introduction xii
List of abbreviations xiii

1 How the law comes into sport 1
What is sport? 2
Amateur or professional: a valid distinction? 3
A two tier system 5
What is law? 6
How is law made? 6
Remedies under the law 7
The balance sheet 8
The Court of Arbitration for Sport 9
Dispute resolution 10
Rules and conventions 11
Codes 12
The legal view of sport 12
Does 'sports law' exist? 14

2 Commercialisation and politics in sport 15
Subscription television 16
How commercialism affects sport 18
The role of government 19
Sport and politics 20

3 The legal nature of sporting organisations 22
Legal personality: the problem 23
The unincorporated voluntary association 23
Incorporation 28
Duties of directors, officers and committee members 30
Duties of directors at common law 30
Duties under the Corporations Act 31
Duties under state associations legislation 32
Corporate governance in sport 33

4 Contracts   35

What constitutes a contract?   35
The parties   38
Remedies   38
Sporting agreements   39
Inducing breach of contract   41
The contract of employment   42
Restraint of trade   43
Unfair contracts   49
Standard form contracts   50
Competition laws   50
Selection   53

5 Sports sponsorship and sporting reputation   56

Types of sponsorship arrangement   57
The formal sponsorship contract   58
Sponsorship conflicts   59
Restrictions on tobacco and alcohol advertising   61
The use of sportspeople in advertising   62
'Right of personality'   63
The Trade Practices Act   64
Passing off   69
Ambush marketing   70
Intellectual property rights   73
Defamation   75

6 The conduct of sporting tribunals   79

Domestic tribunals   80
Legal intervention   81
Disciplinary proceedings   81
The laws of natural justice   82
Running an effective tribunal: the practicalities   90

7 Sports injuries and compensation   91

How do the courts view injuries in sport?   92
When the law becomes involved   92
Recent changes in the law   92
Who gets sued?   94

Negligence 94
Intentional injury: assault 100
Obligations of participants 102
Liability of the manager or coach 105
Pregnancy and participation 109
Liability of sporting bodies 110
Liability of referees 110
Liability of organisers 110
Obligations of the occupier 112
The over-zealous fan 114
Liability of volunteers 115
Good Samaritans 115
Vicarious liability 116
Transmission of infectious diseases in sport 116
Compensation legislation 117
The NSW Sporting Injuries Insurance Scheme 118
Faulty equipment 119
Effect of the civil liability legislation 121

8   Insurance and risk management 122

The insurance crisis and responses 122
Risk management is essential 123
Risk standards 123
What is risk? 123
Concepts of risk management 124
The role of insurance 126
General rules for persons insuring 130
Alternative insurance arrangements 131

9   Criminal liability 132

Standard of proof 132
Criminal law 133
Assault 133
Murder and manslaughter 135
Policy issues 137
Violence in sport 138
The sporting crowd 139
Compensation 139

10 Discrimination and other issues 141

What is discrimination at law? 141
Laws against discrimination 142
Women and sport 145
Discrimination in employment 146
Discrimination in a sporting context 146
Use of facilities 147
Provision of services 148
Discrimination and sporting clubs 148
Penalty in disciplinary proceedings 149
Licensing 149
Single sex sport 150
Determining the sex of competitors 150

11 Sport and taxation 152

Income tax in Australia 153
What is income? 153
Income from outside Australia 156
Exempt income 156
Deductions 157
Capital gains tax 158
Tax averaging provisions 158
Fringe benefits tax 158
Provisional tax 159

12 Anti-doping 160

The problem 160
Why athletes use drugs 161
A brief history of regulation 161
The WADA Code 162
Implementation in Australia 163
WADA Code prohibitions 163
Doping offences in Australia 164
Impact of the WADA Code 167

Notes 169
Table of cases 189
Table of statutes 195
Index 197

Foreword

It is often said that he who ignores history is condemned to relive it. In sport, the administrator or athlete who fails to understand the importance of the law may find themselves reliving 'that' moment many times over as it is contested and re-contested in one jurisdiction after another.

Sport has always been a contradiction of unbridled passion and fixed boundaries. Increasingly it has also become a business environment that can determine athletes' financial futures as well as their places in the record books. International corporations invest their corporate image in sporting codes, sporting events and in individual sportsmen and sportswomen.

As the stakes rise, so to does the likelihood that people will seek to resolve disputes through the legal process.

Too often people in sport have seen this as some sort of intrusion, something foreign to their way of life.

On the other side, those looking to the law have sought to see sport as merely another business that can be classified in normal market terms.

Sport and the Law can assist in the establishment of some common ground between these two views. It also encourages an understanding of the realities we all live with in terms of rights and obligations.

Sports law is a relatively new and therefore quickly evolving speciality. The importance therefore of revising editions of *Sport and the Law* cannot be overstated, any more than can the importance of people within sport taking the time to read such publications.

The law is not a threat to the way we play and administer sport; instead, the law is something that can map out the pathway through the complicated problems which can arise either on or off the field.

In recent years, the National Rugby League has not only weathered some highly publicized drama but has produced record breaking results due not only to the excitement of our sport but our careful adherence to our rules and to the processes that support those rules. These have allowed us to deal with onfield issues with confidence, and to deal with what can at times seem like a minefield of off-field issues in ways that do not unduly interfere with the effective running of the competition.

The law's role in the business of sport has indeed become so critical that some of the early generation of 'in-house' sporting lawyers have become chief executives or commissioners of those sports, a trend evidenced in Australian sport and at both the NFL and the NBA.

It's true that on an emotional level the theatre of sport allows us to suspend our daily existence for a while, but in some ways that also increases the responsibility of administrators to ensure that we do not lose sight of the rights and obligations of those connected with a sporting competition or event.

Being aware of those rights and obligations will also hopefully assist in demystifying much that is often said of sport and the law. Terms such as restraint of trade, passing off, discrimination and natural justice are waved around as some new sporting vernacular at the slightest hint of an argument, and are often argued, even by lawyers, with little attention to the relevant sport's established rules.

Deborah's book represents the most informed and concentrated reference guide to assist us all in exploring those issues.

I encourage everyone involved in sport and in the coverage of sport to read it and to keep it within close reach.

David Gallop
Chief Executive
National Rugby League

Acknowledgments

The first edition of this book grew out of my own interest in sport, and talks given to Rugby League coaches and members of other sporting groups. Peter Corcoran, the late Darryl Chapman, David Weisbrot, Peter Murray and Terry Woods provided comments on the first two editions of the book and I repeat my thanks to them here.

This edition was once again the product of my dealings in sport: legal advice given to sports administrators, organisations and individuals across a diversity of sports; my work on tribunals involving discipline, selection issues, doping and transfer rules; and my close association as board member and legal advisor in a number of sports.

The original trickle of cases and situations has become a torrent which at one stage threatened to overwhelm the original focus of the book, but I trust that the examples included continue to provide useful assistance to the reader. The diversity of legal issues facing sportspeople and sporting organisations is a continual source of amazement to me. In commercial legal practice I saw few problems faced by large organisations which were more complex or distracting than those confronting sporting organisations and their administrators, and many of the issues were the same.

The way forward for sporting organisations is to deal with these issues proactively and effectively as they occur.

Governments would do well, however, to contemplate the commonality of many of the issues and the inefficiency of individual legal advice sought by organisations which rely on government funding. Better anticipation of legal requirements of funded organisations, and advice and assistance, particularly with dispute resolution, would ease the burden on many administrators and allow them to focus on their main game: increasing participation and improving the way sporting services are delivered to participants.

Finally I thank all of my family for their input and support during the preparation of this edition. I particularly thank my children for continuing to expose me to an endless stream of sporting situations to add to my understanding of grassroots sport. It goes without saying that their involvement in an array of different sports has substantially delayed the third edition but immeasurably increased my enjoyment of the area.

Deborah Healey

Introduction

Players, officials and coaches have rights, obligations and potential liabilities, whether or not they are paid for their services. The unpaid sportsperson may at least possess the right to fair treatment by a judiciary or disciplinary committee. A sportsperson injured by the intentional or negligent action of an opponent or other person may take action in court, or may be liable for injury caused. Unpaid officials may have a duty to consider the safety of both players and spectators.

Laws that place responsibility on directors and committee members apply whether or not they are receiving any remuneration for their efforts. The 'amateur' distinction counts for little where issues such as corporate governance are concerned. The sheer numbers of people engaged in sports such as netball and lawn bowls mean that those involved have enormous responsibilities, regardless of the fact that most participants are unpaid. These numbers are set to increase with the focus on active lifestyles, as obesity and an aging population present challenges to the community.

Other sports such as surfing and running have numerous unregistered participants, and the law may also apply to aspects of these. A recreational runner may suffer injury through faulty equipment – running shoes that are not up to the job. A tennis player might aggravate an injury through poor treatment or advice, and be able to sue the treating doctor or physiotherapist or podiatrist. A marathon runner may dehydrate because insufficient drink stations were provided by organisers of the marathon course. A surfer may cause injury through negligent use of a surfboard, and be liable to pay damages to the injured person.

The areas of criminal law, negligence and the principles of natural justice are potentially relevant to most sports. Once a sport pays its players or participants, or where large amounts of money are involved through sponsorship or grants, the potential application of the law increases. Contract law, trade practices, taxation and employment law are some of the legal areas that might apply.

This book attempts to show, through a wide range of possible scenarios, the enormous application that the law can have to sport, and ways in which those involved can deal with potential problems.

List of abbreviations

AFL Australian Football League
AIS Australian Institute of Sport
ANZSLA Australian and New Zealand Sports Law Association
AOC Australian Olympic Committee
ARL Australian Rugby League
ASC Australian Sports Commission
ASDA Australian Sports Drug Agency
CAS Court of Arbitration for Sport
HREOC Human Rights and Equal Opportunity Commission
ICAS International Court of Arbitration for Sport
IOC International Olympic Committee
NRL National Rugby League
SOCOG Sydney Organising Committee of the Olympic Games
WADA Code World Anti-Doping Agency Code

Chapter 1

How the law comes into sport

The law is the method that our society uses to determine the rights of individuals. It touches every aspect of our lives, and sport is no exception. The growth and expansion of professional sport, the fact that so many people now make a living from the sports industry, and a heightened community awareness of individual rights suggest that those involved in sport will increasingly turn to the courts to protect their interests.[1] The Sydney Olympics in 2000 focused the attention of Australians and the world on sport in this country as never before. Australia's success in the Rugby World Cup likewise underscored the importance of sport to the nation and its economy. Developments like the introduction of subscription television turned professional sport on its head, challenging the role of sporting organisations.

Sportsmen and women have long passed the point where they are surprised that the law might apply to them, and they now expect it to protect their rights in circumstances that would not have been contemplated twenty years ago. The application of the law to all aspects of sporting life continues to present a range of legal challenges for sporting organisations, athletes and promoters, and a variety of ideological and emotional challenges for many fans.

The increasing range of complex legislation in areas such as child protection, privacy and discrimination, coupled with new civil liability legislation and an increased focus on risk management, challenge even the best run sporting organisations. For those not in the top tier in terms of sponsorship, or not able to attract funds from the sale of things like broadcast rights, the effects of regulation can be stifling.

This book discusses the rights and liabilities of those involved in sport, whether in a paid or voluntary capacity. It explains the areas of commercial law that are relevant to sporting organisations and individuals. It also provides a useful explanation of some basic legal concepts and principles for the lay person.

What is sport?

While most people could name and describe many sports, defining the word itself is a more difficult task. The Oxford Dictionary defines 'sport' as 'amusement, diversion, fun ... pastime, game'.[2] Sports have been differentiated from games on the basis of the high physical skill factor they involve, and a sociologist has defined sport as

> institutionalised competitive activity which involves two or more opponents and stresses physical exertion by serious competitors who represent or are part of formally organised associations.[3]

The extent to which these factors are present in a sport varies. It is possible to think of many activities that most people would describe as sports, but that do not contain all of them. A more appropriate definition for current purposes would be one encompassing athletic activity, some skill and an element of competition.

Definitions, however, do little to convey the passion that sport arouses in competitors and spectators alike. Many writers have described the place of particular sports in their society:

> To think of football as merely 22 hirelings kicking a ball is merely to say that a violin is wood and cat gut, Hamlet is so much ink and paper. It is Conflict and Art. (JB Priestley)

> Life itself is a game of football. (Sir Walter Scott)

> There is no way to explain that baseball is not a sport, or a game or a contest; it is a state of mind and you can't learn it. (John Steinbeck)[4]

Those involved in sports have held a variety of views on the place of sport in their lives and in society generally:

> I sometimes think that running has given me a glimpse of the greatest freedom a man can ever know, because it results in the simultaneous liberation of both body and mind. (Roger Bannister, the first man to run a mile in under four minutes)

> Winning is not everything, it's the only thing. (Red Saunders, college football coach, 1940)

> Some people think football is a matter of life and death. I don't like that attitude. I can assure them it is much more serious than that. (Bill Shankly, English football manager)[5]

It has been suggested that sport is a national obsession in Australia.[6] While some would dispute this, there is no denying the extensive media coverage that sport of all kinds attracts, or the status afforded our sporting 'heroes'. The euphoria following the success of the Sydney 2000 Olympic bid overshadowed most other news for many days. The 1993 visit of the President of the International Olympic Committee, Juan Antonio Samaranch, and his comments on the Homebush Olympic Pool were widely reported alongside the Liberal Party leadership change. At the time of writing (during 2004), events involving the alleged criminal behaviour of players in several football codes eclipsed coverage of the war in Iraq. Press reports on the behaviour of leading sportspeople and their families rivals the tabloid coverage of movie stars.

Amateur or professional: a valid distinction?

Participants in sport have traditionally been classified as either 'amateur' or 'professional'. The distinction was that professionals could receive a reward for their activities, while amateurs could not. Team sports fostered by the British public school system were the domain of the upper-class male. Those who took part could rejoice in the beauty of sport for its own sake – making a living was usually an irrelevant consideration. It was from these roots that the idea of the amateur 'gentleman–sportsman' sprang.

The amateur view of 'sport for sport's sake' was formed in this environment, and its emphasis on gentlemanly conduct rather than winning led to the establishment of various sporting conventions, some of which still exist today. It is a convention of cricket, for example, that one does not bowl bouncers to a non-recognised batsman.[7] It is a boxing convention that a fighter does not hit an opponent who is on his way down.

The amateur ideal culminated in the modern Olympics, which were first held in Greece in 1896. Olympic rules traditionally defined an 'eligible amateur' as:

> One who participates and always has participated in sport solely for pleasure and for the physical and mental benefits he derives therefrom, and to whom participation in sport is more than recreation without material gain of any kind, direct or indirect.[8]

In the past participation in the Olympics was confined to amateurs, with the rules being strictly enforced by the International Olympic Committee (IOC). One famous case involved Jim Thorpe, US winner of the decathlon and pentathlon at the 1912 Stockholm Olympic Games. Thorpe was stripped of his medals on order of the IOC when it was revealed that he had taken part in some professional baseball matches, and his name was removed from the record books.[9]

In what used to be called the Eastern Bloc countries, athletes were traditionally students, or in the army. In the USA college athletic scholarships provided some support for amateur athletes. Whether these systems offended the Olympic amateur ideal in principle could be discussed. In practice they were accepted.

Times have changed and attitudes have mellowed since the inception of the idea of the amateur. Ingmar Stenmark, 1980 Olympic slalom and giant slalom ski champion, was excluded from the 1984 Winter Olympic Games at Sarejevo by the International Skiing Federation because he was involved in endorsement contracts for ski equipment. The same skier, having similar endorsement contracts, competed in the 1988 Winter Olympics at Calgary, Canada. He was once again an amateur.

Professional sport is not a new phenomenon. It has been suggested that the birth of professional sport occurred in Greece in 594 BC, when Solon decreed that any Athenian who was a victor in the Olympic Games should receive 500 drachmae – the equivalent at the time of a hundred oxen.[10] Other examples of professional sport have occurred throughout history.

Big money professional sports today include tennis, golf and, in Australia as a result of subscription (pay) television, rugby league, rugby union and Australian football. Winners of tournaments may receive hundreds of thousands of dollars in prize money. Players may also be involved in exhibition matches, adding to the takings.

These amounts are complemented by lucrative sponsorship and product endorsement deals. Some of the top world athletes can attract big money. The 1988 Seoul Olympics brought this to public attention in the most dramatic way when it was revealed that Canadian sprinter Ben Johnson, stripped of his 100 metres gold medal for taking anabolic steroids, stood to lose some $10 million in advertising and sponsorship deals. In a more recent example, in 1999 Tiger Woods entered into a five-year promotional deal with Nike for $90 million, considerably more than he had received during his career for playing the sport of golf.[11]

In a more unusual deal, Australian swimmer Ian Thorpe has reportedly been given 1.5 million shares in the company So Natural Foods, which sells soy drinks, canned fish and Thorpedo brand energy water, in payment for his endorsement of its products.[12]

Some sports provide amply for their best exponents; others are played on a semi-professional basis, with players holding another job. In either case, sportspeople have real interests to protect if they are injured, or if their right to play their sport is otherwise affected. The 'sporting economy' of government grants and sponsorship money, even where participants are not paid, increases this trend. The Seoul games provoked a major public discussion in Australia over ways of providing some form of financial support for Australian competitors, many of whom had been obliged to rely on unemployment benefits in order to complete rigorous training schedules. Various schemes for some level of state or federal subsidy were implemented as a result.

Recognition of a change in community perception of the amateur–professional distinction can be seen in the Eligibility Code (rule 41) of the Olympic Charter. The rule states that to be eligible for participation competitors, coaches, trainers and officials must comply with the Olympic Charter and with the rules of the International Federation for their sport; be entered by their National Olympic Committee; 'respect the spirit of fair play and non violence'; and comply with the World Anti-Doping Code.

The by-law to rule 41 provides that each International Federation is responsible for developing its eligibility criteria in accordance with the Olympic Charter, and for applying those criteria along with its affiliated National Federations and the National Olympic Committees. The by-law also provides that

> Except as permitted by the IOC Executive Board, no competitor, coach, trainer or official who participates in the Olympic Games may allow his person, name, picture or sports performances to be used for advertising purposes during the Olympic Games.

> The entry or participation of a competitor in the Olympic Games shall not be conditional on any financial consideration.

Recent versions of the Olympic Charter do not expressly use the word 'professional'.[13]

A two tier system

Of more relevance today is the distinction between sport as a commercial enterprise and sport as grassroots recreation.

Sports that operate in a truly commercial manner are generally well patronised, are the beneficiaries of large sponsorship contracts, are broadcast on television and radio, or have other significant commercial means of funding their activities. Their administrators are well paid, their players or participants are rewarded handsomely for their efforts, and they have access to legal and commercial advice that allows them to fully exploit the potential of the sport or the talent of individual players. Business contributed $480 million in sponsorship to Australian sport and recreation activities in 2000–2001.[14]

Sport at any other level struggles to exist on the goodwill of volunteers and with government support. Total expenditure by all Australian governments on sport and recreation activities in 2000–2001 was not quite $200 million.[15] The paid employees of sport at grassroots level work to put teams on the field and players in international competitions, if relevant. Its officials are often unable to access legal and commercial advice as a matter of course due to cost constraints, which means that they are often tactically disadvantaged by the time they get it. While many argue for sport at grassroots level to 'become more professional' the difficulties often seem insurmountable, and the officials may spend more time on legal issues than they do developing and administering the game. In the absence of large injections of cash or assistance at this level, this situation looks set to continue.

What is law?

The law is a body of rules enacted and imposed by society to determine the rights of its citizens. Law governs relationships between citizens; it also governs the relationship between citizens and their own property, and the property of others. The law governs the way in which society operates in the same way as the rules of a sport govern the way in which it is played.

How is law made?

Law is made in two ways. The first type of laws are statute laws, which are made in parliament. These are the laws that immediately spring to mind when the word 'law' is mentioned. The *Crimes Act*, the *Motor Traffic Act* and the *Privacy Act* are examples of statute laws.

The second type of law is the common law. Common law is made by judges, and it is part of a system whereby judges must follow previous decisions or 'binding precedent'. Put simply, this means that a judge generally must follow an earlier decision of an equivalent or higher court in a case involving a similar set of circumstances.

Australia has a federal system of government, with both Commonwealth and state legislation. No one set of laws is applicable in all areas relevant to sport. If a state enacts a law that is inconsistent with a Commonwealth law, the Commonwealth law prevails. Common law may also differ between the states.

The law of one state is not binding on another, although it may be of interest to a court hearing an issue. Historical links with England and its legal system mean that the decisions of UK courts are looked upon with interest by our courts, but they are no longer binding on our judges. There is also an increasing trend in some areas to look at law from other legal systems such as those of the US or the European Union, but their decisions are not binding on our judges although they may be helpful in resolving issues in our courts.

One important factor to remember is that if there is both common and statute law on a particular point, the statute law overrides the common law. Thus statutes are often passed by parliament to clarify problem areas, or to change the approach to an area previously handled by the common law.

The law is also divided into criminal law and other law (*civil* law). Criminal law deals with breaches of the law sometimes called 'felonies', 'misdemeanours' or 'indictable offences'. A person convicted of a crime can be punished by a fine or imprisonment. The standard of proof required in a criminal case is higher than in other branches of the law. Before a defendant can be convicted of an offence, the judge or jury must be satisfied *beyond reasonable doubt* that the person is guilty. In civil law, where the consequences of losing a case are not so dire – 'life or liberty' are not involved – the case need only be proven *on the balance of probabilities*, a much less stringent test.

At common law, a 'civil wrong' for which the law provides a remedy is called a *tort*.

Remedies under the law

Where a criminal offence is proven, the defendant may be fined or imprisoned. In a civil action, the law provides a variety of remedies for someone who wins a case. It can provide damages for various types of loss suffered, including loss of wages. It can provide an applicant with an injunction, which may be in the form of a restraining order or be positive in form, compelling the other party to perform some action. Breaching the terms of an injunction may lead to a fine or imprisonment for contempt of court. Courts may also make other orders.

Laws differ from state to state. The law applying to a particular situation in one state might be totally different from the law applying elsewhere. For example, an amateur sportsperson from NSW injured in that state might be entitled to more generous remedies than an amateur sportsperson injured in the same way in Victoria.[16] Factual situations sometimes need to be considered carefully to assess which law applies. Given the diversity of laws Australia-wide on, for example, civil liability, determining which law applies in a particular situation involving injury can be very important.[17]

The balance sheet

The law is involved in sport in many ways. Some purists still call for a return to the days when the game was paramount and the money irrelevant, but it is impossible to turn back the clock, and the trend in our society to reality television and spectator sport as a hobby rather than participation suggests that this will not occur.

Sports and sportspeople have used the law to their advantage in many cases. We are long past the time when the involvement of law in sport was limited to liability for a punch on the sporting field. Today the legal issues involved are far broader; and, as will be seen, they extend across the whole spectrum of running a big or small business, depending on the sport involved. The South Sydney Rugby League Football Club, for example, can attest to the utility of the *Trade Practices Act* as a weapon in its war against relegation from a competition. The club's initial win in the Federal Court led to its reinstatement into the National Rugby League competition lest any subsequent competition be delayed or disrupted. Despite the fact that it ultimately lost on appeal in the High Court, South Sydney remains in the competition due in part to the groundswell of public opinion that surrounded the drama of the court hearing and appeals. [18]

Despite the complexity of the laws involved, most cases involve simple questions affected by legal issues such as those described below:

- *Running the game: the sporting organisation*   Issues of control and ownership are generally resolved by considering the legal nature of the body involved and the rules that apply to the game, competition or event. The relevant laws are those of contract and incorporation.
- *Selling the athlete and the game: who owns what?*   Questions about the extent to which a sport controls or 'owns' an athlete, or has the legal right under rules or a contract to restrict the athlete's ability to gain sponsorships or attract other potential sources of individual income, raise matters connected with the content and construction of the athlete's agreement, the employment contract and the rules of the organisation or event. Other legal issues are the ability to deal with sponsorship conflicts, and the protection of the name and reputation of a sport, an individual athlete or a particular event. The relevant laws are generally those of contract and intellectual property.

- *Who gets to play?* Disciplinary issues raise questions of natural justice. Selection issues raise questions of the interpretation of selection criteria, the interpretation of rules governing appeals, and other contract issues. Administrative law issues such as natural justice are relevant. Discrimination law deals with the ability of pregnant women, people with a disability and others to participate in sport, as well as the place of transgender athletes. Criminal law may affect the rights of players to participate.
- *Injury: who pays?* Injury to participants raises the law of negligence, particularly in the context of responsibility.
- *Performance: can I take this one?* Doping involves issues of legislative interpretation and the application of anti-doping policies that are contractually based. The World Anti Doping Code (the WADA Code) is relevant to many sports and their participants.

Ultimately the scorecard on the involvement of law in sport is positive. The advantages far outweigh the disadvantages, despite the continued protestations of some administrators who would prefer to exercise a final discretion without any opportunity for review.

Sporting organisations outside the first tier would benefit extensively, however, from greater guidance from government and regulatory bodies on how best to fulfil their legal obligations, particularly in relation to complex legal areas which they struggle to understand (with good reason) and with which they seek to comply.

The Court of Arbitration for Sport

The courts play a large role in the settlement of sporting claims and disputes, but other forums may also be relevant, and recourse to these alternatives has increased. This is the trend in most areas of law, with the establishment of a number of formal and informal tribunals outside the court system, and the inclusion of dispute resolution mechanisms in documentation governing relationships between parties.

The Court of Arbitration for Sport (CAS) was set up by the IOC in 1984 to settle disputes involving Olympic sports. It is becoming increasingly important in the resolution of sporting disputes. While it is not a court in the same sense as a country's law courts, it provides a forum for resolving Olympic-related disputes and other disputes involving the International Federations that govern the Olympic sports and their members. Other sporting disputes may also go to CAS if the parties agree.

The primary basis for the jurisdiction of CAS is rule 61 of the Olympic Charter, which states that:

any dispute arising on the occasion of, or in connection with, the Olympic Games shall be submitted exclusively to the Court of Arbitration for Sport, in accordance with the Code of Sports-Related Arbitration.

The regulations and by-laws of many International (and National) Federations affiliated with the IOC also give CAS jurisdiction over disputes within their sport, or nominate CAS as the place where appeals go from their internal tribunals – their *appellate jurisdiction*.

In addition, athletes competing in the Olympics are required to sign a standard form Athletes Agreement which says that all disputes arising during the period of the Games will go to CAS. During the period of the Olympics, CAS sets up a special panel to hear disputes arising out of them called the Ad Hoc Division. At the Sydney Olympics 14 cases were heard by the Ad Hoc Division: eight related to eligibility, two to pre-Games drug tests, one to a Games drug test and three to results.[19]

Under the Olympic Athlete Agreement, decisions made by CAS are final, non-appealable (except to a CAS Appeal Tribunal) and non-reversible. This was upheld in *Raguz v Sullivan*, a case involving selection for the Sydney Olympics.[20]

CAS hearings are conducted in accordance with the CAS Code.[21]

CAS does not involve itself with technical questions or areas covered by the Olympic Charter. It determines issues in other areas relating to sport, such as suspension of an athlete for drug use, or contracts for the sale of sporting equipment.[22] It has the powers of an international court of arbitration, with people who have both legal training and experience in sports issues being appointed as CAS arbitrators.

Following criticism about its connection with the IOC, the International Court of Arbitration for Sport (ICAS) was established to administer CAS and ensure its independence from the IOC.[23]

Dispute resolution

Taking disputes to court is generally very expensive. If the sport involved is high profile and wealthy, a court may be the best option. Most sports and the individuals involved in them, however, are not in a position to incur large legal bills. While not generally as expensive as court action, CAS can still be costly because the parties are usually represented by solicitors and barristers. In some situations the legal rules require disputes to be taken to a superior court exercising a particular jurisdiction; for example, anyone who wishes to allege a restraint of trade in NSW needs to take proceedings in the Supreme Court, the only court in that state that can hear such an action.

Even where sports have funds, courts do not always provide the best way of solving a legal problem, particularly where the parties need to work together in the future, as they often do in sport. Dispute resolution is a growing area in general legal practice, with many lawyers now recognising that the use of a formal dispute resolution mechanism is often preferable to traditional legal proceedings. Many lawyers are trained in dispute resolution, and it is becoming an increasingly acceptable alternative to litigation. Some courts have the power to refer matters for mediation or arbitration.[24]

While bodies such as the Australian Sports Commission (ASC) and the various state departments are often called upon to help sort out disputes involving sport in Australia, there is no truly comprehensive national forum to hear disputes in all sports.

There is some legislative recognition of the difficulties faced by the bulk of the sporting community in gaining access to justice. The NSW *Associations Incorporation Act 1984*, for example, provides that all organisations incorporated under it must specify in their rules a forum for the resolution of disputes between members, or between the organisation and members. If an organisation does not specify such a forum the legislation's Model Rules apply, and the place of dispute resolution for the organisation will be Community Justice Centres of NSW.

The development of cost-effective dispute resolution for sport is a matter of great importance, and it needs to be addressed in a way that provides those involved with the means to resolve disputes outside costly court processes, where possible.

Rules and conventions

The rules of a particular sport or game necessarily govern the way in which it is played or carried out. Definite rules are necessary to ensure that a proper contest will take place, although the laws of the land will always override the rules of play of a particular sport.

Those who join sporting clubs and associations may subscribe to a variety of constitutions and by-laws, and they generally intend to be bound by them.

Conventions or unwritten rules, or the rules of 'good sportsmanship', are in a somewhat different category. They are normally legally unenforceable, but those who refuse to abide by them are generally looked upon with disdain by other participants.

Codes

Various codes and by-laws introduced by sporting organisations seek to deal with issues relating to appropriate behaviour by organisations, officials, participants and spectators, including parents.

The Australian Olympic Committee (AOC) has introduced an Ethical Behaviour By-law which focuses on issues such as child abuse, discrimination and harassment, and vilification. The by-law applies to all athletes or officials who receive financial assistance from the AOC, are members of a shadow Olympic team or have been nominated for selection to any team selected by the AOC, as well as to members of the AOC executive, its officers and employees. The by-law sets out a procedure for dealing with such conduct, culminating in a hearing. If a breach of the by-law is established, a person who has engaged in the conduct may be disciplined by measures including suspension or termination of shadow team membership.

Following various allegations of bribery, including those in relation to the Salt Lake City Winter Olympics, the IOC instituted a Code of Ethics that includes the provision:

> The Olympic parties or their representatives shall not, directly or indirectly, solicit, accept or offer any concealed remuneration, commission, benefit or service of any nature connected within the organisation of the Olympic Games. [25]

The code itself espouses ideals including dignity, integrity, use of resources for Olympic purposes only, maintenance of harmonious relations with state authorities and environmental protection.

There is a trend towards codes of behaviour which may be either voluntary or mandatory across the whole commercial spectrum as an alternative to more formal regulation.[26]

The legal view of sport

The commercial growth of sport has led to a radical change in the way in which the courts view sporting clubs and associations, and sports participants. While the local sporting club with its honorary office bearers and three-figure bank account is still very much alive, the legal position in relation to the administration of many other sports has changed irrevocably. Unfortunately, in some cases, the outlook of administrators and others involved has not kept pace with changing circumstances.

Since the first edition of this book was written in 1989, most 'tier one' sports have adapted to the new commercial and legal world in which they operate, although some took longer than others to realise the extent of the change that was needed. Other organisations still struggle to make the change. Administrators must consider whether their own views on governance and legal issues are realistic in light of changing circumstances, particularly in relation to their own potential liability and the liability of their organisation or club. Unless attention is turned to this issue, and the focus of administrators and their employing boards reflects the normal commercial approach to doing business, those involved expose themselves to the full force of the law for inappropriate behaviour and poor corporate governance.

A good example of judicial thinking about sport is the Adamson case,[27] which involved the disputed transfer of an Australian football player. In the High Court, Sir Garfield Barwick (then Chief Justice) stated that he could see little difference between the presentation of a theatrical spectacle and the presentation for reward of the spectacle of a football match played by professionals as a major source of their income and the income of the promoter.

The type of approach exemplified in the Adamson case has led to the characterisation of big budget sports such as Australian football and rugby league by some commentators as the 'sports entertainment business'. The real situation is that sport can be just as much a part of the commercial world as any other multi-million dollar business. Those who would treat sport purely as a commercial venture, however, sometimes fail to appreciate the intensity of commitment of those involved.[28]

The law is about the protection of rights. In this vein, the case of *McKinnon v Grogan*[29] is of interest. The matter involved the way in which the North Sydney Rugby League Club should be run. Courts had traditionally been reluctant to become involved in the internal affairs of voluntary organisations such as sporting bodies. The judge hearing the case, Wootten J, said that to characterise the running of the regulatory institution of a major sport in the community in the same way as one would a group of friends meeting to play tennis was simply inadequate. His Honour stated that those who join the League and subscribe to its constitution and by-laws should be taken to intend to be bound by them. They should also be able to involve the courts, in appropriate circumstances, to have their disputes settled.

A similar approach has been taken in some cases in the UK. In a case that involved the rejection of a female racehorse trainer's licence application, the Master of the Rolls, Lord Denning, differentiated the right of admission to a social club from the right of admission to a jockey club. Social club members had the right to please themselves about admitting newcomers. In the case of a jockey club, however, which exercised 'a virtual monopoly in an important field of human activity', the courts could give redress because the livelihood of the applicant depended on the admission. The club was not bound to admit all applicants, but could refuse admission only for proper reasons. It was not proper to refuse an otherwise qualified applicant solely on the ground that she was a woman.[30]

In Australia, Tadgell J discussed the intervention of the courts in the context of the suspension of a high profile Australian Football League (AFL) player in *Australian Football League v Carlton Football Club Limited*.[31] His Honour stated that the courts were reluctant to interfere because they recognised that there are some kinds of dispute which are

> much better decided by non-lawyers or people who have special knowledge of or expertise in the matters giving rise to the dispute than a lawyer was likely to have.

He added, however, that the courts are likely to interfere where private rights, including rights in property, have been adjudged to deserve protection. His Honour concluded by stating that within that broad category of property

> there is no decision of a private or domestic tribunal with which the courts will refuse to interfere if interference by them be considered necessary for the attainment of justice.

Does 'sports law' exist?

Purists have considered whether there is a separate branch of law which can be called 'sports law', or whether there is just a collection of laws that happen to apply to sports and the sports industry in particular circumstances in the same way as laws apply to the entertainment or tourism industry.[32] The growing importance of CAS in resolving international sporting disputes is hastening the globalisation and development of sports law as a distinct body of legal knowledge.

Chapter 2

Commercialisation and politics in sport

Sport has become an industry in itself. Increased funds are available to sport at all levels, and more people than ever are earning their living from it. The affluence of our society and increased leisure time have contributed to this phenomenon. There is also a general recognition that sports participation is beneficial at all levels, and this has led to increased government funding at both elite and grassroots levels. Where large sums of money are involved, people who disagree over aspects of the arrangements, or who are disadvantaged by injury or by the decisions of others affecting their capacity to earn, will be prepared to go to court to settle their differences.

Before the 2000 Sydney Olympics it was suggested that Australian corporate sponsors would spend $1.2 billion to feature on the chests, waists, feet and eyes of gold medallists, premiership players and international sportspeople. Sponsors wanted to see athletes in the market-place extolling the virtues of their products, especially in the build-up to the Olympics.[1]

Sponsorship funds are keenly sought and fought for at both professional and amateur levels, and for both elite and recreational participants. Their application to paid sport is immediately obvious. Amateur codes also have funds made available to them by way of sponsorship and government grants. This means that many amateur sports are taking an increasingly 'professional' view of their operations, evident first in the use of paid officials and organisers, and second in a more scientific approach to training, the treatment of injury, and performance generally. Many grassroots sports now have the means by which they can implement coaching and development programs for their young athletes. This professionalisation occurs regardless of whether the athletes themselves are actually paid.

The innovations with the greatest effect on sports of all descriptions have been television and, recently, subscription television (pay TV). The broadcasting of sport has proved almost universally popular with viewers. More people watch sport than play it. The favourite sport of a country, or one in which a compatriot is expected to excel, shown on prime-time television, or 'live' by satellite, attracts an enormous audience. One only has to look at the appeal of the Wimbledon tennis finals or the Olympic Games coverage to see the drawing power of major sports. In August 1995 NBC reportedly won the deal for the US television rights to the 2000 Olympics by offering a double package of $US715 million for the Sydney Olympics and $US575 million for the Salt Lake City Winter Olympics in 2002. In Australia, the Seven Network reportedly paid $190 million in 1996 for broadcast rights to the Sydney, Athens and Beijing Summer Games and the Salt Lake City and Turin Winter Games. It has also been reported that the Seven Network aimed for $100 million in advertising revenue for the Athens Games.[2]

The rights to such television coverage, and the sponsorship of such events, are extremely valuable and provide huge sums of money to the organisers. Professionals who take part usually receive substantial rewards for their efforts. The relationship between a professional sports league and its broadcast network is unusual in that it generally involves a contract that runs over many years. The right to sponsor a highly ranked competitor or team may provide exposure worldwide for a sponsor and money for the individual or team, or for an unpaid athlete's organisation.[3]

Subscription television

Developments involving rugby league, rugby union and a host of other sports emanating from the introduction of subscription television in Australia irrevocably changed the way in which sports are owned, run and viewed in this country.

The increase in available air time brought about by subscription television presents opportunities for many smaller sports to be shown. Not all sports, however, will be able to take advantage of the perceived bonanza that subscription television provides; only those that present an attractive product and are able to adopt a comprehensive and professional approach to sports marketing are likely to do so. Subscription broadcasters will also be unlikely to wish to cover sports which have significant exposure on free-to-air networks.

Due to regulations governing advertising on subscription television, subscription fees must be the predominant source of income for broadcasters, which is likely to result in more sophisticated marketing techniques to ensure that sponsors can be involved in sports programming in a meaningful way. Event naming rights, venue sponsorships and team sponsorships are likely to become more important in this environment.

A critical limitation on subscription television coverage of sport is the Commonwealth government's anti-siphoning list. When subscription television was introduced in 1994 the Minister for Communications and the Arts announced that certain major sporting events would continue to be available for broadcast on free-to-air television due to their inclusion on this list. The provisions are aimed at preventing specified events from being 'siphoned off' to subscription television if they are of a kind that the minister believes should be televised free to the public. Events are specified in a notice published by the minister in the *Government Gazette*.[4] Subscription broadcasting services cannot acquire the right to broadcast an event on the list until the national broadcasters or the commercial networks have acquired such a right.[5]

The subscription television industry argues that the anti-siphoning list imposes significant constraints on competition by subscription television,[6] and it has even been argued that it may reduce the amount of sport seen live on television.[7] Amendments to the legislation in 2001 mean that free-to-air broadcasters must offer live rights to others if they have acquired them but do not intend to use them.[8] Events are also automatically delisted six weeks before the commencement of an event if free-to-air broadcasters have been given a reasonable opportunity to acquire the rights. Further changes to the list and processes were announced in April 2004.[9] An updated anti-siphoning list will apply from 2006 to 2010, with additions being the Olympic and Commonwealth Games. Other events have been removed. Events will be automatically delisted 12 weeks before an event is due to occur, rather than the current six weeks.[10]

The effect on sport

There are numerous opportunities for a telegenic sport to use subscription television to its advantage. It has been suggested that some sports teams are routinely able to double the size of their home arena by packaging and marketing their sport in a way that is attractive to local cable operators.[11]

One noted US author has stated that technological developments such as cable and pay-per-view television, while expanding broadcast time and the demand for programming, have affected sport

> because expanded broadcast of amateur and professional events has brought a mixed blessing of greater exposure to the public but decreased attention to individual events as a result of oversaturation of the market. The extent of influence that television has on sports has also changed. Schedules, locations and times of games are readily shifted to adapt to the needs of television.[12]

It is quite evident that changes of this kind are already affecting the timing and organisation of sport. The women's marathon at the 1995 World Athletic Championships, for example, was run in the hottest part of the day to coincide with major television viewing times; this has also occurred during the Olympic Games. The original sport 'manufactured for television' was, of course, one-day cricket, which now also attracts significant numbers of spectators at its games. This was not the case in its early days. Sports such as triathlon have been presented in an 'upmoded' format to improve their television appeal.

It is up to sports administrators to ensure that the integral nature of a sport is maintained or improved and not destroyed, and that the interests of competitors are not prejudiced.

How commercialism affects sport

The increasing involvement of money in sport has led to effects said by some to be negative. The fact that amateur sports are becoming more professional in their approach, and the increasing tendency to provide some type of reward, blurs the distinction between the categories of amateur and professional. In most sports the distinction is no longer maintained.

This question aside, athletes have been accused of placing too much emphasis on money, and adopting an attitude of 'win at any cost'. This is said to be inconsistent with the basic philosophy behind sport. It seems, however, that any change in athletes' competitive attitudes is not simply directed at a larger winning purse for its own sake, but comes about for a variety of reasons:

- For many professional athletes, sport is their job or career. If they do not win, they have not done their job well.
- The perfection demanded of today's finely tuned athlete means that the athlete usually has only a few years at the top in which to maximise income. This may encourage an all-out approach by some.

- Sponsors and broadcasters may pressurise competitors, demanding a marketable product in return for their investment.
- With the advent of the instant replay, competitors may be forced to relive, with adverse comments, a poor or mediocre performance.
- Those who succeed as top-class athletes are characteristically driven by a strong will. Success demands total commitment, adding to the pressure.

Factors such as these may create enormous tensions which erupt on the playing field, leading to allegations of 'unsportsmanlike' behaviour and suggestions that the sport is no longer a 'game'. For the athlete concerned, this may be very true.

The role of government

Governments around the world are involved in sport to varying extents. Involvement takes different forms. The approach of the former Eastern Bloc countries, for example, was very different from that of Australia.

The Commonwealth Department of Sport, Heritage and the Arts is involved in sport in Australia in many ways. Sport and recreation for the disabled, major international sporting events, the development of facilities, the activities of the ASC and the Australian Institute of Sport, recreation, fitness and safety are some of its sports-related responsibilities. Since 2002, Commonwealth and state governments have taken the lead in law reform aimed at reducing the cost of insurance to all members of the community but particularly in a sporting context.[13]

The 1994 Federal Budget allocated $135 million to help Australian athletes to compete with distinction at the Sydney 2000 Olympics. This funding was in addition to the $150 million given to the NSW government for capital works at the Homebush Bay Olympic site, and to some $62.8 million already committed to programs under the umbrella of the ASC. These programs mainly involved staged payments over a number of years. This funding was said to represent an 18 per cent jump in real terms in sports funding.

The amount spent indicated recognition by the government of the importance of sport and leisure in the lives of Australians. Grants also add significantly to the pool of money available to amateur sport.

Long before the Sydney Olympics, in 1980, the Commonwealth government took the step of fostering excellence in particular sports with the establishment of the Australian Institute of Sport (AIS). The establishment of the AIS was seen by many as a knee-jerk reaction to the failure of the Australian team to win any gold medals at the 1976 Olympic Games. A superior level of coaching, world-class facilities and access to sports science and sports medicine support were seen as essential instruments for the development of sporting potential. Some of the sports represented at the AIS are basketball, diving, gymnastics, hockey, netball, rowing, soccer, squash, swimming, tennis, track and field, water polo and weightlifting. Some AIS programs are now decentralised, and there is continuing debate on this issue.

In addition, each Australian state has its own department to take care of sport, and many of the states have developed, and fund, their own state sports institutes and academies.

Sport and politics

It is often suggested that sport should be apolitical, or 'above' politics. There is no doubt that this is a laudable aim in theory, particularly where amateur sport is concerned. The reality, however, is that sport has enormous political impact.

Sport arouses intense feelings of nationalism – witness the surge of national pride following Australia's victory in the 1983 America's Cup and the subsequent media interest in its defence – and governments have exploited this to increase their own standing and power. The attitude of Hitler's government at the 1936 Berlin Olympics is the most notorious example of this. Nationalism may account in part for the size of grants to sport and the emphasis placed on it in some countries.

Apart from nationalism, politics has always had a place in sport. While political boycotts of sporting events generally arouse the ire of the sporting public, they are not a new occurrence. Although the Olympic Charter emphasises that the Games are contests between teams and individuals, and not countries, teams have dropped out of most Olympics since 1928 for political reasons.[14]

Whether it be the boycotting of a particular Games or the cutting of sporting ties with a particular country, the use of sport as a tool in international relations is well established. One case that was the subject of enormous controversy was the sporting boycott of South Africa because of its apartheid policies. Cricket and rugby union football tours of South Africa and overseas tours by white South African teams led to demonstrations, violence and litigation.[15] By contrast, other sports (for example, surfing and tennis) maintained links with that country, leaving it to individuals to decide whether to compete. Entertainers and traders had no restrictions placed on them.

In 1984–85, the Commonwealth Department of Sport, Recreation and Tourism made payments of over $40 000 to athletes who did not compete in the Moscow Olympics and to those who withdrew from third party sporting contracts with South Africa. In 1985–86 almost $14 000 was paid to athletes who withdrew from third party sporting contacts with South Africa.[16]

It is difficult to quantify the effect, if any, that the sporting sanctions against South Africa had on the changes that have taken place there. The end of apartheid, with the election of Nelson Mandela as president, ensured the country's reinvolvement in international sporting events. South Africa took part in the Barcelona Olympics in 1992. The re-entry of South Africa into the international sporting community was complete with South Africa's win in the Rugby World Cup in 1995; and a South African runner won the 1995 City to Surf half-marathon in Sydney.

Political situations can change rapidly, as evidenced by the unravel-ling of the former Soviet Union and the subsequent emergence of a host of 'new' nations at the 1994 Winter Olympics. The transformation of Sarajevo, host city of the 1984 Winter Olympics, into a strife-torn war zone in the 1990s was another example.
The decision by Australian cricketer Stuart MacGill not to tour Zimbabwe in 2004 lest the tour be used by the Zimbabwe government as a propaganda tool is another indication of the close connection between sport and politics.

Chapter 3

The legal nature of sporting organisations

When people band together to further their joint interest in a sport or other activity, there must be some form of rules or agreement to enable the group to operate effectively. The aims and objectives of individual members in any group are not necessarily the same as those of others, and individual objectives are not necessarily in the best interests of the group as a whole. Group aims and objectives must be set out clearly in order to avoid potential conflict.

Large professional organisations are usually well aware of the need to clarify the rights and obligations of members and office bearers. Even non-profit organisations, however, need rules, to cover both everyday matters and the more contentious situations that may occur. The members of these organisations are often motivated by a desire to raise standards in their sport or to foster its growth, but that does not mean they will necessarily agree on the best course of action to take in a particular situation. The fact that money is not involved does not automatically free an organisation from controversy.

The types of guidelines or rules that should be adopted, and their content, varies. The type of organisation concerned, and its objectives, give an indication of the appropriate format. A group may decide to incorporate under the Commonwealth *Corporations Act 2001*, in which case certain documents are required by law; a few basic rules may appear sufficient for the purposes of a small non-profit club. However, they may not adequately cover unforeseen situations, and members and office holders may find themselves incurring liabilities far beyond their expectations.

Changes in the status and budgets of sporting organisations have resulted in an increase in the number of reported legal decisions involving unincorporated associations. A failure of organisations and officials to keep pace with financial developments may prove disastrous in terms of the liability of the individuals involved.

Legal personality: the problem

A continuing difficulty when sportspeople and organisations are involved with the law is the question of 'legal personality'. This involves the types of persons and groups that the courts will recognise for legal purposes.

The law recognises natural persons and various statutory 'persons', but it does not recognise a group that just gives itself a name. It will, for example, recognise Joe Brown, an individual, and Broken Hill Pty Ltd, a body incorporated under companies legislation. It recognises the IOC, a body incorporated under Swiss law as a non-profit society with legal status.[1] However, a group of people who join together for a common purpose – such as playing a sport – and form a tennis club or a district swimming club usually constitute what the law calls an 'unincorporated voluntary association'.

Problems may arise when such a group seeks to legally enforce some right that it believes it has, or when someone else seeks to recover damages or compensation from the group. Can the group enforce a sponsorship agreement the terms of which have not been fulfilled? Who is liable if a member breaks a leg on a tennis court owned or leased by the tennis club? From whom should the tradesman seek to recover if his account for work carried out on the club premises goes unpaid? Who does the professional sportsman sue for unpaid prize money or guaranteed air fares or accommodation costs? Is a junior soccer club liable for injury to a child during a game it has organised?

The unincorporated voluntary association

There is no legal requirement for an organisation to become incorporated unless it has profit as one of its purposes.[2] If a non-profit organisation such as a sporting club does not become incorporated, however, it does not exist in the eyes of the law as an entity apart from its separate members. This means that the club may not enter into a contract, sue or be sued in its own name, or take part in any legal proceedings on its own behalf. Thus the Bondi Beach Parachuting Club, for example, exists only in the eyes of its members.

The courts have devised a variety of ways of getting around the problem to determine the rights and liabilities of parties. However, the approach taken in any particular case will depend on the facts involved. This means that the outcome will not be certain, and liability may not fall where those involved in the running of the organisation would have chosen or expected.

Where the organisation itself would have been liable had it been incorporated, the court can usually find someone involved with the organisation who should bear the responsibility. Sometimes, for example, committee members have been found to be liable, jointly or severally, for a debt or an award of damages at law.[3] 'Jointly or severally' means that an amount may be recovered from all or any one of those named. In other cases, all the members are found liable. The ease of determining who the actual members were at the relevant time may be important here. Where contractual liability is concerned, the length of time between the formation of the contract and the raising of the matter in dispute has been of particular relevance in determining who should be liable.

Sometimes the courts have simply been unable to find anyone who should take the responsibility when all the facts have been taken into account. This means that rights or liabilities that were intended to accrue to the organisation have had no effect.

An unincorporated association cannot hold property[4] (outright or in trust) or sign a lease.[5] Where the ownership of group property has been in question, the courts have sometimes vested it in those who were members at the time of the formation of the group, or when the group was dissolved.

A good sporting example of this situation involved the Carlton and Fitzroy football clubs.[6] The Carlton Cricket and Football Club was a company limited by guarantee (that is, it was incorporated); the Fitzroy Football Club was an unincorporated body. The clubs had agreed that the Fitzroy Club would be allowed to play some matches on the Carlton ground at Princess Park. The agreement was signed by the president and secretary of the Fitzroy Club on behalf of the members in accordance with its constitution and rules.

The Fitzroy Club decided to withdraw from the agreement. When the Carlton Football Club tried to enforce it, the court held that there was no such entity (or 'legal person') as the 'Fitzroy Football Club'. This being the case, and when all the circumstances were considered, there was no contract that could be enforced against it or its members.[7]

In the course of the judgment, the position of unincorporated associations was described by the judge in a way which highlights the problems which the law has in recognising them:

> In a broad sense a sporting club is like a crowd which is interested in some operation or some incident. In ordinary language one says of such a crowd, although it had been first seen some hours before, that

'the crowd is still there', when in fact the individuals constituting it may be entirely different persons, and it is only the object of their interest that has remained the same. Because the object of interest has remained unchanged that appears to give the crowd a continuing identity which in fact it does not possess.[8]

This approach might mean that an agreement considered important by a club may be unenforceable by it if the club is not incorporated.

Liability of committees

When considering whether it is the committee members (or other elected officials) or the membership as a whole who are liable, the court generally tries to ascertain the intention of the group, based on its constitution and rules. Whether group intention is ascertainable, and what it is, depends on all the circumstances.[9] The general principle, however, is that those who accept office must accept the responsibilities and liabilities that go with their positions.

Formulation of proceedings: who do you sue?

The unincorporated association may also create enormous problems in terms of the formulation of legal proceedings, resulting in a waste of time and money for all concerned. For example, a Canterbury Rugby League player, Wayne Peckham, took proceedings in 1972 seeking workers' compensation payments under the *Workers' Compensation Act* (NSW) for injuries sustained at club training. His initial proceedings were taken against the Canterbury District Football Club, an unincorporated body. The court found that there was no such legal entity. Peckham reformulated his proceedings, and took them against the individual committee members with whom he had originally contracted in 1969. The injury occurred in 1972, however, and a new committee was in office. The court decided that Peckham should sue the committee which was in office at the time of the injury. When Peckham did so, he finally recovered compensation.[10]

Rights created by club constitutions and rules

What actual rights and liabilities are created by the constitution or rules of an unincorporated association?

This may not seem to be particularly important in isolation, but it becomes very important when one considers its practical significance. If the rules of a club state that elections must be held every year, for example, but the president and secretary decide that there is no need to hold them one year because they are going to win anyway, can other members force them to hold the election? Can a member who is

entitled on the face of the rules to nominate for an office in an organisation have the nomination refused for reasons not contained in the
rules? Even if the reason for the refusal is contained in the rules, can
the member complain if the ruling seems unfair? What of member
complaints about issues such as the application of club funds? If
members have a complaint about how a club is being run, and its officials refuse to listen, or matters are not resolved in a satisfactory way,
can they go to court to enforce their rights?

If the rules of the association form a binding contract between the
members and the association, a simple way to enforce members' rights
would be to take the matter to court claiming breach of the contract.
Do the constitution and rules contractually bind the members, and do
they create a contract between the members and the association?
(Contract law is considered in detail in chapter 4).[11]

When a body is incorporated under the *Corporations Act*, its constitution forms a contract between the members and the incorporated
body.[12] There are, however, conflicting views as to whether this is the
case with an unincorporated body, particularly when it is a body
formed for recreational purposes like a social or sporting club.

While contract may not be the only basis for creating rights for
members of an unincorporated association,[13] the rules of the association are the most obvious indication of the way in which the founding
members intended the organisation to be run.

In a 1934 case involving another category of unincorporated voluntary association, a political party, the High Court looked at the
effect of the rules of voluntary associations. The situation in *Cameron
v Hogan* involved the refusal of a Labor Party branch to endorse the
Premier of Victorian as an election candidate, and his eventual expulsion from the party. The High Court concluded that there was no contractual or other basis on which the plaintiff could claim relief in the
circumstances. The court described the position of voluntary associations and their members in the following way:

> They are for most part bodies of persons who have been combined
> to further some common end or interest, which is social, sporting,
> political, scientific, religious, artistic or humanitarian in character,
> or otherwise stands apart from private gain and material advantage.
> Such associations are established upon a consensual basis but, unless
> there were some clear positive indication that the members contem-
> plated the creation of legal relations *inter se* [between themselves],
> the rules adopted for their governance would not be treated as
> amounting to an enforceable contract.[14]

This High Court logic has never been overruled, but it has increasingly been viewed as being out-of-date in its approach to the social club situation.

In other decisions, the courts have found ways around it. In a case involving a dispute about how the North Sydney District Rugby League Football Club should be run, the judge commented that *Cameron v Hogan* had been decided a long time ago. His Honour saw the court's role in the voluntary social (or sporting) club situation in a vastly different manner:

> I consider that citizens are entitled to look to the courts for the same assistance in resolving disputes about the conduct of sporting, political and social organisations as they can expect in relation to commercial situations. If it is not forthcoming, a vast and growing sector of the lives of people in the affluent society will be a legal no man's land, in which disputes are settled not in accordance with justice and the fulfilment of deliberately undertaken obligations, but by deceit, craftiness, arrogant disregard of rights and other means which poison the institutions in which they exist, and destroy trust between members.[15]

The intentions of the members will thus be the most important factor in determining whether a contract exists in relation to the rules of an unincorporated association. If a contract does exist the members will be able to enforce the rules through the courts. All the surrounding circumstances must be considered carefully to ascertain the intention of the members.[16] The constitution and rules of the organisation will obviously be of particular importance in this situation.

Relationship between the levels of an organisation

An interesting question raised by a decision to expel a club from the Sydney Rugby Union competition concerned the relationship in contract law terms between the governing body of a state organisation and the clubs at grassroots level within that organisation.

An invitation to the Drummoyne Club to participate in the Sydney club competition for three years was reversed following the competition's restructure. The Drummoyne Club was a member of the Sydney Rugby Union, which was in turn a member of the NSW Rugby Union. The judge refused to enforce any agreement between the Drummoyne Club and the NSW Rugby Union on the basis that there was no contract between them, although there was a contract between NSW Rugby Union and Sydney Rugby Union, and between Sydney Rugby Union and the club. (His Honour found that the club could not be excluded on other grounds.)[17]

What should a constitution contain?

Whether or not the members of an organisation decide that incorporation under any form is necessary, the constitution or rules should try to provide for both the purpose and the operation of the body. While every eventuality cannot be foreseen when the constitution is drafted, there are some situations that will always occur. Provision may be made for other possibilities by including a rule that entitles a proportion of members to call a general meeting. Legislation governing incorporation may dictate minimum content.

Provisions that will always need to be covered in the rules relate to:
- membership qualifications and admission procedure
- cessation of membership
- election of office-bearers
- powers of committee members
- possible group indemnity of office-bearers
- application of group funds
- winding-up of the group.

Protection of non-contractual rights

Contractual rights are not the only rights that the law recognises. The law has recognised other rights that may be enforced by club members and aspiring members, and that do not depend on contract. They tend to relate to narrower areas of justice and fairness, however, and are not as easy to enumerate as those contained in a written set of rules.

Two important areas in which courts may intervene illustrate the fact that the rules of an organisation do not totally determine its rights and liabilities and those of its members:
- The courts require that decisions made in relation to suspension or fines be made fairly. This involves the legal area of natural justice (or procedural fairness), which is discussed in chapter 6.
- The courts have long taken particular care to protect the right of an individual to work (discussed in chapter 4). Even non-members of an association may have a right to membership if the right to work in a particular industry or area depends on it.

Incorporation

Many sporting bodies have become incorporated in an attempt to alleviate the sort of legal identity problems discussed above. If profit is an objective, the organisation generally *must* be incorporated under the *Corporations Act*. Other organisations may choose to incorporate under state laws dealing with incorporated associations.

All incorporated organisations need to be aware of the changing nature of the responsibilities that parliaments are imposing on organisations and the individuals who run them. The laws imposing these responsibilities apply to all organisations once they are incorporated, whether or not they have paid officials or participants.

Incorporation as a company

Organisations that have as one of their objects the 'acquisition of gain' must generally be incorporated under the *Corporations Act*. Sports that incorporate under this Act generally do so by forming what the law calls a *company limited by guarantee*.

Most types of companies are made up of shareholders who hold shares. A company limited by guarantee, however, has members rather than shareholders. A member of a company limited by guarantee is involved in the functioning of the company in much the same way as a shareholder but, unlike a shareholder, does not pay in any capital. If a company limited by guarantee is wound up, however, and it has not enough assets to pay its debts, each member is liable to pay the amount of the guarantee specified in the constitution (or by agreement) or, for older companies, the memorandum (see below). Members cannot be required to pay more than this. Past members are generally not liable.

The names and types of constituent documents that a company must have have changed over the years with changes in the legislation. Older companies may still have a *memorandum* and *articles*. Newer companies may have a memorandum alone or, after 2001, a constitution.

Incorporation as an association

If financial gain is not one of an organisation's objects, it may choose to incorporate under the associations legislation of its state, which provides a relatively simple, cheap means of incorporation.[18] The required documents are called *objects* and *rules*.

The NSW Act, for example, provides for the incorporation of bodies having a set of objects and rules, a non-profit principal purpose and more than five members. Fundraising is not precluded, but it should not be the main purpose of the organisation. The minister may refuse to incorporate an organisation as an association if it is considered inappropriate. The Act requires that various matters be included in the rules, and if a required matter is not dealt with, the Model Rule provision covering that issue is imported into the rules of the organisation. Following the recent insurance crisis there is no longer a requirement for the maintenance of a $2 million insurance policy for all NSW associations, although clearly public liability insurance is highly desirable from a risk management perspective.[19] The organisation must lodge an annual financial statement with authorities.

The laws governing incorporated associations in other states and territories are in some cases stricter, and in other cases more lenient, than those operating in NSW. All states have their own requirements as to the contents of the rules of associations. In every state an association may decide to transfer to the status of a company.

Duties of directors, officers and committee members

Whether or not a company has a truly commercial nature, directors and others must take reasonable steps to ensure that management of the organisation is carefully monitored.

The National Safety Council case[20] in 1991 indicated quite clearly that a director must keep abreast of a company's affairs, particularly if there are reasonable grounds to suspect that the company will not be able to pay its debts. In that case the non-executive chairman of a company limited by guarantee was found to be liable for $96 million in debts of his company, although his honesty was not in question, because he did not involve himself enough in its affairs.

The duties of directors can be divided into those imposed by the common law, and those imposed by the laws incorporating the organisation, either the *Corporations Act* or the associations laws of a particular state or territory.

Duties of directors at common law

The difference between common law and statute law was discussed in chapter 1.

Directors have always had a duty to exercise reasonable skill and care, and 'fiduciary duties of good faith', at common law. A fiduciary duty arises from the existence of what the law calls a *fiduciary relationship*, which exists whenever one party has duties or obligations imposed on it because it has been entrusted with powers that may be exercised for the benefit of another. In the case of a company, a fiduciary relationship exists because a company is an artificial person that can only act through its directors. The position of director exists for the benefit of the company, and the director's powers must be exercised only for the benefit of the company.

At common law, then, directors must act in good faith and for the benefit of the company. They must also act with 'due diligence' (that is, they must act reasonably and with skill). This means they must become familiar with the company and how it is run.[21] They must not allow their own or anyone else's interest to come before the interests of the company, or make use of their position to gain a personal advantage or an advantage for someone else. They must not misuse confidential information, and must not take business opportunities that ought to have been taken by the company.

In any situation where a director has breached one of these duties, it is not a defence to say that no dishonesty was involved or that the company did not suffer any loss. If there is a breach of duty, the director is liable to the company for any profits obtained by the director, or losses suffered by the company. A company can, however, forgive the acts of a director.

Duties under the Corporations Act

The duties owed by directors and other officers under the *Corporations Act* are similar but not identical to those owed at common law. An important distinction between the common law and statutory duties of directors is that the latter may have both civil and criminal implications. Civil penalties generally require a civil standard of proof; that is, breaches must be proven on the balance of probabilities.[22] Criminal penalties can be fines of up to $220 000 or imprisonment for five years or both.[23] A criminal standard of proof is required in this case; that is, breaches need to be proven beyond reasonable doubt. Penalties for contraventions of the *Corporations Act* include disqualification from the management of a corporation as well as monetary penalties.

For the purposes of the *Corporations Act* 'officer' is defined to include a director, secretary or executive officer of a corporation.[24]

The Act requires directors and other officers to exercise the degree of care and diligence that a 'reasonable person' in a similar position would exercise having regard to the corporation's circumstances.[25] They must act 'in good faith in the best interests of the corporation' and 'for a proper purpose'.[26] This includes some consideration of the position of creditors. If the officer is 'reckless' or 'intentionally dishonest' in relation to this duty, criminal liability can be imposed.[27]

Officers and directors must not improperly use their position, or information obtained through holding or having held that position, to either 'gain an advantage for themselves or someone else', or 'cause detriment to the corporation'.[28] A person who makes improper use of their position or information gained through it can be subject to both criminal and civil penalties.

The *Corporations Act* also prohibits insolvent trading.[29] 'Solvency' means the ability to pay all the company's debts as and when they become due, rather than a surplus of assets over liabilities.[30] Directors who do not prevent their companies from incurring debts while insolvent, or who make companies insolvent, are personally liable for these debts in some circumstances. If there were reasonable grounds to suspect that incurring the debt would make the company insolvent and the director was aware of those grounds or ought reasonably to have been aware of them, the director may be personally liable.[31] If the director had reasonable grounds to expect that the company would remain solvent, or that a competent person was monitoring solvency and keeping the director informed, the director may not be liable.[32]

Duties under state associations legislation

The discussion on common law duties of directors is also relevant to committee members or council members of associations. However, the legislation governing the operation of associations differs greatly between the states, and very different responsibilities are imposed on associations by the different laws. Those involved in the running of these bodies must be aware of the contents of the legislation of their state – failure to comply with the relevant legislation may involve significant fines or, at worst, personal liability for debt.

New South Wales

There is no specific duty of diligence for directors contained in the NSW Act,[33] but there is a prohibition against insolvent trading.

Officers can be personally liable for debts incurred by an association in some circumstances. 'Officer' is defined to mean a committee member, the public officer, the secretary, the treasurer, the executive officer or an employee of the association.

Where an association has been, or is being, wound up, where its incorporation has been cancelled, or where it is unable to pay its debts, it becomes a *division 3 association*. If a division 3 association incurs a debt and immediately beforehand there were reasonable grounds to expect that it would be unable to pay its debts as and when they fell due, *or* there are reasonable grounds to expect that if it incurs the debt it will not be able to pay its debts as and when they fall due, committee members at the time the debt is incurred are guilty of an offence and liable jointly and severally for payment of the debt. A person incurring a debt in these circumstances may not be indemnified by the association.[34] Defences are possible where the debt was incurred without a committee member's express or implied authority, or where at the time it was incurred the member did not have reasonable cause to believe that the association would not be able to pay its debts.

By definition, an association is only unable to pay its debts if a court order or judgment in favour of a creditor is returned unsatisfied in whole or in part.[35]

Acts intended to defraud creditors or for a fraudulent purpose are expressly prohibited, and anyone knowingly concerned in such conduct is guilty of an offence and liable to be fined, imprisoned or both.

South Australia

The South Australian Act provides that officers of 'prescribed associations' must act honestly and with reasonable care and diligence. Insolvent trading is a criminal offence.[36]

Associations with gross receipts in excess of $200 000 or any greater amount prescribed by regulation are 'prescribed associations'.[37] 'Officers' include committee members, the secretary, treasurer or public officer, or those concerned in the management of the association. This means that managerial employees are caught by the provisions.

The threshold turnover figure excludes many associations from the ambit of the legislation. The question of the standard to be applied to officers of those associations excluded is, therefore, unanswered. The setting of a standard so similar to the common law in the legislation appears to preclude the application of the common law provisions in South Australia.

Other states and territories

Other states and territories do not specify duties of directors, except that the Western Australian legislation requires disclosure of pecuniary interest and states that directors may not participate in decision-making where they have a pecuniary interest. The ACT legislation has similar provisions, and also prohibits improper use of position.[38]

Corporate governance in sport

Issues of corporate governance in Australia have been put in sharp focus in the first years of the twenty-first century by developments involving companies such as One.Tel, HIH and James Hardie. According to the ASC, corporate governance is determined by:

- how an organisation develops strategic goals and direction;
- how the board of the organisation monitors the performance of the organisation to ensure it achieves these strategic goals; and
- ensuring that the board acts in the best interests of the members.[39]

In the view of the ASC there are five major principles of corporate governance:

1 clear delineation of governance roles
2 effective governance processes
3 effective governance controls
4 governance improvement, and
5 member responsiveness.

Better run organisations require leadership, integrity and good judgment. They are more effective decision makers, and are transparent, accountable and responsible in their activities and resource allocation.

Chapter 4

Contracts

The contract is one of the basic units of the legal system. An individual may enter into numerous contracts in day-to-day activities without realising that a contract has been made. Buying a home involves a formal contract of sale. Buying a bus ticket, riding to a bus stop and getting off sees the completion of a less formal, but still valid, contract.

If an individual agrees to play a sport for a club or to coach a team for reward there will usually be an agreement between the parties – often in the form of a contract of employment. An agreement by an organisation to sponsor an athlete, a team or a sport also usually involves a contract. One of the most important sporting contracts of recent years was the Host City Contract between the IOC, the AOC and the City of Sydney which entrusted the organisation of the Games of the XXVII Olympiad to Sydney on the basis of its bid documents, which were thus given contractual force.[1]

A contract is a particular type of agreement between two or more parties, containing promises by each party that they intend to be enforceable at law.

A brief summary of contract law principles follows. The principles are then applied in a discussion of some aspects of contract law that can be relevant to sport.

What constitutes a contract?

It is commonly thought that a contract must be in writing, but this is not so. An oral contract may be just as binding as a written contract. The big advantage in having a written document is that once it exists it is much easier to prove that there is a contract and what it contains.

Contracts may also involve a combination of oral and written terms. The fact that there is a written contract does not mean that the contract is confined to the document. Oral assurances made before signing a contract may be classified as *terms* (part of the contract), or *representations* (not part of the contract), depending on the circumstances surrounding the formation of the contract.

While all contracts involve agreement between the parties, not all binding agreements are called contracts. In one publicised dispute, Ivan Henjak, a player with the Canberra team in the NSW Rugby League competition, signed a document called a 'statement of intent', which stated that he would negotiate terms to play with the Newcastle team in 1988. Henjak then signed an agreement to stay with the Canberra team for the 1988 season. Although the first document was not actually called a contract, Henjak did agree in it to negotiate terms with the Newcastle Club. His signing with Canberra made playing for them impossible. Henjak reportedly agreed to compensate Newcastle.

Contracts do not even have to be negotiated by the parties. Terms and conditions written on the back of a ticket to a football match, for example, may constitute the terms of a contract between the purchaser of the ticket and the match organisers.

Contracts themselves contain various essential elements. There must be an *offer* and an *acceptance*, and there must also be what is called *consideration*. The terms of the contract must be *certain*, and the parties must *intend* to form a legally binding agreement. The parties must also have the legal *capacity* to make a contract. Finally, the purpose of the contract must be legal.

Offer, acceptance and consideration

If I say, 'Would you like to buy my car for $5000?' I am making an offer. If you reply, 'Yes, please', you are accepting my offer.

Consideration is what might be called the value of the bargain – in the example, $5000. It is essential to the existence of an enforceable contract; that is, one that the law will recognise and enforce through the courts.

Consideration does not have to be the true value of the bargain, but it must be real and not what the law terms 'illusory'. If the car mentioned was valued at $10 000 in the marketplace, $5000 would be real consideration. One cent would not be.

Certainty

The terms of any agreement must be sufficiently certain. A claim for breach of contract by the Jordan Formula 1 Grand Prix racing team against Vodafone in relation to a million dollar sponsorship agreement allegedly concluded by car phone failed when the court found that no binding agreement had been reached. While there was evidence of various discussions and meetings, decisions reached were too incomplete and uncertain to constitute a binding contract.[2]

Intention

Before a legally enforceable contract can exist, the parties must *intend* their agreement to be legally binding. Suppose someone says, 'If you can do that, I'll give you a thousand dollars,' both parties knowing that the offer is not to be taken seriously. In such a situation, no binding agreement will exist. The actual intention of the parties is what is relevant here; it will be ascertained from all the circumstances.

Capacity

The parties to a contract must have the legal *capacity* to enter into a binding agreement. Minors (people under 18) lack the capacity to enter into certain contracts. Others who *may* lack capacity in some circumstances include people affected by alcohol or drugs, and people with an intellectual disability or a mental illness. Until round the mid-twentieth century, married women lacked capacity at law to enter into a contract

The position regarding minors and the enforcement of contracts is particularly complicated, and differs from state to state. The issue is relevant to sport in many situations because of the great numbers of participants under 18. The purchase of a ski lift ticket by a minor is an example of the type of situation that might arise. If the ticket contains a clause exempting the operator from liability for injury and property damage, and the young person is injured and breaks his skis, the enforceability of the contract term would be in issue.

The general rule at common law was that a contract made with an 'infant' (a minor) was voidable at the minor's option, depending on the nature of the bargain. This meant in effect that if the minor wanted the contract to be binding after thinking about it, or when it came to be enforced by either party, the minor could choose to treat it as binding or not. Some contracts at common law were valid unless the minor repudiated them before reaching the age of 21. Some 'beneficial contracts' were exceptions, being considered valid by the courts.

The common law has been altered in certain respects by laws relating to particular types of contracts in each state.

The *Minors (Property and Contracts) Act 1970* (NSW), the most sweeping legislation of its kind, comprehensively regulates the whole area in NSW. In that state, contracts signed by a minor are presumed to be binding unless the minor, due to youth, lacks the necessary understanding. Contacts for the minor's benefit are presumed to be binding. The legislation of other states often applies in some areas only.

In recognition of the difficulties concerning contracts with minors, the 2004 Olympic Team Agreement contained an acknowledgment by a team member under 18 that the agreement was for the minor's benefit and that selection was conditional on parents or guardians signing an acknowledgment attached to the agreement. In that second acknowledgment the parents agree that the agreement has been read by the minor and by them, that it is for the benefit of the athlete, and that they have received legal advice on the content. Whether this would result in the agreement being construed by a court as being for the benefit of the minor in all cases is not entirely clear. The law governing the agreement is stated to be the law of NSW.[4]

Illegal agreements

The law refuses to enforce an *illegal* agreement. A well-known old case involved an agreement between two highwaymen to split the proceeds of a robbery. When one tried to enforce the agreement the court refused, stating that a contract to commit a crime was unenforceable.

The parties

There must be parties to a contract. Ascertaining the actual parties to a contract has provided quite a few legal problems for those involved in sport, as discussed in chapter 3. The change in the nature of sport from an amateur to a more commercial context has been fairly swift. Many associations have been left with a status and constitution that are incongruous with their present character, and have failed to recognise the need to protect office-bearers in a changed legal climate.

Remedies

If the terms of a contract are breached, one or other of the parties may turn to the courts to enforce it, or to seek other remedies. Depending on the particular circumstances, possible remedies include:
- an order that the defaulting party fulfil their part of the agreement
- a declaration that the contract is at an end, with damages being awarded to the party suffering harm
- a declaration that the contract is still operative, with damages awarded to the party who is not getting exactly what was agreed on.

Sporting agreements

Players may make a variety of different agreements in the course of their sporting activities. All these involve the concept of a contract discussed above. The actual rights and obligations of the parties involved, as embodied in the terms of the particular contract, will vary in their degree of complexity. Some of the types of contracts that may be found in sporting situations are discussed below.

Contracts to perform

The professional sportsperson may contract to play exclusively for one body or club, signing an agreement involving a large consideration (payment) and a commitment to perform for a specified number of years. Such a deal may involve a detailed contract setting out the rights and obligations of the parties. This contract may actually constitute a contract of employment, and the law relating to that area may apply to it. This possibility is discussed below.

Depending on how the sport in question is organised, the player may agree to participate in a particular event or activity, or a series of events. This contract will obviously operate for a more limited period of time, but may still involve a document of some complexity.

Where a sportsperson simply agrees to play a sport for a particular club or organisation the traditional 'amateur' type of situation is involved. Here a legally enforceable agreement is rarely concluded in relation to any commitment to play. The law sees the major reason for this as being a lack of the intention to create legal relations, and a 'domestic' arrangement results.

An amateur event may involve a contract where the competitors pay an entry fee and agree to abide by set rules. Such was the situation in *Clarke v Dunraven*.[6] Two members of a yacht club entered a club race having given written undertakings to abide by club rules. One rule was that any yacht disobeying any of the rules was liable for 'all damages arising therefrom'. In breach of a rule of sailing, one of the yachts ran into another yacht, sinking it. The court found that there was a contract upon which the owner of the damaged yacht could sue the other yacht owner.

Management contracts

Professional sportspeople often sign long and detailed management contracts under which it is agreed that particular people or organisations will represent their interests in negotiating and generally overseeing their sporting activities.

Sponsorship contracts

The general popularity of sport and sportspeople, and the amounts of money involved in the marketing of goods and services in our society, have already been mentioned. These factors contribute to the degree to which sportspeople are in demand as product image makers and endorsers. Many sports, even 'minor' sports, have one or more sponsors, and sporting organisations, teams and individuals may all be involved in sponsorship arrangements.[5] All these arrangements will involve a contract. Descriptions such as 'professional' do not assist in determining the existence of a legally binding contract – many well-known amateur athletes are sponsored by clothing, footwear or sporting goods manufacturers. Many amateur sports groups are sponsored. Even children's sports may find sponsors.

Other sporting contracts

The types of contracts discussed also apply to coaches and other paid officials, such as trainers, who are involved in particular sports. Where these individuals develop their own high profile or reputation for excellence, they may find themselves in demand for endorsements and other types of advertising contracts.

The Olympic Team Agreement

Participation agreements may form contracts even if the participants are not being paid to compete, because by signing the agreement they secure significant advantages, which constitute the essential element of consideration. The Olympic Team Agreement (a detailed document covering matters from general conduct to anti-doping and athlete sponsorship) is a type of participation agreement. The Olympic Team Agreement for the 2004 Olympics was 16 pages long; with additional schedules, it totalled 47 pages in all. (The 2000 Olympic Team Agreement was 40 pages long, with 25 clauses and six schedules.)

Athletes signing the 2004 agreement received $1000 in August 2004. They agreed to abide by the Olympic Charter, and acknowledged the receipt of various listed benefits received from the AOC (the other party to the contract). The terms involved strict limitations on the extent to which an athlete's personal sponsorships could be publicised during the Olympic period, and athletes were required to notify the AOC of their sponsors. They agreed not to bring the sport, AOC or the team into disrepute, and to comply with the WADA Code and various ethical codes. They also released the AOC from all

liability for any injury, regardless of whether or not it had been negligently caused.

Most of the agreement ran from the time of signing until midnight
on the day of the Closing Ceremony, but a significant number of
clauses continued indefinitely. These mainly related to issues such as
insurance, use of the team uniform, marketing and promotional activities, acknowledgments concerning the application of disciplinary
procedures, agreements not to sue for injury or loss caused by anyone
in connection with the administration, management or operation of
the team or Games participation, and dispute resolution. The agreement also included a schedule of benefits for loss or injury suffered.[7]

Analysis of agreements of this kind reveal significant restrictions
on the personal freedoms of athletes in return for their participation.[8]

The Olympic Charter sets out a number of eligibility conditions
and declarations to be contained in the Olympic agreements to be
signed by athletes, coaches, trainers and officials in Australia. They
relate to issues such as:

- agreement to comply with the Olympic Charter, the WADA Code
  and the IOC Code of Ethics
- agreement to be filmed, photographed and recorded for the
  purpose of promotion of the Olympics
- agreement to refer disputes exclusively to CAS
- rules governing trade mark identification on clothing and equipment.[9]

Inducing breach of contract

Organisations, agents, promoters and others must not encourage
someone to breach a contract in order to get the person to enter into
a new agreement. Anyone doing this would be open to action for what
the law calls 'inducing breach of contract'. The action may be proven
if the other party to the original contract can show that:

- the person allegedly inducing the breach knew of the contract,
  intended to prevent it being carried out, and took direct action or
  committed an unlawful act to induce the breach; and
- the original contracting party suffered damage as a result.

Damages may be awarded against the person inducing the breach
regardless of whether an action is also available against the party who
breaks the contract.[10] Such an action was successful in *Greig v Insole*,
discussed below, where World Series Cricket players took action
against the English cricket authorities.

An injunction was granted under this legal category to Super League in July 1995 to prevent the Australian Rugby League, NSW Rugby League and Bob Fulton (an Australian coach) for six months from entering into any agreement with any Super League contracted player or from taking steps to induce players not to participate in the Super League competition.[11]

The contract of employment

The nature of many professional sporting contracts means that they are classified as contracts of employment at law. The growth of the sports industry and the availability of large amounts of money for its best participants mean that many sportspeople are in a position to make a very comfortable living from their sport.

The existence of an employment relationship (which used to be called at law a 'master–servant' relationship), as opposed to the sport-sperson being an 'independent contractor', imposes a number of obli-gations on the employer. At common law, an employer is vicariously liable for the acts or omissions of an employee. This means that the employer is liable regardless of whether the employer was personally involved or at fault. The employer must provide a safe system of work, and is also generally liable for personal injury suffered by an employee where there has been a breach of a statutory duty.

At common law, a variety of rights and obligations accrue to both parties to an employment relationship.[12] These may be varied by the terms of a written agreement. In addition to these, terms of an employ-ment contract may come from statutes, industrial awards or enterprise agreements, or be implied by common law or practice.

Determining whether a worker is an employee or an independent contractor is sometimes a complicated process, and a number of tests have been evolved by the courts for use in such situations. The ability of the employer to 'control' the activities of the worker is the most important.[13] Generally, it would appear that the sportsperson who signs up with a particular organisation for a period of time to perform a variety of activities falls into the category of an employee. Thus an Australian Football player who signs with a club and agrees to attend training, play in all matches for one or more seasons and make himself available for a variety of promotional activities on behalf of the club is probably an employee. A tennis player who agrees with the Tennis Australia to play in the Australian Open tennis tournament, with potential prize money of a given sum, is an independent contractor. These examples illustrate the operation of the 'control test'. The footballer would be coached by a club coach, and other facilities would be made available to him to improve his fitness and ability. He would receive detailed pre-match and training instructions. The tennis player, however, would probably have his own coach, and be left more or less to his own devices in his attempt on the title in question.

While a detailed explanation of the law of employment is outside the scope of this book, the matter of termination of employment should be considered carefully by employers, and employees should be aware of their rights. A maze of common law and statutes is applicable, including the Commonwealth *Workplace Relations Act 1996* and various state Acts.

The Commonwealth and all the states now also have legislation dealing with occupational health and safety that spells out certain obligations of employers and employees.

Restraint of trade

Everyone has various rights at law, and one of the most important is the right to work. The courts have traditionally recognised that this right is something that should not normally be taken away from a person, although this recognition involves existing legal doctrines and no separate action is available for the right to work as such.

The doctrine of restraint of trade is aimed at protecting a person's right to work, and promoting free and competitive economic conditions. The doctrine provides that all restraints of trade are *prima facie* void; that is, generally not permissible. A restraint will be permitted, however, if it is reasonable in the interests of the parties to the transaction as a whole, and in the public interest. Whether a person has received adequate compensation for a loss of rights is relevant here.[14]

Clauses that restrain trade may be included in a contract. They are normally found in contracts for the sale of small businesses. A contract for the sale of a butcher shop as a going concern, for example, will often include a term to the effect that the vendor will not start another business of the same type in the same or an adjoining area for a certain period of time. When called upon to consider such terms, the courts will look to see whether what has been agreed upon is reasonable. The vendor receives payment for giving up a right to work in the area for a particular length of time, but the restraint must be no more than a reasonable protection for the purchaser. The reasonableness of the protection is considered in light of the clientele of the business and the consideration paid.

Terms that 'restrain trade' may also be found in the constitutions and rules of sporting clubs and associations. In relation to sport, the control of labour markets by way of transfer rules, pooling of players and other means has traditionally been justified on the grounds of

> the attainment of sporting equality and the survival of their sport. They argue that in the absence of such controls the rich clubs would secure the most skilled players, and through their continual domination of the competition, spectators would lose interest in the sport.[15]

Examination of the areas in which these restrictions operate shows that they rarely result in a more even distribution of competition successes for participating teams. They may, however, result in ill feeling and litigation between players and rule-makers.[16] Many interesting sporting cases have revolved around the imposition of restrictions on participants by sporting organisations. Such restrictions have usually been enshrined in association rules and have limited the ability of sportspeople to move from club to club, even to obtain entry to competition or employment, or to take advantage of other opportunities that arise because of their skill and sporting reputation.

There may also be attempts through club rules to fetter comment by insiders on the conduct of officials or other aspects of a sport. Such restrictions are usually included for the 'good of the game', but may not be for the good of participants.

Some cases of interest are discussed below.

Restraint in a contract
In a case involving baseball in the ACT, the employer argued that there was an implied oral option in the agreement. The court found that this would constitute an unreasonable restraint of trade in that it would allow the club to dispense with the player's services for two years without remuneration, yet could prevent him from playing major league baseball in Australia.[17]

Zoning and transfer restrictions
In relation to professional sport in Australia, most restraints that have come before the courts appear to have been contained in the rules or by-laws of sporting organisations. The most important recognition of the right of the courts to intervene in this type of situation can be found in the well-known High Court case of *Buckley v Tutty*.[18]

The case involved the transfer and retention system operating at that time in the NSW Rugby Football League competition. A Sydney player, Dennis Tutty, wished to leave the Balmain Club, which wanted to retain his services. The club placed a very high transfer fee on him, as it was entitled to do under League rules. Tutty complained of this for two years in a row, and actually sat out for an entire season. At this stage, Tutty's contract with the club had expired, but the transfer fee placed on him was still prohibitive.

The High Court held that the laws of the League in this situation were in restraint of trade. They prevented professional players from making the most of the fact that there were clubs prepared to bid for their services, and they were actually a fetter on the right of a player to seek and engage in employment. The existence of the League appeals system did not operate to make the restraints reasonable.

The case broke new ground in Australia, because Tutty was not actually a party to the contract of which he complained. The contract in question was the rules of the League, the parties to it being the League and the Balmain Club.

Another player, John Elford, took proceedings at the same time. He had been placed on the retention list by the Western Suburbs Club, but his contract with the club had not yet expired. The High Court held that the laws in question were not unfair in respect of the unexpired contract in all the circumstances. Elford was still committed to play for the club by his contract, whereas the only thing that had kept Tutty at Balmain was the restrictive League rules.

The zoning rules of the Victorian Football League (VFL) were the subject of court consideration in *Hall v Victorian Football League*.[19] Peter Hall wished to play for the South Melbourne Club, but he was residentially bound to the Collingwood Club. The rules, coupled with the VFL clearance and appeal system in operation at that time, were found to restrain trade. The same result was reached in relation to similar VFL rules in the Adamson case,[20] and in a decision involving the Sydney Swans Club and a player, Silvio Foschini.[21] Rules relating to the transfer of a Sheffield Shield cricket player between states have also been found to be in restraint of trade.[22] Soccer's retain and transfer system was at one point described as 'embodying a slave trade'.[23]

More recently, the rules of a country district rugby league competition that restrained non-professional players for up to four years from moving to a club that was prepared to pay them a small amount per game were found to be a reasonable when considered in the light of the legitimate objects of the competition.[24] The court applied

Buckly v Tutty and stated that the issue of 'reasonableness' was not dependent on such issues as equality of bargaining power between the parties, or the adequacy of remuneration. In a contrasting decision, residency rules applying to a part-time player in an elite netball competition were a restraint of trade that the All Australia Netball Association was unable to establish were reasonable.[25]

Player drafts

Another type of rule that has been found to be in restraint of trade in particular circumstances is the player 'draft'.

The Australian Football League (AFL) has a draft system that has not, to the writer's knowledge, been challenged in court.

In 1990 the NSW Rugby League established a scheme based on the AFL draft. An 'internal draft' applied to players who had previously played in the Premiership competition, and an 'external draft' to all others. A salary cap ceiling had previously been placed on player payments by the League for each club, based on the club's financial position. Players were entitled to nominate some conditions, but not the club for which they wanted to play.

At first instance, the court found that the draft was reasonable. This finding was overturned on appeal, when the Full Federal Court found that the scheme went too far. It had the greatest effect on players, infringing their right to choose for whom and where they wished to work. The Full Court emphasised that special circumstances would be required to justify such a scheme.[26]

Monopoly restrictions

While some organisation rules seek to control a sport's labour market for the purpose of maintaining fair competition, others have sought to maintain the monopoly the ruling body has in the competition itself by placing restrictions on player involvement with other groups.

The dispute between the Kerry Packer organisation and the governing establishments of cricket in the UK and Australia is a case in point. *Greig v Insole*[27] involved the rules of the UK cricket authorities and their decision to ban from test cricket, retrospectively, all players who had agreed to play with the Packer group. The rule changes were found to be in restraint of trade. While the cricket boards argued that the rule changes were instituted to protect the game and were necessary in the public interest, the court found that they went too far.

Exclusionary practices

In another cricket case a former Australian captain, Kim Hughes, took action against the Western Australian and Australian authorities on a number of points, one of which related to restraint of trade. His action followed his disqualification from district cricket on his return from a 'rebel' cricket tour of South Africa. The Western Australian Cricket Association and other state cricket associations had initiated proceedings in the Victorian Supreme Court to prevent the tour by Hughes and other players. Those proceedings were resolved between the parties. The ban was placed on the players following the resolution. Hughes complained that it had been a term of the settlement that no further action would be taken against the players. The court found that the ban was in restraint of trade. It went beyond what was necessary to protect the legitimate needs of the body concerned and was against the public interest, which lay in the opportunity to see first class cricketers in action. Other potential income-earning activities of Hughes were irrelevant to the restraint of trade question.[28]

The *Trade Practices Act* may also be relevant in the context of exclusionary practices. The definition of 'exclusionary provision' in the Act (s. 4D) provides that persons in competition with one another may not agree to prevent, restrict or limit the supply or acquisition of goods or services from another person. Although Hughes argued that this provision applied in his case, it was found not to be the case as the bodies involved were not 'trading corporations', which was necessary for the application of the provision at that time.

An important English decision, *Nagle v Fielden*,[29] involved the exclusion of a woman horse trainer from that occupation. The rules of the Jockey Club provided that no-one could train horses to race at their meetings without a licence. The club also had a policy of refusing to grant licences to women. A woman who appeared to be qualified had been refused a licence. Although there was no contractual relationship between the trainer and the Jockey Club, the court intervened to protect her right to work, and stated that the rules, which had the effect of excluding a person from employment, must not be exercised arbitrarily.

Attempts to suppress insider criticism

Other rules are imposed by governing bodies to restrict 'insider' comment that is critical of an organisation's policy or conduct. This would seem to be reasonable to some extent for the protection of the sport as a whole, and it is assumed that such reasonable restrictions would be tolerated by the courts. Attempts by an organisation to gag all critical comment, on the other hand, would be against public policy, and would not be upheld by the courts if a restraint of trade was involved.

A relevant case was *Beetson and Masters v Humphreys*.[30] Following prolonged adverse criticism in the media, the NSW Rugby Football League passed a rule that purported to ban those involved in the game from writing newspaper columns about the sport unless they were professional journalists. The rule covered referees, coaches, district officials and players. Arthur Beetson, a well-known player, and Roy Masters, a well-known coach, took proceedings claiming that the rule was invalid. Before the matter went to court, the rule was modified to provide that anyone could write if the League was notified, as long as the article did not criticise the League or its referees. The League argued that the rule was for the good of the game.

The court held that the rules in question were too wide, that they affected too many people and that they were for too long a period of time. The court invalidated the rules, emphasising that critical comment did not endanger the very reputation of the League. In so doing, it stated that the League was entitled to make rules to protect the interests of members and the welfare of the game itself, and that this right was not restricted to merely protecting the competition which the League was running. In this case, however, the rules went too far and were in restraint of trade.

Reasonable restraint

It has been suggested that the administrators of various sports are aiming at the 'orderly marketing' of their commodity by imposing restrictive rules and by-laws. Restrictive rules and constitutions have also been said to

> impinge upon the rights of the individuals who provide by far the greatest contribution to it, that is the players and athletes themselves.[31]

Major sporting organisations must accept that the courts will recognise a public interest factor that must be considered when framing rules of this kind. Reasonable restraints must be possible and it would seem that these should be worked out between players and associations. This end can be achieved by collecive bargaining, as now happens in some sports such as Australian football and rugby league.[32]

Unfair contracts

A contract between a sportsperson and the entity by whom that person is paid may constitute a contract of employment. The High Court has held that, for example, professional Rugby League players are employees,[33] although the court recognised in the Super League case that this might not always be the case.[34] Whatever the exact form a contract of this type takes, it may be that some industrial legislation will apply to it. The NSW *Industrial Relations Act 1996* allows the hearing of 'unfair contracts' cases in relation to employment, and a similar law applies in Queensland. Extensive powers are given to the NSW Industrial Relations Commission to intervene where contracts are unfair, harsh, unconscionable, or against the public interest, or provide for inadequate remuneration, or are designed to avoid award provisions.

In a decision involving a Rugby League player, Ed Sulkowicz, the commission declared that a contract made between the player and the Parramatta Club was void. The contract was for two years and provided that Sulkowicz would be paid $15 000 per season once he was graded. At the beginning of the second year, the club informed him that he would not be graded that year, and purported to free him from any contractual obligation. Sulkowicz maintained that the club owed him $15 000.

The club relied on the contract as a whole, arguing that it gave them the right not to grade the player. Sulkowicz had been required to complete a heavy pre-season training schedule, and the judge found that a contract which placed this burden on him, and then purported to leave the club free not to grade him, was one-sided. Sulkowicz was awarded $15 000.[36]

Clearly there are some limits on the extent to which unfair burdens can be imposed upon sporting 'employees' by their employers.

The unfair contracts provision of the NSW *Industrial Relations Act* was used to attack the failure of the Australian Rugby League (ARL) to select Canberra players signed by Super League, in one of the several actions that sprang from the setting up of a rival rugby league competition in Australia. Counsel for the ARL argued that the signing by the players in question (Stuart, Daley, Clyde, Walters and Mullins) had caused considerable damage to the ARL, while the players themselves had been richly compensated for a detriment that they ought to have foreseen.[37] Ultimately, the judge found that this was unfair in that, among other things, it limited the freedom of players to contract by using existing contracts as a sanction. It also was against the public interest in that it denied the public access to players of the highest skill.[38] Following the decision, ARL selectors still failed to include a Super League player in the 1995 World Cup tour.

Four Canterbury players also took action, seeking to have their ARL contracts varied to provide that Canterbury compete in the ARL competition and not the Super League competition on the basis of unfairness by Canterbury in relation to the negotiating process with Super League.[39]

The level of benefits payable under the *Sporting Injuries Insurance Act*, which covers professional sportspeople in NSW,[40] was also challenged under this provision. The court found that they are not so inadequate as to be unfair.[41]

Standard form contracts

Professional sporting contracts are often what are called *standard form contracts* drawn up for use in a particular sport.

Standard form contracts are common in all walks of life. They are usually on a printed form that contains spaces for various particulars to be filled in. A contract to buy a house (known at law as a contract for the sale of land) is a good example of a standard form contract.

Standard form contracts are often criticised. They are usually drawn up by the party with the most bargaining power, and they may deprive the other party of real agreement in that there is little choice as to most of the contents – standard form contracts are usually presented on a 'take it or leave it' basis.

While not all of them are unfair, it is important to remember that they may be used to impose disadvantageous conditions on the 'weaker' of the parties.

This is not always the case. Standard form contracts may have some advantages when they are drawn up by a body like the governing body of a sport, which has the interests of both club or association and player in mind. The use of a standard form contract may remove the need to negotiate every minor issue, so that time and attention may be focused on matters of importance or disagreement.[42]

Competition laws

Other provisions, notably those in the Commonwealth *Trade Practices Act*, a law designed to foster competition in the marketplace, may be used to challenge the rules or conduct of sporting organisations.

Application of the provisions of the Act to the ARL–Super League dispute emphasised the extent to which commercial law is now an integral part of the sporting equation. Claims by one side or the other in that case involve issues of anti-competitive arangements (s.45) and misuse of market power (s.46).[43]

Ultimately the Full Federal Court found that 'commitment and loyalty' agreements signed by all ARL clubs contained exclusionary provisions prohibited by the *Trade Practices Act* (s.4D). An exclusionary provision is an arrangement between competitors that has the purpose of restricting or limiting the supply of goods or services to, or acquisition of goods or services from, particular persons or classes of persons. The clubs met with the ARL to discuss the Super League proposal and signed agreements designed to prevent any of the clubs from choosing to participate in a rival competition. The Full Court was prepared to find an arrangement between all the clubs even though each of them only signed an agreement with the ARL.[44]

The same provision was used by the South Sydney Rugby League Club to address its removal from the National Rugby League (NRL) competition. After the dispute between Super League and the ARL was settled, the parties agreed to create a unified competition that would have 14 teams in 2000. Only teams that satisfied certain criteria would be included. South Sydney was excluded, and claimed that there was an arrangement between News Limited, the corporation behind the Super League, and the NRL that had the purpose of excluding particular persons or classes of persons. The High Court ultimately found that there was no exclusionary provision because there was no exclusionary purpose by the parties, and the provision was not directed at particular persons or classes of person.[45]

Other provisions in the *Trade Practices Act* prohibit price fixing, resale price maintenance (attempting to specify a minimum price for the on-supply of goods or services) and secondary boycotts. In 1994 the Trade Practices Commissioner issued a press release stating that in the previous 12 months there had been 'a significant number' of trade practices matters 'involving sport-related instances of resale price maintenance, price fixing and boycotts', citing as examples the boycott of a new competitor by a sports trophy supplier and the stipulation by a lawn bowls supplier to retail outlets that lawn bowls could not be sold below a specified price. The commissioner reminded the sport industry that maximum penalties under the *Trade Practices Act* at that time were $10 million for corporations and $500 000 for individuals. The commissioner stated: 'Sport is a big industry in Australia and will be monitored assiduously by the Commission'.[46]

In another use of the *Trade Practices Act*, an applicant for membership of the Indoor Cricket Federation (NSW), whose centre was only three to five kilometres from that of an existing member, complained and sought an injunction when entry was deferred by the federation, which had previously said that this proximity would not affect any membership application. The judge found that the federation was acting in trade or commerce even though it was an association (not a corporation), which was essential to the application of section 52 of the *Trade Practices Act*, and that misleading conduct had occurred.[47]

The *Trade Practices Act* also prohibits *exclusive dealing*, which is dealing with another party on the basis of a nominated condition that reduces competition. For example, customer and territorial restrictions in licensing and sponsorship agreements may fall within the ambit of section 47 of the Act if they have the purpose, effect or likely effect of substantially lessening competition. Fila, a sportswear company licensed to distribute AFL products, introduced a selective distribution policy which meant in effect that Fila refused to supply retailers who stocked the products of other AFL product licensees. This conduct fell within the provision. Between the time of the conduct and the hearing Fila appointed administrators and withdrew its defence. A penalty of $3 million was imposed in view of the deliberate nature of the conduct, the fact that it was implemented by the managing director and the fact that the company was warned by the AFL that there could be a problem with the policy. The conduct was also a misuse of the company's market power in the market for licensed apparel for each AFL team.[48]

Other parts of the exclusive dealing provisions of the *Trade Practices Act*[49] prohibit a person from dealing with another on condition that the goods or services of a third party are also acquired (or refusing to deal without acceptance of such a condition). This type of conduct is called *third line forcing,* and it is currently prohibited regardless of its purpose or effect. Action was taken against the Australian Rugby Union (ARU) by a company engaged in corporate hospitality when the ARU refused to supply tickets to it for corporate hospitality off-site because it was not an ARU-appointed operator. The company argued that the ARU refused to supply admission to the stadium for its customers because they had not agreed to acquire a corporate hospitality package from IMG, the authorised provider. The claim was dismissed in this case, but it shows the broad reach of the provisions.[50]

Selection

The development of selection policies and the disputes that arise from their application raise interesting practical and philosophical questions, such as:

- Is participation in events such as the Olympics a right or a privilege?
- Can athlete selection be totally objective?
- What say should the athlete have in the process?

Ultimately the selection process is aimed at arriving at the best participant or team to represent the sport, but this factor is often lost in a complex process and is in any event often a very subjective determination.

Selection disputes generally revolve around the agreement or understanding between a sport and its athletes about what athletes need to do to be eligible for selection, although such agreements can be attacked on grounds relating to such matters as discrimination and restraint of trade.

The selection policy of a sport may create a contract between a sport and its athletes. Other legal areas may also be relevant, depending on the way in which the criteria are developed and applied. Whether the courts will become involved in selection issues will depend on questions such as whether the parties intended to create a legal relationship (and hence whether there is a contract) and whether the court overcomes its disinclination to become involved in a domestic sporting matter. Issues such as the potential for financial gain and the nature of the event will influence the decision.

Is there a contract?

Depending on how selection criteria are drafted, there may be no contract between the parties. This was the situation in *Forbes v Australian Yachting Federation*,[51] which involved the selection of a yachting team for the 1996 Olympics. The Australian Yachting Federation had formulated detailed selection processes, but changed these in the course of the lead-up to selection. The process depended on team results, but one team split up and there was contention about the way in which the team results could be used by the individuals concerned. The policy was silent on this issue. The court found on the facts that there was no contract between the parties because there was no true offer and acceptance, and the fact that the criteria expressly provided for alteration indicated that there was no intention to create legal relations. The misleading or deceptive conduct provisions of the *Trade*

Practices Act and the NSW *Fair Trading Act* did not apply because the federation was not a trading financial corporation and the representations were not made in trade or commerce.

Santow J did accept that the federation had made representations on which athletes had relied, and that it must have known that they would do so. The plaintiffs had wasted money in following the superseded criteria, and his Honour ordered compensation on the basis of *equitable estoppel*.[52] The nomination of the other athletes was, however, upheld. This case is an example of a situation where there was some legal remedy despite the absence of a contract.

The case also provides a good example of the tension between the need to provide a clear indication to participants of the criteria to be used and the risk arising from an organisation's failure to provide for all eventualities and some reasonable flexibility.

Striking a balance

The tension between the need for certainty and the need to provide for unforeseen events was highlighted in 2004 by Ian Thorpe's failure at the selection trials to qualify for the 400 metres freestyle at the Athens Olympics. Thorpe was the current Olympic champion, but he false started at the selection trials and thus did not qualify to defend his title. The selection criteria of Australian Swimming contained no discretion to cover those circumstances. It was only because of the generous withdrawal of fellow athlete Craig Stevens, who had qualified, that Thorpe was able to (successfully) defend this title.

The challenge in formulating selection criteria is finding a balance between certainty for the athletes and discretion in the sport to nominate the athlete likely to perform best in the event regardless of the criteria. The appropriate mix of subjective and objective criteria often depends on the nature of the sport and whether or not it is a team or individual selection. Issues such as personality and ability mix are critical to selecting a workable and effective team.

Improving selection processes

Following cases like the Forbes' case, which was financially disastrous for the Australian Yachting Federation at the time despite its victory on most legal points, administrators sought to make criteria more objective and certain, and this approach was implemented leading into the 2000 Olympics. The AOC formulated a standard approach to selection criteria and assisted Olympic sports with selection processes with a view to fairness and certainty for athletes and organisations.

The AOC selection document provided a careful process involving an internal appeal mechanism followed by appeal to CAS, in combination with a clause that purported to remove the ability of the court system to hear selection appeals. The chief executive of the AOC, John Coates, encouraged '...anyone who feels the criteria that they have been training and participating towards hasn't been followed to pursue their rights.'[53] This approach led to a situation where appeals by non-selected athletes prior to the Sydney Olympics appeared to be out of control. Press reports of the selection disputes were emotive.[54]

The actual statistics for the period are as follows: 638 athletes were selected for the Sydney Olympics. There were 42 appeals from original selections to internal sport tribunals, and 12 further appeals to CAS. Only three appeals were ultimately upheld by CAS. In retrospect, although the appeals took up time and cost money, the overall number was small relative to selections as a whole, and in most cases the original decision of selectors was upheld.

During this time the jurisdiction of CAS under the process and the athlete's agreement was confirmed in *Sullivan v Raguz*.[55] It is likely that a very detailed and fair process was instituted by the AOC both to improve certainty for both athletes and sports, and to increase the likelihood of upholding exclusive CAS jurisdiction. Exclusive CAS jurisdiction is advantageous in terms of speed and cost.

Following the Sydney Olympics the AOC commissioned a report canvassing options for reducing the number of disputes involving selection.[56] The Australian and New Zealand Sports Law Association (ANZSLA) in conjunction with the ASC issued guidelines for selection in 2002 aimed at certainty and consistency. The guidelines emphasised proper communication of selection policies to athletes, consideration and counselling for those not selected and seeking input from experts before problems arise.[57]

Selection for the Olympics is governed by the AOC's Olympic Team Selection By-Law. The by-law provides a detailed process under which the National Federation notifies first a shadow team, then a final team, to the AOC, choosing the athletes in accordance with nomination criteria previously made known to them. The AOC applies selection criteria, and has the ultimate right of selection. Once an athlete is named by the AOC, a standard form Olympic Team Membership Agreement is signed.

There were few selection disputes leading up to the Athens Olympics, suggesting that the processes have been significantly improved.

Chapter 5

Sports sponsorship and sporting reputation

Increased media and marketing interest in sport has seen continued growth in the number of sponsorships, both of sports and of individuals involved in them. Events such as the Sydney Olympics and the Rugby World Cup underlined the commitment of business to this form of promotion.

Sponsorship agreements sometimes involve the use of sportspeople or a team or sport in promotional advertising. Sponsorship may involve the mere wearing of the sponsor's clothing or the use of labelled equipment as a statement in itself about the product quality.

The money available to athletes under sponsorship arrangements is, in most sports, far more than they can earn through participation in the game. Athletes are generally enthusiastic about promoting themselves, and seek to exploit their fame and reputation to the maximum. Most sporting organisations rely on their ability to present sponsors with a number of marketable participants so as to maximise sponsorship opportunities.

The importance of high profile athletes to business is clear. A good example of a concrete advantage to a product is the sale of 50 000 mobile phones by Vodafone Live! in the three weeks after the Manchester United player David Beckham began endorsing the product.[1]

Every citizen has a right to protect name and reputation. The high degree of public interest in sport and its participants means that those involved in sport, as individuals, teams or organisations, often need protection for their names and reputations. Sportspeople have often resorted to the law where a name has been used in an unauthorised or misleading way, or where a slur has been cast on a reputation.

The areas of law discussed below apply not only to individuals, but also to a sport itself. If, for example, a newspaper were to suggest that all participants in a particular sport were drunks, or that a sport was unduly violent, the reputation of that sport might be affected. The Canterbury Bulldogs Rugby League Football Club reportedly lost sponsorship deals valued at some $1.3 million with potential sponsors including retail chain Bing Lee and Bluescope Steel following rape allegations about several players. Ultimately no charges were laid.[2] If a newspaper article were to suggest that a sporting event was 'fixed', it might reflect on the players, the sport itself and its officials. Sports and individuals involved in allegations of match fixing have been acutely aware of the potential for reputation and sponsorship disaster. These issues have generally been treated promptly and seriously by sporting organisations.[3]

While the law can be used to protect those involved in sport, sportspeople must also be aware that they have obligations in relation to advertising and endorsements with which they are involved. These obligations are in addition to those which might be expressly written into their contract.

The ability to take legal proceedings may depend on whether the potential applicant has 'legal personality'.[4] None of the remedies discussed below is restricted to individuals, although defamation proceedings die with a natural person, and they are difficult for organisations. There are, however, limits on the extent to which a 'right of personality' can be protected under Australian law, and these are discussed below.

Types of sponsorship arrangement

The sponsorship of sport takes many forms. Those sponsoring a sport or an athlete may do so for various reasons, and the nature of any arrangement between the parties will differ according to its purpose.

The most basic form of sponsorship might involve a gift of money or equipment to a struggling association or a particular individual. This type of arrangement involves a kind of patronage. The gift of a new tennis net to the local school by a parent or a manufacturer is merely an act of generosity and would generally imply no obligations on the students except perhaps to enjoy its use, unless there was some additional understanding between the parties.

Even the next small step up from this uncomplicated type of arrangement, however, might see some obligations implied on each party. A promising young surfer given a free wetsuit or surfboard by a local manufacturer would usually agree in return to wear the suit or use the surfboard in local competitions. The surfer would thus provide the manufacturer with a form of free advertising for the product as the result of an informal agreement that is to both parties' advantage.

A similar type of arrangement might be the supply of jumpers or uniforms to a junior soccer or netball team by a local retailer on condition that they are emblazoned with the retailer's name. Even in the absence of a formal agreement, one might assume that if the behaviour of the players is not reasonable and brings the sponsor's reputation into disrepute, the arrangement would be terminated.

The formal sponsorship contract

More complicated types of sponsorship agreement involve a written contract between the sponsor and the organisation, team or individual involved. A sponsorship agreement may involve a particular event, or be for a particular time period. It has been stated that the sponsorship of sport has the following dimensions:
- It provides a captive audience.
- It allows continuous involvement.
- It provides entertainment value.
- It ensures audience participation.
- It provides opportunities for promotional activities as well as direct marketing programs.[5]

Seen in this light, the advantages of sports sponsorship to the sponsor are obvious. The general advantages to those being sponsored are also clear. While the details will vary according to the market pull of the individual or sport concerned, it must be assumed that no-one would enter into such an arrangement unless it involved some advantage.

A sponsorship agreement is a form of contract, and as such it is governed by the laws of contract that were discussed in chapter 4. Some other points of importance will be mentioned here.

A sponsorship contract should be drafted clearly, setting out the rights and obligations of the parties. Both the length of time that the agreement will operate (the *term*) and any amount of money involved should be stated clearly.

Sportspersons contemplating individual sponsorship agreements should make sure that these do not conflict with their association or club rules and are not inconsistent with any written players' contracts that they have.[6]

Sporting organisations looking at particular sponsorship agreements should ensure that the agreement does not remove major aspects of control from their organisation. The substitution of the judgment of a commercial body for that of a body formed for the advancement of a particular sport may not be a positive move. At the 1984 Olympics, for example, the marathon was run to coincide with the 'prime time' closing ceremony. Athletes complained about the timing of the event, arguing that it was not the best time of the day for it to be run. Athletes finishing the race after a certain time were not allowed to finish in the stadium, but had a different finishing line so that proceedings would not be disrupted.

Some of the issues that should be considered for inclusion in a sponsorship contract include territory, category exclusivity, signage, broadcast rights, intellectual property licences, virtual advertising and the protections that can be included against ambush marketing and sponsorship conflicts.[7]

Sponsorship conflicts

The nature of sport in this country means that the potential for conflict over sponsorship is great. Sport exists at individual, club, district, state, national and international levels. Each group in the hierarchy seeks to maximise its sponsorship opportunities, but must coexist with the others; each attempts to carve out its own sponsorship territory and to establish its marketability. These relationships can be tricky, with all parties jockeying for positional power and seeking to control their operations and their own sponsorship arrangements. The fact that each organisation has its own rules, and perhaps a standard form employment contract with restrictions on sponsorship, complicates life for all involved.

Rules and standard form contracts generally impose restrictions on the extent to which players and teams can engage sponsors. Contract law governs the dealings between them, and it can be extremely complicated to determine the conflicting obligations of each party. Issues of restraint of trade may arise if restrictions imposed on the right of an individual to contract are unreasonable in the circumstances.

The rules of the IOC complicate the issues for Olympic sports and competitors, with restrictions such as those which provide that competitors may not allow their names to be used during the period of the Olympics in a context that associates the person with the Olympics. Olympic sponsorship potential is maximised for the IOC during that

period, and the sponsors of organisations and individuals are con-
strained lest athletes face IOC sanctions. Speedo is a major sponsor of
Australian Swimming, but the AOC gave Ian Thorpe and two other
athletes permission to wear the body suit of other manufacturers in the
Olympics on the basis of its affect on their swimming performance.[8]

There have been numerous examples in the press of situations
where marketing and sponsorship conflicts have arisen in major sports
or in connection with prominent participants. Vodafone sponsored
the ARU team for a number of years. The 2003 Rugby World Cup,
however, was sponsored by Telstra, and World Cup games were held
at Telstra Stadium. Following the World Cup, Vodafone decided not
to renew its sponsorship. A venue change for the 2004 NRL semi-final
between the Broncos and the Cowboys to North Queensland was
achieved only after cooperation between venues and conflicting sponsors. In 1994, Commonwealth Games chief Arthur Tunstall reportedly threatened to send athlete Jane Flemming and swimmer Keiran
Perkins home from the Commonwealth Games if alleged ambush marketing of the Games' sponsors continued.[9] A dispute arose in 1994
between Australian Swimming and a number of prominent Australian
swimmers over the proposed signing of the swimmers to a four-year
$1.2 million contract in conjunction with one of Australian Swim-
ming's existing sponsors, Uncle Toby's. Swimmers sought more flexibility in their sponsorship arrangements. Having the 160 swimmers
signed up, however, particularly the high-profile team members, was
important to the sport's financial preparation for the 1996 Olympics.
Ultimately the Uncle Toby's sponsorship was not renewed.[10] Uncle
Toby's subsequently organised its own surf Ironman Series, presumably in an attempt to maintain greater control over the rights to a water
sport.

Conflict resolution

Conflicts in situations of this kind are resolved in many ways, but resolution is generally heavily influenced by the bargaining power of the
parties involved. It is clear that concessions are more readily made for
high-profile athletes. Athletes generally try to accommodate the
system where a high-profile event is involved. The sponsors of individual participants generally concede that an athlete's failure to
achieve Olympic selection, for example, will not result in any residual
value for that sponsor. The sponsorship contract will only fulfil its
potential from a sponsor's point of view if the athlete in question continues to perform at the highest level.[11]

Restrictions on tobacco and alcohol advertising

Restrictions on the advertising of cigarettes, tobacco and alcohol on radio and television may curtail or limit sponsorship arrangements with their suppliers.

Restrictions on advertising material relating to cigarettes and tobacco have existed in Australia for many years. A range of legislation applies to various aspects of the tobacco industry. Some states restrict the age at which consumers may purchase cigarettes. Radio, television and print advertisements for cigarettes or other tobacco products are prohibited under the Commonwealth *Tobacco Advertising Prohibition Act 1992*, which operates alongside state legislation but overrules state Acts if there is any inconsistency.[12]

Accidental or incidental accompaniment of broadcasts is allowable as long as the broadcaster does not receive direct or indirect benefit from the broadcast.[13]

The traditional tobacco company sponsorship of sporting events, with the mention of company names, the display of logos, the playing of music associated with the company and half-time entertainment aimed at highlighting aspects of sponsorship, has been considered by the Australian Broadcasting Tribunal and the Federal Court. The question of whether material constitutes advertising will be assessed by the court in all the circumstances.[14]

The prohibition on tobacco advertising is very broad due to the expansive definition of 'advertisement'.[15] An 'acknowledgment of assistance or support', however, is allowable.[16] Sponsorship itself is not prohibited, but the strict regulations limit the benefits usually associated with sponsoring.

Some exceptions were traditionally made for events of international significance, or where an event would otherwise be lost to Australia. In the past, notices under the provisions allowing these exceptions have been published for events such as the Adelaide Grand Prix and the *One Australia* Challenge for the Americas Cup. Conditions may be imposed by the minister.[17] Publication (not including broadcasting) of tobacco advertisements in connection with a sporting or cultural event is allowed subject to ministerial discretion until 2006. No application can be made for a new event except in very limited circumstances.

Penalties for breaches of these prohibitions are high.

Breweries account for the sponsorship of many major sporting events in the Australian calendar. There are various program standards (in the form of mandatory Codes of Practice) which may impact on the advertising of alcoholic products.[18] There are also relevant voluntary Codes of Practice. The Commercial Television Industry Code of Practice, for example, provides that a direct advertisement for an alcoholic drink may only be broadcast during certain adult classification periods and accompanying live sporting events during weekends or public holidays. Under the code, a program sponsorship announcement on behalf of a brewing company or other liquor industry company that does not directly promote the purchase or use of an alcoholic product is not, however, a direct advertisement for an alcoholic drink.[19]

The use of sportspeople in advertising

The popularity and standing of sportspeople in the community at large means that they are not only extremely newsworthy, but also particularly attractive as a means of endorsing or creating publicity for a product. This attractiveness is enhanced by the apolitical, clean-cut, uncomplicated image of the average sports star. The pursuit of excellence in sport is generally seen by marketers as a type of 'wholesome endeavour'. The association of a product with symbols of wholesome excellence is seen by marketers to be extremely positive.

Where companies sponsor sports, participants are often involved in the sponsor's advertising. Cricketers were involved in advertisements for Mercantile Mutual when it sponsored the Mercantile Mutual Cup. Esso used the Australian netball team in its advertising when it was a sponsor. At the same time, individual sportspeople may have sponsors independent of their team, and this is generally acceptable under team contracts if the individual sponsor does not conflict with a team sponsor. Former Australian Rugby League captain Brad Fittler had an individual sponsorship with Aussie Home Loans.

Aside from this distinction there are different categories of sporting endorsement, with different implications for those involved. Endorsements are sought for products that may be used in the sport for which the participant has become famous. If Lleyton Hewitt is the number one tennis player in the world, people will want to buy the Lleyton Hewitt tennis racquet, or the racquet that Lleyton himself uses. If Lleyton says 'I always wear Brand X tennis shoes because they help my game', many people will take him at his word and attribute part of his success to the shoes. A Steve Waugh cricket set or cricket game obviously suggests that Steve Waugh thinks it is good. Waugh, being a former international cricketer, is assumed to know a good cricketing product when he sees it. Running shoes advertised by Olympic Gold medallist Cathy Freeman would also fall into this category.

Sportspeople are also used simply to attract attention to a product through their popularity – this type of advertising is called 'character merchandising'. Swimmers Ian Thorpe and Grant Hackett have appeared in advertisements for a breakfast cereal, as has the Australian Rugby Union team, the Wallabies. The Sydney Roosters Rugby League team have appeared in advertisements for shampoo.

The marketing advantage that flows from the endorsement of a product by a sporting personality, and the amounts of money involved in such practices, may lead to disputes between the parties. The potential advantage from the use of a famous name may even lead to unauthorised use of that name.

These situations apply not only to sports competitors, but to coaches, referees and officials, depending on their level of public exposure, or, in the case of a newsworthy item, on the type of item and the degree of public interest in the sport involved.

Coaches, players and officials have rights to use and to protect their names and reputations at law. They also have an obligation to make only truthful statements when endorsing products. In particular, sportspeople endorsing goods in an area in which they are expert should make sure that they make only truthful statements. A statement by Lleyton Hewitt that he always used a particular brand of tennis racquet because it was the best, or by Cathy Freeman that she considered brand X running shoes the best for marathons, would carry great weight in the minds of consumers of those products.

'Right of personality'

Australian law does not provide the comprehensive legal 'right of personality' that exists in the US,[20] where it helps sportspeople protect their names and reputations. That law, which prohibits the use of another's identity for commercial advantage without permission, has been used to protect Bette Midler in relation to her distinctive voice,[21] Tom Waits in relation to his voice,[22] a television hostess from the use of a lookalike robot,[23] and a well-known basketball player from the use of his former name.[24]

Australian athletes depend on a combination of laws to protect their rights in situations of this kind.

The Trade Practices Act

The *Trade Practices Act* may be used by consumers or by those selling goods to prevent unfair practices in the marketplace. One part of it is specifically aimed at protecting consumers. While some of the sections are targeted at certain types of unfair practices, more general sections are aimed at preventing the use of misleading statements or unfair conduct in advertising and in other transactions. The Australian Constitution imposes some limits on the application of the *Trade Practices Act*. The states, however, have enacted mirror fair trading legislation.[25]

One of the reasons the *Trade Practices Act* is so useful is that people other than consumers are entitled to bring actions for breach of the Act if consumers are likely to be affected. This is because the Act states that 'any other person' may take action, and the courts have read this to mean exactly what it says.[26] Trade competitors often take action to stop their rivals making untrue or misleading claims about a product, which benefits both consumers and themselves. Consumers may bring actions if they have been misled; affected sportspeople may bring actions to prevent consumers being misled; competitors of those advertising sporting products or using sports personalities for endorsements may bring actions to prevent consumers being misled.

Section 52 of the Act is the one most relied upon in this area. It prohibits a corporation 'in trade or commerce' from 'engaging in conduct which is misleading or deceptive or is likely to mislead or deceive'. If the court finds that the section is breached, it may grant an injunction to prevent any future breach. If anyone suffers loss or damage as a result of behaviour that breaches the section, damages may be awarded in compensation. The court may make orders for corrective advertising – the publication of advertising that corrects an earlier false impression.[27]

The courts have found that 'mislead' in section 52 means 'lead into error'.[28] Conduct that leads people into error or is likely to do so, therefore, falls within the meaning of the section. 'Conduct' covers a very wide area of behaviours.[29] Whether conduct is misleading is assessed by the court hearing the case, taking into account its effect on the people who would be its target audience – those likely to see it.[30]

Section 53 of the Act prohibits the making of representations that are misleading or false. The word 'representation' includes words and other things that convey an impression to those who see them. These things might be photographs, illustrations or diagrams. Separate parts of the section are aimed at particular types of false or misleading representation. Representations suggesting that goods or services have sponsorship or approval that they do not have, for example, are prohibited by section 53(d), which is particularly relevant in this context. This would include representation that an athlete or organisation is connected with a product, service or other organisation when it is not.

Breaches of section 53 constitute criminal offences, punishable by fines. By contrast, people found to have breached section 52 have committed a civil offence, and cannot be fined. The difference is reflected in the standard of proof required for a conviction (see chapter 1). As section 52 breaches are subject to a lesser standard they are easier to prove, and actions under section 52 are far more common than actions under section 53. If the Australian Competition and Consumer Commission takes action under the Act to punish someone who is in breach of its provisions, it will often seek a penalty for a breach of section 53.

A consideration of some section 52 and 53 cases involving sport will show how wide the scope of the sections is, and how useful they may be to both fans and those seeking to protect themselves.

'Real' cricket

Australian sports fans may remember the situation which became known as the 'cricket war'. A company involving Sydney businessman Kerry Packer organised a series of cricket matches, and contracted with many players who were playing traditional test match cricket for Australia and other countries at that time. The breakaway 'World Series Cricket' group described the matches in advertisements as 'Super Tests' played under 'Test Match conditions'. Accompanying pictures showed players in action for their various countries.

Robert Parish, the chairman of the Australian Cricket Board at the time, sought an injunction claiming that the advertisements were likely to mislead readers into thinking that the games in question were organised by the Australian Cricket Board. The court found that the public would be likely to be misled (s. 52) and that the advertisement did represent the matches as having characteristics which they did not have (s. 53). An injunction was granted to prevent future advertisements from being worded in the same way.[31]

'Authentic' helmets

A manufacturer sold cricket helmets in a box that featured the words 'test match' and pictures of two well-known cricketers wearing helmets; the boxes also proclaimed that the helmets were 'endorsed by international superstars'. The helmets featured in the pictures were those of another company. The second company complained that the wording on the box, coupled with the pictures, suggested that the helmet in the box was worn by test cricketers, when it was not. Purchasers might buy the helmet in the box thinking that it was the one manufactured by the second company, which was not the case. The court agreed, and orders were made preventing the sale of the helmet in that type of box, and infringement of the registered design of the manufacturer bringing the action.[32]

Status of a boxing match

The tickets for a boxing match in Brisbane advertised the fight as a 'Heavyweight Boxing Championship of Aust'. Tony Mundine, at the time recognised by the Australian Boxing Federation as Professional Heavyweight Champion of Australia, took proceedings against the promoters. Mundine was not involved in the match, and he sought orders from the court preventing its advertisement in those terms. The court agreed with Mundine, and made orders preventing the bout from being advertised in that way.[33]

Champs meet every night

A sports promoter and its advertising agency were fined for an advertisement appearing in a newspaper for the 'Rio International Challenge' tennis tournament. The advertisement read 'Lendl v McEnroe – Nightly at 7.30', when in fact the tournament was a round-robin event and it was only ever envisaged that the two players would meet once. The court found that the representations were clearly of importance to those proposing to attend the tournament, and fined the agency $4600 and the promoter $2000 for breach of section 53(aa) of the *Trade Practices Act* (relating to misrepresentations in relation to the standard or grade of services).[34]

Swimming pool endorsement

Tracey Wickham, a former world record-holding distance swimmer, complained that a pool company which she had originally authorised to use her name and photographs for promotional purposes was trading under the name 'Tracey Wickham Pools', and was doing so after the termination of their agreement. The court found that this was the case, and that the use of her name also misrepresented that the company had her continuing approval.[35]

'Backstabbing' team members

In a case that went to court but never went on to a full hearing, Kim Hughes, a former Australian cricket captain, took action against a newspaper claiming that its articles were defamatory and also in breach of section 52 of the *Trade Practices Act*. The articles were headed 'Mutinous elements threaten to destroy Australian cricket' and 'A team divided – gallows await yesterdays heroes' and included a cartoon caricature of Hughes, then captain, playing cricket with a knife through his back. The court found that this type of matter could fall within the Act, but did not decide whether it actually did in this case.[36]

Use of champion in unauthorised photograph

Gary Honey, a former Commonwealth champion long jumper who had represented Australia many times, took action in relation to an unauthorised use of his photograph. A photograph of Honey competing in the Commonwealth Games was used without his permission on a poster by Australian Airlines, and distributed free of charge in schools. His name was placed on the bottom of the poster. Permission was granted by the photographer under the *Copyright Act* as the creator of the photograph. A non-profit religious group approached the airline and was given permission to use the photograph on one of its publications. Gary Honey took action based on misleading conduct and passing off but failed; the judge found that the essential aspect of the photograph supported participation and excellence in sport and nothing more, and did not warrant the finding of approval, sponsorship or endorsement. The Commonwealth Games being an amateur competition, it was not easy for the public to draw the conclusion that there was some kind of commercial connection between the parties.[37]

Misrepresentation of sponsorship or connection

Swimmer Keiran Perkins, through his management company, complained about a Telstra insert in a Brisbane newspaper at the time of carrier preselection. The insert showed Perkins beside a pool wearing a cap with a Telstra logo. Perkins argued that the advertisement indicated that he supported Telstra in the ballot. Telstra had a sponsorship agreement with Australian Swimming to sponsor the Telstra Dolphins swimming team, but Perkins was not a member of the team. The Court of Appeal found that the conduct was misleading because it implied Perkins' consent and that he supported Telstra in the preselection. The court concluded that the conduct reduced Perkins' ability to commercially exploit his reputation.[38]

Goods with same name

The Nike sporting goods company had registered a Nike trade mark in Australia for footwear and clothing while a Spanish company had registered a Nike trade mark for cosmetics and toiletries. The sporting goods company claimed that this constituted misleading conduct. Evidence that Adidas, another major manufacturer of sporting products, had introduced fragrances that were often placed side-by-side with the Nike products proved to be particularly important. The High Court agreed with the trial judge that placing 'Nike Sport Fragrance' in the same area in pharmacies was likely to deceive members of the public into believing that the Nike fragrance was in some way promoted or distributed by the sporting goods company, or with its consent or approval.[39]

'Showdown' matches

South Australian Brewing sponsored both the Adelaide Football Club and the Port Adelaide Football Club, which competed in the AFL competition. Matches between the two clubs were commonly referred to as 'Showdown' matches, and South Australian Brewing promoted Showdown 7, 9 and 10 in conjunction with its West End beer. It was the registered owner of the trademark 'Showdown' in respect of sports events, and had exclusive pourage rights at the ground where the matches took place.

Carlton & United Breweries (CUB) ran competitions in connection with three of the Showdown matches as part of its promotion of its Victoria Bitter beer. Winners won tickets to the games in a special box licensed to CUB. CUB had a non-exclusive licence to use AFL intellectual property, including the logos and playing apparel of the two South Australian clubs, for promotional and advertising purposes. It also had sponsorship agreements with both captains, and used them in its advertising.

South Australian Brewing alleged that CUB had infringed its trademark, passed off its own goods and services as those of South Australian Brewing, and falsely represented that there were various associations between CUB, Victoria Bitter beer and the Showdown matches. It also alleged that CUB beer was available at the ground.

The court found that the 'head to head' picture of the two captains constituted representations that CUB was a sponsor of the two clubs, and that the clubs had authorised its promotion. This was despite the contractual arrangements, which could not override section 52. CUB was ordered to stop that part of the promotion.[40]

Website Olympic representations

The Seven Network complained that News Limited engaged in misleading or deceptive conduct and misrepresentations on websites that used the words 'Athens Olympics', a representation of the Olympic torch and a banner and countdown to the Games in close proximity to its names and business-related logos. Seven argued that the use constituted representations that News Limited was authorised to broadcast the Olympics, or sponsored the Athens Games or those involved in it, or that the websites were approved. Other broadcasters advertised the Olympics in similar ways. Ultimately the court found that the *Trade Practices Act* was not contravened in the circumstances.[41]

Olympic rings

Telecom New Zealand published an advertisement featuring the word 'Ring' five times, positioned as the Olympic rings and in similar colours. Other wording indicated that with Telecom mobile a person could take their phone to the Olympics. The New Zealand Olympic Committee claimed that the advertisement breached provisions in the *Fair Trading Act* because it suggested a connection or association between the company and the Olympic movement. The court found that the average reader of the advertisement would not be misled.[42]

Passing off

An action for *passing off*, at common law, may prevent the use of one's name or some other factor that misleads the public by suggesting that, for example, goods being sold are those of another or are associated with that person. Calling your restaurant 'Greg Norman's Steakhouse' or your shop 'Pat Cash's Sports Store' when the business has no connection with the named person would be passing off. In these circumstances, the person whose name or reputation had been used could apply for an injunction to prevent further use and sue for any loss or damage suffered if there was an intention to deceive.[43]

To prove passing off it must be shown that 'goodwill' exists in the business, that the defendant has made a misrepresentation that there is a connection between it or its goods and the plaintiff or the plaintiff's business, and that the plaintiff's business has suffered or is likely to suffer damage as a result of that misrepresentation, usually by damage to reputation or loss of customers.

Formula One driver Eddie Irvine, for example, was successful in a claim against a radio station for using his likeness to promote it when there was no connection between them (in circumstances somewhat similar to those of the Keiran Perkins case discussed on page 67).[44]

An action for the tort of passing off is somewhat similar to some types of section 52 case. The situations of Tracey Wickham and Tony Mundine, mentioned earlier, might also be actionable under passing off law. The two types of action are similar in some applications but not completely interchangeable. Section 52, for example, will only apply if there is the actual possibility of deception of consumers, and not just confusion as to the source of two similar products or the degree of connection between them. It may, however, be invoked by *anyone at all*, as long as the activity complained of has the capacity to mislead or deceive members of the public.

The remedies available for passing off should also be compared with those available for breaches of section 52 of the *Trade Practices Act*. They are similar, but the right to injunction and the type of orders that might be made are narrower for passing off. 'Account of profits' is available for passing off.

Ambush marketing

Ambush marketing involves a situation where a sponsor of an organisation or event finds that its advertising advantage has been diluted by some action of a major competitor, often undertaken at far less expense. Not only do ambush marketers diminish the advantage that the sponsor has paid to establish, but they also hitch a free ride on the drawing power of successful organisations and events in that they are able to establish an association with them without cost. They contribute nothing to the overall good of the organisation or event, but are advantaged because it has taken place.

There are no fixed categories of conduct that constitute ambush marketing, but examples of situations that might fall within the description are:

- showing conflicting advertising material alongside that of a substantial sponsor
- someone who has no real connection with an event cashing in on its popularity by buying advertising time during the broadcast of the event and advertising in a way that implies a connection with it.

The crux of ambush marketing lies in the particular contracts surrounding the event or persons involved. These may be, for example, contracts made between the sponsor and the sport or team, or between the sport and a television station.

Ambush marketing is not in itself unlawful, and ambushes which do not break any law are difficult to combat. Marketers can engage in clever campaigns suggesting that a non-sponsor is somehow connected to an event without breaching any law. Laws such as the *Trade Practices Act* and the Fair Trading Acts of the states prohibit the making of representations that are untrue or that suggest some affiliation, approval or sponsorship that does not exist, but ambush marketing need not involve conduct of this kind. Some of the most successful ambushes are effected with some subtlety merely by positioning, or by the vague implication of a connection. It is very difficult to prevent such ambushes occurring if they are not illegal except by careful planning and control.

A famous ambush involved the use of the slogan 'Remember that to visit Spain you don't need a Visa' by American Express when Visa was a sponsor of the Barcelona Olympics. Other organisations have attempted to gain advantage by engaging in promotions of an 'Olympic' nature around the time of the Olympic Games. The use of the Olympic insignia is governed by the *Olympic Insignia Protection Act 1987*. These campaigns, however, have been cleverly constructed to draw on the reputation of the Olympics without infringing the Act. Where there is no breach of that legislation or the *Trade Practices Act*, there is little to prevent campaigns of this kind.

The AOC regularly acts to protect itself from situations which it considers to involve ambush marketing. For example, it commenced proceedings against Toyota Motor Corporation Australia Limited in 1994 alleging ambush marketing. The AOC claimed that Toyota's advertisements in relation to the Winter Olympics in Lillehammer represented that Toyota had contributed to the funding of the Australian team, was a sponsor of the competitors, and was affiliated with the team, among other complaints. Eventually the dispute was settled by consent and the proceedings discontinued.

In another example of ambush marketing, Peugeot was an official sponsor of the Rugby World Cup, but the official vehicle supplier to the Wallabies ran advertisements showing the team cramming into one of its cars, and the advertisements of competing car manufacturers were aired during broadcasts of rugby matches in a scenario that left people wondering who the official sponsor was.[45]

There is added potential for ambush where broadcast rights are offered in addition to sponsorship. The emergence of new viewing and interactive media platforms, as well as the capacity for virtual advertising, increases the likelihood of ambush in these contexts and

underscores the need for a careful analysis of contractual arrangements to minimise the risks to sponsors.

Ambush marketing can often be prevented by careful drafting and
negotiation of contracts. Once again the negotiating power of a
sporting organisation in this situation will depend on its drawing
power. Some organisations are only too grateful to receive any media
coverage and are unable to make demands of a telecaster, even if it
embarrasses the organisation in a sponsorship sense. For an organisation in this position, it will be a question of determining the lesser of
two evils. Where an organisation has leverage, however, it should
ensure that difficulties relating to ambush marketing never occur.[46]

Protecting Olympic symbols

Protecting the properties of an organisation or an event reduces the
capacity for ambush marketing.

The *Olympic Insignia Protection Act* gives the AOC control of the
use in Australia of the Olympic rings symbol, certain terms such as
'Olympic' and the Olympic motto, and nominated Olympic designs.
The purpose of the Act is to allow the AOC to make maximum use of
symbols associated with the Games for the purpose of fundraising for
participation in the Games through the licensing of some of the designs
and the symbol. The Act provides both copyright and design protection in respect of specified Olympic properties. Various provisions
relating to court proceedings make it simpler for the AOC or a licensee
of any of these properties to take legal action.

The Act was amended in 1994 to widen the protection it offers.
Under the amendments, the Olympic torch and flame designs and
other properties are protected for a period of time around each Olympics. Both Australian business names legislation and *Corporations Act*
regulations prevent the use of various Olympic names when people
register businesses or corporation names.

Before the Sydney Olympics, the Commonwealth government
enacted new legislation to prevent ambush marketing and safeguard
sponsorship revenue by protecting words and symbols associated with
the Sydney 2000 Olympic Games and the Paralympic Games. The
Sydney 2000 Games (Indicia and Images) Protection Act 1996 protected
additional words such as 'Sydney Games', 'Sydney 2000' and many
other combinations, including the general catch-all

> any visual or aural representation that, to a reasonable person, in the
> circumstances of the presentation would suggest a connection with
> the Sydney 2000 Olympic Games or Sydney 2000 Paralympic Games.

Similar protections have been put in place for the Melbourne Commonwealth Games in 2006.[47]

Similar Victorian legislation protects defined 'Grand Prix insignia', including words such as Grand Prix and Formula One that suggest association with the Grand Prix events run in Victoria. Penalties are up to $100 000 for a breach, with a power to seize offending goods.[48]

Intellectual property rights

Successful merchandising depends on the possession of property rights that will enable the prevention of piracy. These rights are conferred by laws that protect registered trade marks, designs and copyright. Licensing of rights, including brands for use in products as diverse as apparel, sporting goods and food, and the development of creative products such as films, computer games and other items can be a significant source of income for the owner of intellectual property.

The increasing incidence of ambush marketing, the push among sports to license their indicia to sponsors and for merchandising, and situations that have arisen in relation to the branding of particular sports show that the creation, development and maintenance of intellectual property has become particularly important in the commercialisation of sport. Golf in the US, for example, registered 8327 trade marks between 1996 and 2001.[49]

Registered trade marks

A trade mark distinguishes the owner's goods or services from those of another, indicates their source, serves as an indication of their quality and represents the goodwill of its owner.[50]

Trade marks are protected in Australia by registration under the *Trade Marks Act 1995*, although unauthorised use of an unregistered trade mark can be prevented if the laws dealing with passing off or misleading or deceptive conduct have been breached. The *Trade Marks Act* refers to trade marks as signs, and defines a sign to include a broad number of symbols and devices as well as words and names.[51] To be registered the mark must be a distinctive badge indicating the origin of goods or services, and must not be merely descriptive. A mark will not be registered if it is deceptively similar to another mark.

A mark is registered in respect of a particular class or classes of goods or services, and is infringed by anyone who, not being the registered proprietor, uses the mark or a similar mark in relation to that class of goods or services. Trade mark registration takes a considerable time, although priority and protection date from the application.

Devices, logos, words and combinations of words and devices can be registered as a mark providing that the mark is 'distinctive' of the goods or services in respect of which registration is sought. Signatures and likenesses have been registered as trade marks.

Once a mark is registered, the proprietor may take action to prevent use by others without permission. A good example involved Arsenal Football Club, which had registered its name, nickname and two devices as trade marks in several classes. Arsenal took action to prevent a supplier of football merchandise items including souvenirs and memorabilia that used the registered trade marks. The court found that the supplier's use of the marks jeopardised the guarantee of origin that the marks conveyed despite the fact that they also were badges of support and loyalty for the team.[52]

Ian Thorpe successfully applied to register the trade mark 'Thorpedo' in relation to sportswear despite the previous registration of the mark 'Torpedoes' by another company that manufactured clothing.[53]

Copyright protection

The *Copyright Act 1968* provides substantial protection for an author of literary works or of drawings, photographs and other depictions that qualify as 'artistic works'.[54] Copyright also exists in relation to sound recordings, films, television broadcasts, sound broadcasts and published editions of literary, dramatic, musical or artistic works. To invoke the *Copyright Act*, work must be first published in Australia and the 'author' must be a citizen or resident of Australia.

Copyright generally exists for the life of the author plus 50 years; copying during this time without the consent of the owner is unlawful. Copyright arises automatically, and there is no system of registration.

In the case of an infringement of copyright, the owner of the copyright (or the owner's exclusive licensee) may obtain an injunction restraining the infringement and either damages or an 'account of profits'. All infringing copies become the property of the copyright owner, who is thus entitled to obtain orders for the delivery of infringing copies not already sold and 'conversion damages' in respect of copies that have been sold.

The Sydney Organising Committee of the Olympic Games (SOCOG) took action against a supporter of animal liberation to prevent the use of a logo depicting a hen in a cage with five eggs resembling the Sydney 2000 Olympic logo on t-shirts and badges used for fundraising for an animal liberation organisation. The court found that the logo infringed the SOCOG copyright and that the offending goods had been sold and not given away as was suggested, and granted injunctions preventing further conduct.[55]

It is important for sporting organisations to understand that to become owners of copyright works such as logos created on their behalf, there must be an assignment of copyright by the commercial artist or company that created the logo.

Copyright is also relevant in relation to broadcast rights. A case involving a popular television program showed the difficulties inherent in re-broadcasting excerpts from someone else's program without consent, including excerpts from sporting events such as a try or a putt even on a news program. Channel Nine alleged that Network Ten infringed its broadcast copyright by recording and re-broadcasting excerpts from its programs and showing them on 'The Panel'. The High Court found that for the purposes of the *Copyright Act*, a 'television broadcast' should be defined as a substantial portion of the relevant program or advertisement (not all the judges agreed). The majority said that to find otherwise would expand the ambit of copyright monopoly beyond the interests that the legislation was intended to protect. The extent to which re-broadcasting can take place now awaits a determination of what is 'substantial' in this context.[56]

Registered designs
Design protection confers a monopoly over the use and exploitation of a registered design. Protection under the *Designs Act 2003*[57] depends on the registration of something that is new and distinctive. Features of shape, pattern or ornament fall within the Act, whether or not they are dictated by the function of the item to which they are applied. Protection lasts for up to ten years, and confers a monopoly that gives the registered owner exclusive right to apply the design to an article or to license others to do so.

Patents
Patents are governed by the *Patents Act 1991*, and give the inventor the exclusive right to exploit an invention for a limited period of time. There are a number of devices and inventions in sport that have been patented or have patent potential. Gear such as improved golf balls and basketballs, for example, can be patented.[58]

Defamation
Individuals who are well-known in the community become newsworthy, regardless of the reason for their fame (or notoriety). Such is

the interest in sport and its participants that there is often great media interest in both the on-field and off-field activities of sport's biggest 'stars'. Celebrity news sells papers. The glamour involved in high-profile sports means high demand for any news about the individuals involved. Positive publicity may be useful to the person involved and to promoters, as it usually increases the drawing power of the competitor. Negative publicity may have the opposite effect.

The effect of unfounded allegations of dishonesty on the reputation of a referee or umpire would be particularly damaging. It was reported several years ago, for example, that actions for damages were pending against particular coaches from the Australian Institute of Sport in relation to the administration of drugs to young institute students. While the coaches allegedly involved may not have been well known outside their own sport, the allegations were widely publicised.[59] Untrue but newsworthy claims about famous sportspeople have resulted in proceedings aimed at true reporting. Defamation proceedings have often been taken by sportspeople who feel that their professional reputation has been injured by media reports about their conduct on or off the field.

An individual is entitled to protection against defamatory material. A defamatory statement at law is 'one which tends to lower a person in the estimation of his fellow men by making them think the less of him'.[60] Defamation generally involves material that satisfies this description in referring to the person who is complaining about it. Defamatory material must have been 'published', which generally involves the communication of the material to at least one other person. Material that may be defamatory includes words, pictures and other representations.

The law of defamation is complicated and is inconsistent throughout the country. Each state and territory has enacted legislation that departs to some extent from the common law.[61] Plans to implement a uniform law of defamation in Australia were originally abandoned when the various state attorneys-general were unable to agree on basic defamation issues, but a new proposal is currently under discussion.

In some jurisdictions, publication of defamatory material may be lawful if it is true. Other jurisdictions require both that the material be true and that publication be in the public interest or have a public benefit. Material constituting 'fair comment' – that is, a statement of opinion about a matter of public interest – may also be allowed. There are other defences for fair and accurate reporting of some public events and communications about government or political matters.[62]

A full apology where material has been negligently published provides a defence in some jurisdictions.

Note that section 52 of the *Trade Practices Act* may also apply to a statement or comment that relates to the behaviour or characteristics of a person and/or organisation if it is likely to mislead or deceive consumers. An advertisement for a sporting event that untruthfully disparages another event, for example, might lead to an action under section 52. The situation involving Kim Hughes mentioned on page 67 involved a claim for defamation as well as breach of section 52.

The following are examples of some sporting defamation cases.

Sportsmanship in issue
Ian Chappell sued Mirror Newspapers over an article that was critical of his sportsmanship and reputation. The other side suggested that he already had a tarnished reputation and had suffered no damage.[63]

'Thrown' cricket match
Clive Lloyd, a former West Indian Cricket captain, sued over an article implying that he and his team had 'thrown' the final qualifying match in the 1981–82 one-day series of cricket matches in order to assure Australia of a place in the finals against it. The article had been titled, 'Come on dollar, come on'. Lloyd recovered $100 000 in damages.[64]

Protection of status
A prominent English amateur golfer sued a chocolate manufacturer who had used a caricature depicting the golfer with a pack of its chocolate. The golfer sued the company successfully on the basis that people would think that he had agreed to the advertisement for gain, which would have affected his amateur status.[65]

Fitness and ability
Les Boyd, a Sydney Rugby League footballer, successfully sued Mirror Newspapers, which had published an article stating that he was 'fat, slow and predictable'.[66]

Naked photograph
A sporting defamation case that received a huge amount of publicity was the Andrew Ettingshausen case.[67] Ettingshausen, a high-profile rugby league player and sometime model, claimed that the publication of a photograph, unauthorised by him, of him in the shower which appeared to show his penis was defamatory. Initially the court awarded the player $350 000 against the publisher of the magazine.

On appeal the finding of defamation was upheld, but the amount of damages was said to be excessive. A new trial was ordered to reconsider the damages issue.

Performance of referee

A radio broadcaster, Alan Jones, raised issues including bias in relation to the performance of a referee, Bill Harrigan, in an interview he conducted with the head of the NRL. A jury found that the comments were capable of defaming the referee. Defences including truth and comment were rejected.[68]

Criticism of disciplinary tribunal

Members of the NRL judiciary claimed that comments made by a well-known former player and media figure, Phil Gould, in relation to a particular disciplinary decision of the NRL Judiciary Tribunal were defamatory. The comments had been made on a radio program and in a newspaper article, and were said to be defamatory because they suggested that the tribunal members had, among other things, acted perversely and corruptly and so unfairly that players could not expect to get a fair hearing.[69]

The conduct of sporting tribunals

Most sports involve activity within a framework of rules, which are normally called the rules of the game. Other rules relating to the way in which sporting organisations conduct themselves and matters such as eligibility and licensing of players or officials are usually contained in the constitution of a corporation, association, organisation or club. Rules relating to a single event are generally contained in guidelines especially drafted for that event.

The interpretation of all these categories of rules is normally undertaken by the governing body of a sport or the organiser of an event. Tribunals are set up to interpret rules and to discipline players or officials who are in breach of rules, or of codes of conduct. The anti-doping policies of the Olympic sports in Australia, for example, nominate CAS as the tribunal for determining disputes arising from breaches of the policy, as does clause 10 of the 2004 Olympic selection policy. Most sports have set up tribunals to hear disputes relating to their members.

It is of the utmost importance that those involved in drafting rules to be used by a sporting association ensure that they are clear. Clarity in rule drafting minimises the number of situations where problems arise. The rules need not be complicated. They should be put simply and clearly, and aim to cover the day-to-day running of the body.

The rules should make fair provision for those actually engaged in the sport as well as those running it, and should attempt to cover matters that are likely to occur in the life of the association concerned.[1] If these precautions are taken, the sport's disciplinary body should be able to function with certainty and a minimum of recourse to the courts.[2]

Traditionally the courts have been reluctant to become involved in the squabbles of club members, and have demanded that there be some infringement of a tangible right before they would grant relief.

Domestic tribunals

The disciplinary bodies of all sports are known as *domestic tribunals*, because they are responsible for administering and enforcing the rules of the sporting association, not the laws of the land.

The rights of individuals may be affected by the decisions of domestic tribunals. A player who receives $500 per match and is suspended for 15 games loses a substantial sum of money. A jockey who is suspended for a year may lose the whole of his livelihood for that period. This is not to condemn all cases where such harsh penalties are given, but to point out the real severity of some penalties, and underline the importance of fair and proper disciplinary proceedings.[3] Non-monetary consequences such as loss of social life may also be involved.

While the courts have shown some reluctance to intervene in the proceedings of unincorporated associations and the way in which they are run, it seems that they will usually be prepared to intervene to protect livelihood, or where there has been a flagrant breach of the principles of natural justice.[4] The growth of commercial interests in sport has led to increased inclination on the part of courts to adjudicate in this type of situation.[5]

The standards of fairness and the rules of procedure that have been set down for domestic tribunals are not as rigid as those that the courts themselves are bound to observe. It would be unreasonable to expect a body hearing complaints involving breaches of players' rules of conduct in lawn bowls to adopt the same procedures as a court of law. The procedure must be appropriate to the actual circumstances.[6]

Setting up domestic tribunals

Domestic tribunals set up to hear sporting charges and disputes may be constituted under special legislation or be provided for in the rules of the association involved.

The nature of a sport and its importance in the community may mean that it is appropriate for its governing machinery to be set up under legislation. In this case the regulations governing disciplinary proceedings have statutory force. The racing industry in NSW is an example of this situation. Racing is governed by legislation because it is an important industry, and it is imperative that it be seen to be run fairly and openly.

The legal requirements of fairness vary, depending on the nature of the sport involved and the circumstances surrounding the matter under consideration, but basic standards must be observed by even the most informal body.

Legal intervention

Courts generally become involved in the domestic proceedings of an association if the association does not comply with its own rules and a party approaches the court. This may happen in one of two ways. The first involves the organisation making decisions that are beyond its power under its own rules. Decisions of this kind are known at law as decisions that are *ultra vires*.[7] The second situation is one in which the organisation interprets its own rules incorrectly.

In the Williams case[8] both the judge at first instance and the Court of Appeal accepted that the courts had a right to intervene in a tribunal decision in some circumstances despite the fact that the player contract provided for the matter to be determined by the AFL Tribunal to the exclusion of the courts. The case involved a penalty for interfering with an umpire. The player and his club argued that the allegation of interference was not supported by the evidence. A majority of the Court of Appeal allowed the appeal on grounds which included that the trial judge had usurped the role of the tribunal in assessing the evidence, and that there was evidence to support the tribunal's finding.

The rules themselves may not be enforceable by the courts; for example, because they are against public policy. Restraint of trade and the right to work, discussed in chapter 4, are relevant here. The organisation's rules in the case involving a licence application by a woman horse trainer were found to infringe the applicant's right to work, and the court would not enforce them.[9]

Courts will also intervene if a decision made by a domestic tribunal is deemed to be unfair because it does not accord with the principles of natural justice (or procedural fairness, as it is also known). These are discussed below; basically they involve someone's right to know what they are charged with and to have their side of the case heard.

There have been circumstances where the courts have declined to review the decisions of domestic tribunals. In the Aga Khan case[10] a horse owned by the Aga Khan won the Oaks at Epsom, but traces of a prohibited drug were found in a veterinary inspection after the race. The horse was disqualified and the trainer fined. The Aga Khan sought judicial review of the penalty. The court declined to hear the matter.

Disciplinary proceedings

Disciplinary proceedings, at their most basic level, may involve the exclusion of a player from a sport and deprive the player of the enjoyment involved in participating in the game.

On another level, the increased earnings now available in sport, whether by way of contract payments, endorsements and appearance money, or through the possibility of full-time employment for both players and officials, have created a great potential for financial loss that did not exist when all players followed a strictly amateur code.

Even where athletes are not professionals, disciplinary proceedings can have a big effect on their careers. One case that brought this home was the disqualification of the first woman home in the 1987 Sydney Wang Marathon. The woman was disqualified because it was alleged that she was being 'paced' by a male runner, which was not allowed. Although she admitted that the man had run with her, she was adamant that he had been following her, that she did not know him and that she had even asked him to stop following her. After further consideration of the matter, the organisers of the race reinstated the runner.

The runner in this case was not a paid athlete, but had she been disqualified her time would not have been considered when representative teams were being selected. A disqualification would also have had an adverse effect on her reputation as an athlete.

The laws of natural justice

It is a general proposition of law that decisions affecting the rights of citizens must be reached only after a fair hearing. The laws relating to a fair hearing are known as the laws of natural justice or procedural fairness. They apply to all courts and tribunals, including 'domestic tribunals'. The laws of natural justice give the accused person protection by asserting that:

- the person accused of misconduct should know the nature of the accusation made
- the person should be given an opportunity to state their case
- the tribunal should act in good faith.[11]

Enforcement of the laws of natural justice is not so strict where voluntary associations and domestic tribunals are concerned as when courts are adjudicating the law of the land. This is because the parties in the case have agreed on the tribunal involved, or have chosen to abide by association rules that provide for its operation. The more onerous the penalty that could be imposed, however, the more care should be taken by the tribunal involved.

Different standards of natural justice apply depending on the surrounding circumstances and the type of tribunal involved.[12]

The right to a proper hearing

The first two elements of natural justice mentioned above fall within what is legally called the *audi alterem partem* rule – the accused must have a proper hearing. The hearing must be conducted according to the rules of the association concerned. What constitutes a proper hearing depends on all the facts and circumstances. Basically it means that representations must be heard from both sides and all the evidence against the accused should be on the table.

The accused must have proper knowledge of the actual charges that have been laid. It is not good enough to be given general information relating to the matter – details of the specific charge laid and the relevant rule or rules of the association should be given. It would not be enough for a tribunal to inform a player that the charge was 'bringing the game into disrepute' under a particular rule if the player had no idea of the conduct to which the charge related. A request for a player to appear before a tribunal 'in respect of hitting X' would also be insufficient if there were several rules that the conduct could relate to and the particular rule was not set out. If tribunal proceedings brought out evidence suggesting that a further charge could reasonably be made against a player or official, the tribunal would be wise to note the fact and perhaps adjourn until the accused could consider the ramifications of the additional charge. Proceeding to a decision on an additional charge without more notice might bring the decision of the tribunal into difficult waters.

The accused must have proper notice of the hearing. The hearing of charges against a person who is not present generally means that their side of the matter is not dealt with properly. (This does not of course apply where the accused has received proper notification of the proceedings and has no reason for not attending.) If the accused has a prior legitimate commitment, then the tribunal would be wise to wait until attendance is possible in order to avoid future complaint.

Notification of proceedings

Notification of the time and place of the hearing of any disciplinary proceedings is important. In a case involving a Rugby League player, the court held that the player, Les Boyd, had not had a proper hearing before a General Committee set up as a disciplinary body.

Boyd was the coach of the Cootamundra Rugby League Club's first grade side for the 1985 season. He allegedly used abusive language to a referee after a match. The District Committee sent Boyd notification of a meeting which had been called to discuss the matter. Boyd both telephoned and wrote to the committee to say that he would be unavailable for the meeting due to a prior work commitment. He requested complete details of the allegations made against him. The meeting was held, and Boyd was fined $500 in his absence.

Relying on legal advice, Boyd did not pay the fine. A meeting was held to discuss the non-payment. Boyd had notice of the meeting but did not attend, on legal advice. He was fined a further $500. He was also disqualified as a member of the football club until he paid the fines. This disqualification meant that he was not entitled to play rugby league football anywhere in the world. Boyd had a contract to play for an English club during the following season.

Boyd was asked to attend a further meeting to discuss the situation. Before the hearing was held, he applied for an injunction to restrain the committee on the basis that he had been denied natural justice. After the match at which the incident was said to have occurred, he had resigned from the football club, and he also now claimed that the committee had no jurisdiction to deal with him.[13] The NSW Supreme Court held that Boyd had not been given a proper chance to present his case. The committee had gone on with the initial meeting even though its members had known that Boyd could not be present. The meeting had been held even though there was no urgent necessity to determine the matter at that particular time. The committee had also failed to give him sufficient particulars of the charge against him.[14]

Following this decision, it seems that it is important to make sure that the person who is to appear before a disciplinary body is given every opportunity to attend. If a person who is to appear cannot attend for a good reason, and there is no need to determine the matter quickly, the hearing should be adjourned until they can be present. The court in the Les Boyd decision was possibly influenced by the fact that the prior commitment involved his full-time employment, while the disciplinary matter arose only out of a semi-professional sporting matter. What is reasonable in any situation will depend on all the facts.

Having decided that the first hearing was invalid, the court did not have to consider the effect of Boyd's non-appearance at the second.

The right to representation

Those called before a disciplinary tribunal do not necessarily have the right to be represented by a lawyer.[15] The courts are unwilling to turn a domestic tribunal into a quasi court of law and, for that reason, will not imply a right to representation where the rules do not grant it. Where disciplinary proceedings are conducted in a fair way by people who have a good knowledge of the sport and the rules concerned, the courts are generally satisfied.

If the rules of an association provide for legal or other representation, it should of course be allowed; otherwise, a breach of the rules will have occurred.

Those drafting rules should consider whether the disciplinary proceedings of its domestic tribunal warrant a right to representation, and whether this right should extend to legal representation before it. Many sporting organisations shy away from legal representation, fearing that matters might take a legalistic and complicated turn once lawyers are involved. Others decide that the ramifications of potential suspension, particularly where a great deal of money is involved, warrant the intervention of legal representatives.

Where the rules state that representation is not allowed, they will not generally be overridden by the courts. This will, however, depend on all the circumstances. In a case relating to disciplinary action against an English soccer club, the point was made that if a charge is very serious, it may be that legal representation is proper and should be allowed.[16] Where the rules are silent on the issue, whether the courts will allow representation depends on the nature of the proceedings.[17] In a case where a 15-year-old who made his living as a snooker player was allowed only limited legal representation at a disciplinary hearing that suspended him for two years, the court denied the right to review. The judge stated that, while it was unclear whether proper representation had been given, ultimately the boy had not suffered.[18]

In a cricket case involving ball tampering where the judge refused to review a tribunal decision, he stated that he saw nothing complex about the issues of the hearing and was satisfied that they were best understood by cricketers.[19]

Procedure at hearings

Both sides to any proceedings should generally be allowed to cross-examine (question) the witnesses of the other, unless this is excluded by the relevant rules. Material not available to both sides should not be used by the adjudicators in reaching a decision.

In another case involving procedure, *Boyd v Humphreys*,[20] the laws of natural justice were held to have been infringed by the NSW Rugby Football League Judiciary Tribunal. In this case, Les Boyd was charged with gouging an opponent's eyes and stomping on his head in a game. He appeared before the League Judiciary Tribunal, which replayed videos of the incident and found him guilty. He was suspended from four competition games and fined $200. He applied to the court for various orders on the ground that he had been denied natural justice.

The court found that this was the case. It appeared from the transcript of the tribunal proceedings that Boyd had repeatedly denied the accusations and finally had said that only another player, John Harvey (the alleged victim), could prove his innocence. Harvey had not been asked to appear. Although Boyd did not in so many words ask for Harvey to be called, the court held that the tribunal was well aware that he was needed. As no steps were taken by the tribunal to call him, the court held that Boyd had been denied natural justice. It is essential to the principles of natural justice that there be a proper presentation of the case and that had not happened here. The court made orders to the effect that the decision of the tribunal was void.

The tribunal of the Sydney Rugby Union came under scrutiny in a 1991 case, when it questioned a player on the pretext of inquiries it was making into the issue of player inducements generally. At the end of the inquiry the player, who had not known that he was under investigation, was disqualified for a significant period. He was informed of his suspension and right to appeal by mail. He took the Sydney Rugby Union to court; the judge found that there had been no compliance with the rules of natural justice. The failure to tell the player that he was being investigated or notify him of the charge was described by the judge as a 'flagrant breach of the rules of natural justice'.[21]

'Proper' penalty

Once a person has been found guilty of a charge, there should be an opportunity to address the tribunal on penalty. A range of penalties should be specified in an association's rules. When considering the appropriateness of a penalty to a particular offence, the tribunal must consider fully the effect of the penalty on the guilty party. A long suspension, for example, brings a loss of income to those paid by the match.

An appeal by Springbok player Johan le Roux against a penalty of 19 months on the ground of excessive penalty following his biting the ear of his opponent, New Zealand Rugby captain Sean Fitzpatrick, was dismissed by the courts. This was despite the great disparity of penalty with similar cases involving other players.[22]

Good faith, unbiased judges

The third element of natural justice indicated above is that the tribunal should act in good faith. This means that those hearing the case should not have an interest in the outcome, or be biased.

Where domestic tribunals are concerned, there needs to be actual bias shown before a decision can be attacked. This is in contrast to courts of law, whose decisions can be contested where either actual or suspected bias can be shown. Bias was argued in one racing case that involved a man named Maloney, who was charged with using obscene language during an annual coursing association reception.[23] Maloney had a long-running feud with a particular committee member, who was on the committee hearing the charge. Maloney did not object at the time. The court found that this 'suspected bias' on the part of the member was not sufficient to affect the committee's decision.

If Maloney could have proven that the member had told another person that this was his chance to 'get even' with Maloney, or some similar remark, actual bias could have been shown.

Members of a disciplinary tribunal or committee must enter into the hearing with an open mind. It would be improper, for example, for an adjudicator to be the person who had made the accusation, or to give evidence in the proceedings.

In Maloney's case two committee members had been present at the alleged incident, and it was held that their knowledge of what actually went on did not disqualify them from hearing the charge. It would have been a different matter if they had given evidence to the committee before taking part in its decision-making process.

Conduct prejudicial to an organisation

Where the conduct of a person who earns a living from sport is concerned, it has been suggested that the courts will consider the issue in a similar way to the High Court in its approach to procedural justice.[24] Catch-all rules such as those which prohibit athletes from behaving in a manner which 'brings the game into disrepute' are common. In deciding whether a tribunal has incorrectly applied a rule of this kind, mere disagreement with the finding is not sufficient to overturn the decision.[25]

Decision-making

Three other principles to emerge from the cases are:
- Those who are not members of the committee should not generally be present when decision-making occurs.[26]
- A tribunal should not surrender its decision-making function to another.
- Decisions should be made on the evidence before the tribunal. Past reputation, for example, should not be relevant.

The burden of proof in disciplinary proceedings generally lies on the person making the allegation, and is the civil standard of proof having regard to the seriousness of the consequences.[27]

In *Dale v NSW Trotting Club*[28] it was alleged that the tribunal had surrendered its function when the legal counsel who had been called in to assist the tribunal 'took over' the running of the disciplinary proceedings. On appeal, it was found that this had not occurred. The tribunal was permitted under the rules to be represented in an appeal; this was all it had done in calling in counsel.

Compensation for tribunal decisions made in error

Wilson v Hang Gliding Federation of Australia[29] involved a claim for damages for breach of contract against his association by a member who had been disciplined. Wilson conducted a hang-gliding business. The Hang Gliding Federation exercised functions in relation to pilot and instructor licensing under civil aviation laws and an agreement with the Civil Aviation Authority. Wilson's licence was cancelled by a disciplinary tribunal following his failure to answer letters of complaint from the association. A judge found that the tribunal decision was outside its power and also procedurally unfair as it took irrelevant considerations into account. The judge did not award the damages sought.

The Court of Appeal only considered the question of damages. For different reasons from those of the first judge, it found that there was no continuing obligation in the arrangement between the association and its members to ensure the tribunal made fair decisions. In any event, there was no evidence that Wilson had suffered any loss.

Tribunals are usually set up as bodies independent of the organisation. Whether an organisation would ever be liable for the conduct of its tribunal will depend upon how it is set up under the constitution, but it would appear to be unlikely. The issue of whether tribunal members could ever be personally liable is one which does not appear to have been determined, but could arguably be overcome by including a clause limiting liability.

Jurisdiction of the courts

The courts have generally held that to agree in association rules to completely oust the jurisdiction of the courts will be void as being against public policy.[30] This does not mean the courts will always intervene – they have recognised that some types of dispute are better dealt with by non-lawyers or people with special knowledge or expertise in relation to the dispute. However, where there are private rights

that deserve protection, the courts will interfere to reach a just outcome.[31] Where the process used is fair and reasonable the courts are
less likely to intervene.[32]

In the Greg Williams case, for example, the player contract
included a term stating that the player would be bound by the various
rules and regulations of the AFL and any determinations of the AFL
Commission. The AFL Tribunal was set up with a non-lawyer laying
charges on behalf of the AFL, and with no legal representation allowed
to a player before the tribunal. There was a clause in the contract
stating that tribunal findings were final and binding.

Williams had been suspended for nine weeks after physical contact
with an umpire, and he and his club sought relief through the courts.
Williams and the Carlton Club argued that the obligations under the
rules to have charges tried in the tribunal was matched by a right to
have the charges determined properly and in accordance with the rules
of natural justice. The judge at first instance intervened despite the rule
which tried to oust the jurisdiction of the courts.

The Court of Appeal allowed the appeal by majority, with the
judges taking three quite different approaches to the issue.[33] All
members of the court looked carefully at what had been agreed
between the player, the club and the AFL. The AFL argued that
because of the agreement the court could only declare the tribunal's
decision of no effect if there was no reasonable basis in fact or law for
making it. Williams and the club argued that there must be a minimum
standard of rational evidence to support the decision. Tadgell JA
found that the trial judge had actually usurped the role of the tribunal
in his analysis of the evidence before it and its findings. Hayne JA concluded that the tribunal's finding was open to it on the relevant rule.
Ashley AJA, dissenting, found that the court had jurisdiction to look
at the matter, and agreed with the trial judge that there was no material
upon which the tribunal could have made the decision.

It seems that domestic tribunals may provide that the principles of
natural justice will not apply to them. Even with such agreement,
however, if issues of right to work, as opposed to mere membership of
a social club, are at stake, a court might be expected to intervene.[34]

The intervention of the courts in a matter of domestic discipline
does not mean that the decision of the court is substituted for the
original decision. The court will merely state whether or not the
original decision was made in a fair manner. If it was not made in
accordance with the rules of natural justice, the court will say so and
the matter will go back to the original tribunal for reconsideration.

This is what happened in *Boyd v Humphreys*, mentioned above. The court found that there had been a breach of natural justice and the matter was sent back to the domestic tribunal for rehearing. Boyd was found guilty of the charge at the rehearing.

Running an effective tribunal: the practicalities

Sporting tribunals are unusual. Generally there is a commitment to the sport by both the participants and the tribunal members. Often those involved are unpaid. Participants before tribunals often have much to lose aside from money if a determination is incorrect or inappropriate. The odds are that those involved will need to continue to work together or participate in the sport. Participants must not only get a fair hearing but must also believe that they have been given one, even if they are unhappy with the ultimate outcome.

Procedures set down for tribunals must be appropriate to the organisation and the actual circumstances. Disciplinary tribunals, for example, serve a different purpose from tribunals set up to review selection processes. Rules about the admission of evidence should be clearly set down and made known to the parties before the hearing. The prospect of an effective process is increased by clarity in the constitution, tribunal rules and procedures to minimise the number of situations where problems might arise. Regular review of rules to ensure that they are workable and reflect the way in which the organisation operates in practice is essential.

An effective chairperson should know the rules and procedures and follow them closely. They should have knowledge of or expertise in the sport, because it lends credibility to the conduct and outcome of the tribunal's proceedings. The chair should also allow the parties to feel part of the process. It may be wise to have a lawyer involved, but the proceedings should not be made overly legal. To some extent these decisions will depend on the severity of the consequences.

There are many ways in which an effective tribunal outcome could be measured. One might be whether or not the parties are happy; but this is unlikely to be useful, since one party will generally lose. Another measure may be the absence of further appeals. Possibly the best outcome is one in which the loser believes that the tribunal considered all the evidence appropriately and fairly, despite losing. An effective tribunal may be one that enhances the credibility of an organisation, and does not, by functioning in an unpredictable or inappropriate manner, bring the organisation into disrepute.[35]

Chapter 7

Sports injuries and compensation

All sporting activity brings risk of injury. Every sport has its own risks, from pulling a muscle through insufficient warm-up before a race, to breaking a leg while skiing, to striking the board while diving. In some sports, officials and spectators may also be at risk.

Some risks are brought about by the very nature of a sport. If these injuries happen, no-one need be at fault. Long distance running seems to cause back and shin injuries because of the amount of pavement pounding involved. Both snow and water skiers often break legs and arms because of the speed at which they travel and the potential to lose control.

Sometimes sporting injuries are caused by other people. A broken limb caused by a punch or a trip is in a different category. Such injuries may well be avoidable. The negligence of participants, organisers or the owner of the venue at which a sport is conducted may cause injury.

It is important for people involved in sport to understand that there is no automatic legal protection just because an accident or injury occurs in the course of a sporting event. Looking at decided sports cases, it seems that most types of sporting activity have landed in the courts. There have been cases involving snow skiing, water skiing, trampolining, hockey, all types of football, cricket, swimming, golf, motor racing and horse riding,[1] to name a few. In many cases the person injured was entitled to compensation. The application of the law in this area is far from theoretical.

Everyone involved in sport at whatever level and in whatever capacity should be aware that many injuries are avoidable and that risks can be minimised. Those who have power to do so should take the necessary steps to prevent injury. In a twist on sporting negligence, it was reported in 1995 that the owners of the racehorse Aragen, destroyed after a race, sued the jockey of a rival horse that they claimed knocked her over. The owners alleged that the jockey of the competing horse was negligent. The jockey was disqualified for two months following the ride. The owners claimed damages covering the prize money of the race in question plus loss of the mare's potential earnings as a racehorse and brood mare.[2]

This chapter looks at the various remedies that may be available to people injured in or around sport, and considers the potential liability of those involved in sport for injuries that occur.

How do the courts view injuries in sport?

In a case relating to the liability of rule-makers in rugby union, the High Court recognised the inherent risks in sport. Gleeson CJ:

> The only way to avoid all risk of injury is not to play at all. No doubt the rules could be altered in many respects to make it safer but people playing or watching rugby football have other priorities.[3]

At the same time, the High Court also recognised that participation in sport involves responsibility.[4]

When the law becomes involved

Compensation for injuries in sport is a complex matter. Sometimes the injured person cannot get compensation, because the injury is part of the risk involved in the sport and is not caused by anyone. In some circumstances, compensation may be provided by the common law of tort (see chapter 1), which involves one person suing another for damage suffered. The damage must result from the action of the person who is sued or the failure of that person to act. The main areas of tort apply to sporting situations are *negligence* and *assault*.

In other situations, compensation is provided by laws that have been enacted for that specific purpose. Workers' compensation laws, for example, may apply to professional sportspeople.

In NSW, some compensation may be provided to participants under a special Sporting Injuries Insurance Scheme. Other states do not have this type of scheme.

Recent changes in the law

There have been significant and well publicised recent changes to the laws dealing with civil liability for personal injury in the whole of the country.

Government and community perception over the past few years has been that damages awards in personal injury cases have become unsustainable as the main source of compensation for those injured through fault.[5] A growth in the number of personal injury actions was perceived, and many people expressed the view that the courts were becoming more liberal in their interpretation of traditional negligence concepts in order to compensate the injured.[6] These factors were combined with an 'insurance crisis', during which one important public liability insurer collapsed and several other insurers withdrew from the Australian market. Not surprisingly, the cost of premiums for third party insurance appeared to rise dramatically. In some cases insurance became unavailable for particular organisations or ventures.

As a result of many of these factors, major reforms to the common law of tort and related areas were undertaken by the Commonwealth and the states. The Commonwealth commissioned a report which has become known as the Ipp Report, after its chair Justice Ipp.[7] The views of NSW Premier Bob Carr, when introducing the new legislation, are fairly representative of government views throughout the country. The premier described the amending Bill as '...a triumph for commonsense', although he acknowledged that '...Parliament will be debating some of the most fundamental changes to the law of negligence ever made'. The premier also said:

> I want this Parliament to seize the opportunity to wind back this culture of blame. If we do, we will help to preserve the community's access to socially important activities. Our community deserves our best efforts to preserve the Australian way of life.[8]

It was intended that the legislation should be uniform across the country, but its content and timing has varied as between states and the Commonwealth. In some cases reforms have been passed but are not yet operative. Precise information on the situation in each state is beyond the scope of this book, and readers will need to ensure that they look at particular sporting issues from their own state perspective. Nevertheless, many of the issues being addressed in the new legislation are common.[9]

The Commonwealth also amended the *Trade Practices Act* and other laws to bring them into line with state and territory developments on civil liability.[10]

The laws attack the burgeoning costs of public liability from a variety of angles, in some states imposing tougher requirements on lawyers to act ethically, in some making simple procedural amendments.

Generally, the states have legislated to:
- reduce the type of damages available for personal injury both absolutely and by way of caps and thresholds
- reduce the period of time during which proceedings can be commenced
- limit claims where the victim is intoxicated, drugged or engaging in criminal activity.[11]

The focus here is on NSW legislation, which generally follows the recommendations of the Ipp Report (and which is similar to that of Queensland). Other jurisdictions are similar in some respects, and reference is made to some parts of the legislation in other states. Over time the legislation will affect the outcome of new cases. Until then the existing cases are still of interest, and many are discussed below.

Who gets sued?

The groups of people liable for causing injury in a sporting situation will generally be:
- other players or participants
- the organiser of an event
- the manager or coach of a team or individual
- the 'occupier' at law (this category is described below)
- spectators
- volunteers
- 'good Samaritans'.

These categories will be considered with emphasis on practical situations to show that the potential for liability is quite broad, often far beyond the expectations of people in these groups.[12]

Negligence

'Negligence' has been described as 'conduct that falls below the standard regarded as normal or desirable'.[13] The term does not refer to an act or omission that involves intention, but to behaviour that fails to measure up to a certain standard. From a legal point of view, this means that to prove a case of negligence it is not necessary to prove that the person responsible for injury or damage actually intended to cause the injury or damage. Intention is always difficult to prove in court. In cases of sporting injury, negligence is often the most suitable type of claim because injury is often caused by careless disregard for the safety of an opponent or someone else, rather than by a desire to actually hurt that person.

The law of negligence is complex. An action generally depends on establishing that a 'duty of care' was owed to the injured person, and proving that damage resulted from (or was caused by) a breach of that duty of care.

The amount of damages that can be recovered through the courts may be reduced if it can be shown that the injured person did not take reasonable care to avoid the injury.

Duty of care

Before any liability in negligence can be established, the injured person must show that they were owed a 'duty of care' by the person who caused the injury. Establishing this depends on demonstrating some relationship between the parties. The question the courts ask is whether the relationship was such that the defendant (the person being sued) should have realised that the negligent act could lead to the damage suffered.

The law relating to the establishment of a duty of care was set out in the 'neighbour principle' in a famous negligence case, *Donoghue v Stevenson*,[14] which involved injury suffered by a person who consumed a bottle of soft drink containing a decomposed snail. In that case, Lord Atkin defined the relationship necessary to constitute a duty of care as involving

> persons so directly affected by my act that I ought reasonably to have them in contemplation as being so affected when I am directing my mind to the acts or omissions which are called in question.

This test depended on the reasonable foreseeability of the result. The test proved difficult to apply in certain situations, and the Australian courts have evolved other tests based on Lord Atkin's principle.[15]

It has been held, for example, that players owe each other a duty of care. In the sporting context, and depending on the circumstances, one might also find that the organisers of a sporting event owe a duty of care to participants and spectators, and that coaches owe a duty of care to both their own and opposition players.

How careful do you have to be?

Once a duty of care has been established, consideration of whether the duty of care has been breached involves what is known at law as the 'standard of care'. This is the *degree* of care that ought to be applied in particular circumstances. How much care do you have to take to avoid injuring your opponent or a fellow player?

The test for the required standard of care is how a reasonable person would have behaved in the same situation – that is, whether the result of the action was reasonably foreseeable, and whether reasonable steps were taken to prevent injury occurring. An accident may be reasonably foreseeable without being likely or probable.[16]

Sporting competitors are expected to go all out to win. This is acceptable from a legal point of view in considering the degree of care required, as long as competitors do not deliberately break the laws of the game or act in a foolhardy manner.

If a duty of care is established, a person who is being sued must take the injured person as they find him or her. This means that if the injured person is particularly susceptible to injury for any reason, that does not help the defendant when damages are being awarded.[17] If a person is more severely injured in a netball brawl because, for example, they have a particularly thin skull, the person causing the injury is not excused. Or if a ball in a golfing accident destroys the good eye of a person who had only one eye to start with, damages are awarded on the basis that the victim is now totally blind.

Categorisation of risk and duty under the legislation

Under NSW civil liability legislation, a person will not be negligent in failing to take precautions against a risk of harm unless the risk was foreseeable and not insignificant, and in the circumstances a reasonable person would have taken precautions against the risk.[18] In determining reasonableness a court must consider the probability that harm would occur if care was not taken, the likely seriousness of the harm, the burden of taking precautions and the social utility of the activity creating the harm.[19] The fact that the risk could have been avoided by doing something a different way, and the taking of remedial action, does not of itself affect liability.

The NSW civil liability provisions categorise risk. The courts have not always been consistent in their characterisation of risks, and it may take some time before the application of the definitions in the legislation to particular circumstances is clarified by the courts.

The legislation in NSW creates separate types of risk, and sets out how those risks will be treated. Most relevant in a sporting context is that persons who engage in recreational activities as defined by the legislation will now be expected to take some responsibility for the decision to participate in the activity.

In South Australia, the duty of care is modified by a registered code for providers of high risk recreational activities.[20]

Inherent risks

Inherent risks are risks that cannot be avoided by the exercise of reasonable care. Under the civil liability legislation in NSW there is no liability for inherent risks.[21]

Obvious risks

Under the NSW law an 'obvious risk' is one that would be obvious to a reasonable person or is patent or is a matter of common knowledge. A risk can be obvious even if it has a low probability of occurring, or it is not prominent, conspicuous or physically observable.[22]

A defendant now has no duty to warn of an obvious risk, the presumption being that obvious risks are accepted.[23] Injured persons are presumed to be aware of obvious risks unless they prove on balance that they were not aware. Awareness of the type of risk is sufficient even if the person is not aware of the precise nature, extent or manner of occurrence of the risk.[24]

This does not apply if the injured person requested advice or information about the risk from the defendant, if the defendant is required by law to warn about the risk or if the defendant is a 'professional' and the risk is of death or personal injury. 'Professional' is not defined, so it is not clear whether this exception applies to people such as professional coaches. The main purpose of its inclusion in the legislation was to clarify the position in relation to professionals such as doctors.

Causation

In order to win damages in a negligence action, an injured person must be able to show that the breach of duty caused the injury. While this may seem fairly simple and a matter of common sense, it is often difficult to decide in a complex set of circumstance. If the patient had not been in hospital following the accident, the doctor would not have operated and caused further injury. Did the original accident cause the patient's subsequent injury? The test used by the courts is called the 'but for' test: would the plaintiff's injuries have been suffered but for the defendant's negligence? If the plaintiff would have been injured in any event, the defendant did not cause the plaintiff's injury.[25]

Under the civil liability amendments in NSW and some other states, there is a new approach to causation. The first question to be asked is whether the negligence was a necessary condition of the occurrence, and the second is whether it is appropriate for the court to extend the liability to the harm caused.[26] The courts are given a discretion about whether or not to extend liability to the particular situation.[27]

Waivers and exclusions: the problems

The most important changes for sport involve the new position on risk warnings in 'recreational activity' and the strengthened ability of those providing recreational services to expressly contract out of liability.

Many cases, particularly in relation to swimming and diving, have revolved around the question of whether warning signs should have been erected in circumstances where there were known dangers and a warning might have prevented injury.[28] Classic cases of a dive into shallow or dangerous waters and in relation to other recreational dangers have been considered by the courts.[29] The cases have considered whether there was a positive duty to warn in the circumstances.[30]

Traditionally courts have been reluctant to allow sporting organisations, facility owners and others involved in sport to escape liability for injury where negligence was involved. This has been the case even where risk warnings were used or where contracts between the parties purported to exclude liability, except in the clearest of cases. The *Trade Practices Act* exacerbated this position, because until the civil liability legislation it was impossible to contract out of the requirement to provide certain services with due care and skill.[31]

Other problems in this area have arisen with minors because of laws limiting their ability to contract (see chapter 4), and the difficulty of proving they were capable of understanding risk warnings.

Waivers and parental permission forms for students, team members and other participants did not generally exclude liability. They were useful in making participants and their parents (if children were involved) aware that activities were undertaken with some risk.

The courts were more inclined to uphold exclusion clauses and waivers in some sporting circumstances over the last ten years. In one case, a pupil injured on her first parachute jump was denied relief on the basis of a very comprehensive exclusion clause in both her contract for training and her membership of the Australian Parachute Federation. The pilot of her drop plane was found to be negligent, but as an agent of the school she was specifically covered by the exclusion.[32]

In another case, a man training as a body builder with a persistent injury made it known to a gym. His instructor was negligent and the purpose of an exclusion clause signed by him was misrepresented, but he was denied relief by the court when he severely aggravated the existing injury. The exclusion clause was found to be effective to protect the gym and its employees even though the gym had neglected to follow its own routine for persons who identified themselves in written documentation as being at particular risk of injury.[33]

Waivers and exclusions under the civil liability legislation

All the states have introduced legislation aimed at enforcing waivers and reinforcing the assumption of the risks of a sport.

The legislation in NSW specifically affects what it defines as 'recreational activities' and 'dangerous recreational activities'.

'Recreational activity' includes:

- any sport whether or not organised;
- any pursuit or activity engaged in for enjoyment, relaxation or leisure; and
- any pursuit or activity engaged in at a place (such as a beach, park or other public open space) where people ordinarily engage in sport or any pursuit or activity for enjoyment, relaxation or leisure.[34]

A person does not owe a duty of care in respect of a recreational activity if it is the subject of a risk warning.[35] 'Risk warning' is defined very broadly to include both oral and written warnings, but to be effective a risk warning must be capable factually of warning participants. The warning need not be specific to a particular risk, but may be more general. It must have been given on behalf of the defendant or the 'occupier'. A risk warning must not have been contradicted by anything said by or on behalf of the defendant. Risk warnings could be contained on signs or in documentation such as tickets or other contracts provided in relation to the activity.

A risk warning may now be given to the parents or carer of a child or other person who is incapable of understanding such a warning.[36]

A defendant is not entitled to rely on a risk warning if the plaintiff was required to engage in a recreational activity.[37] This may have implications for areas like compulsory school sport.

A 'dangerous recreational activity' means a recreational activity that involves a significant risk of physical harm.[38] It is not clear whether significance will be measured by likelihood of injury or potential severity of outcome.

A defendant is not liable in negligence for harm suffered by another as a result of the materialisation of an obvious risk of a dangerous recreational activity engaged in by the injured person, whether or not the person was aware of the risk.[39] The application of this provision will depend upon whether an activity is characterised by a court as being a 'dangerous recreational activity' and whether the particular risk is 'obvious'.[40]

Express right to contract out under the legislation

The civil liability legislation in NSW specifically acknowledges the right of parties to a contract for recreational services to make their own agreement on liability. People are not prevented from reaching an agreement about their rights and obligations, even for the elimination of due care and skill by the party providing the services. Terms of a contract stating that a person has accepted the risk may now be effective, although it is to be expected that the courts will still insist that the terms of any such contract are clear and have been accepted by the injured party. The *Trade Practices Act* has also been amended to allow this contracting out, although the definition of recreational activity in the Act is different from that in NSW and in other states.[41]

The extent to which the courts are prepared to enforce terms excluding liability will be one of the most important legal developments arising from the legislation.

Summary of the NSW civil liability provisions

The most important provisions affecting sporting activity in NSW can be summarised as follows:

- There is no liability in negligence for inherent risks.
- There is no obligation to warn of obvious risks.
- There is no duty of care for recreational activity where a risk warning has been given.
- There is no liability in negligence as a result of the materialisation of an obvious risk in a dangerous recreational activity regardless of whether or not the injured person knew of the risk.
- The parent or guardian of a minor or incapable person may receive a risk warning on behalf of that person.
- Persons may contract to expressly eliminate due care and skill in the performance of a contract.
- A volunteer will not be personally liable in negligence when acting in good faith and within the scope of duty (see page 115).

Intentional injury: assault

The tort applicable to sporting situations that involves intention is assault. Traditionally, 'assault' involved the threat of violence to another person, and 'battery' (or 'trespass to the person') was the actual infliction of the injury. These days the word 'assault' is commonly used to cover both aspects. The tort of assault involves:

- the direct application of force by one person upon another
- no consent by the person who is hit, and
- injury as a result.[42]

It is clear from the definition that those sports commonly known as 'contact sports' offer many potential instances of assault in a single game. The question of consent in this case, however, does not mean a formal consent between all participants. By competing in a game, a participant impliedly consents to those things that are inherent in the sport. A footballer impliedly consents to the 'assault' involved in each tackle. A netballer or tennis player does not consent to the same type of conduct. They would, however, consent to the degree of force inherent in their respective games. Collisions between doubles players in a tennis match are a normal part of that sport. Behaviour 'normal' to the particular sport will be covered by implied consent. Consent may also be implied for some acts that are outside the laws of the game.

Participants do not generally consent to undue violence.[43] It is obvious that difficult questions will arise if ever legal action is taken for injury occurring during a karate tournament.

In a case involving Australian football, a player sued a member of the opposing team. Evidence showed that the opposition player deliberately struck him on the head with an elbow, causing serious injury.[44] It was claimed that, because foul play was common in Australian football, the injured player had impliedly consented to this type of behaviour. This defence was rejected and damages were awarded. The evidence was found to have shown only that foul play sometimes occurred. Strong evidence of constant practice would have been needed to show that consent had been given to a blow like the one in issue.

The judge also distinguished between rules made for the protection of players and those made to improve the game. A penalty relating to player safety awarded by a referee will be relevant to a tort action. Activity that is actually within the rules of the game may still end up in court, depending on how it occurs.

An important case involving assault on the football field confirmed the application of the tort in an area where an action (tackling) permitted by the rules was performed in a dangerous manner (outside the rules) and resulted in serious injury to the tackled player. One rugby league player, Bugden, tackled another, Rogers, illegally. The trial judge found that this constituted an assault, as although the activity of tackling was permitted under the rules, the tackle causing the injury was illegal and dangerous. The judge awarded almost $69 000 in damages to Rogers. Bugden's club was found to be vicariously liable for the injury, a concept that is discussed later.

Both sides appealed. On appeal, the judges upheld the findings of assault and vicarious liability. In addition, Rogers was successful in receiving awards of 'aggravated' and 'exemplary' damages.[45] Aggravated damages are generally awarded due to the high-handed, malicious, oppressive or insulting nature of the act concerned. The appeal court agreed with Rogers that he had not been awarded any damages to compensate him for his frustration and anger at the nature of the tackle, and awarded him an extra $8000. Exemplary damages, which are awarded in situations where the defendant has acted in disregard of the victim's rights, amounted to $7500. Importantly, the court warned sporting employers that if a club authorised such an illegal and dangerous act, it might be the subject of a substantial award of exemplary damages.

An action of a similar nature, taken by a former Footscray player against the Melbourne Club and a player, was reportedly settled.[46]

Obligations of participants

Both negligence and assault may be relevant to participants.

The courts have stated that players or competitors may owe each other a duty of care.[47] The rules of a sport may be relevant to the determination of this duty, particularly if they relate to safety. Whether negligence can be established will depend on whether or not the defendant has behaved in the manner of a reasonable competitor.

In an important High Court sporting case concerning negligence,[48] the facts were that a skier was injured in a collision with a stationary boat. The skier sued the driver of the towing boat. The High Court held that even though those engaging in a sport undertake the inherent risks of that sport, this does not absolve participants of all duty of care. The driver of the boat had been negligent in this case. The court emphasised that each case must be decided on its own circumstances.

In one English football case, a player sued in negligence for damage caused when his leg was broken in a tackle. A referee in the match had described the tackle in the following way:

> The slide tackle came late and was made in a reckless and dangerous manner, by lunging with his boot studs showing about a foot/18 inches above the ground ... In my opinion the tackle constituted serious foul play and I sent the defendant from the field of play.[49]

Negligence: the test

Frazer v Johnston[50] confirmed that participants owe each other a duty of care, and set out a simple test for determining whether a participant has breached the duty of care owed in particular circumstances.

The case involved a collision between two jockeys. Finlay J found that top jockey Malcolm Johnston 'caused his horse to cross dangerously close in front of the two horses further inside of him ...', compressing the horses and causing a fall in which Frazer was injured. This behaviour was not in accordance with the rules of racing. Johnston had failed to take reasonable care for the safety of fellow jockeys, and a reasonable man would have foreseen the risk.

The court readily found that Johnston owed Frazer a duty of care and ordered him to pay $121 490. Finlay J considered decisions that set out the test for breach of duty as being whether a reasonably careful man would have acted in that manner in the circumstances, and translated it into a test of Johnston's conduct in the following terms:

> So it becomes in the present case the reasonable man riding as a licensed jockey in a horse race. Those circumstances do not negate the duty on the part of the defendant to take reasonable care to avoid a foreseeable risk of injury to the other jockeys ... That single standard of care remains. But it does shape what the reasonable response of a man in that situation could be. He is sitting astride a horse probably weighing between 1000 and 1200 pounds and travelling up to forty mile per hour ... In short, what is reasonable will vary with the circumstances in which the parties are involved.'[51]

On appeal it was argued that the duty of care in a sporting situation is a duty not to cause foreseeable danger, and differs from other tests for duty of care. Following trends in other High Court cases, the Court of Appeal rejected this different test, opting instead for an approach in sport similar to that adopted in all other negligence cases.[52]

In another case a golfer was severely injured in a charity golf day when a ball hit him on the head. The Court of Appeal confirmed the decision of the trial judge that a second player had breached his duty when he hit the ball without ensuring that it was reasonably safe to do so. The behaviour was outside accepted golfing behaviour, and the risk of being hit in this way was not inherent in the game of golf.[53]

Liability between participants: assault

A participant is potentially liable to another participant for assault.

Almost all sports involve the potential for this type of action. When considering assault in a match, however, the type of assault where a player hits another out of frustration or anger must be contrasted with the type of 'assault' caused by forceful play. The first type is no different from an assault occurring anywhere else, and will be treated as such by the courts. The second type creates more difficulty, because the question of whether there was consent to the behaviour must be considered. As noted above, this entails consideration of the rules of the game, general conditions of normal play and all other circumstances.

Injury to spectators caused by participants

The participants in any sport must have some regard for the spectators at a sporting event. Depending on the nature of the sport, attendance may be fraught with danger. It is clear that it would generally be more dangerous to attend the speedway than a tennis match.

The courts have recognised that participants will attempt to do their best to succeed, stating that 'the best tradition of sporting endeavour' will not be penalised.[54] In the case in which that statement was made, a photographer was injured at a horse show by the winning horse when he got in its way in the actual ring while photographing. The court found that both the rider involved and the organisers had taken sufficient precautions in the circumstances.

By way of contrast, a participant who injures a spectator while doing something that is clearly not part of a sporting activity will be liable according to ordinary tort principles. Questions of implied consent will not be relevant. A football player who flings into the crowd a boot taken from an opponent's foot would be an example. Another would be a tennis player who flings a racquet into the crowd in disgust, injuring a spectator. If this seems far-fetched, consider the following example involving former tennis star John McEnroe:

> [In] the US Open in 1983, McEnroe had a temper tantrum he may regret. In an incident captured by the television cameras, McEnroe threw sawdust in the face of a front-row fan who was, in McEnroe's opinion, too forthright and vociferous in rooting for McEnroe's opponent. This incident has given rise to litigation which is pending as of this writing.[55]

There are numerous examples of situations where spectators have recovered damages for injury caused by participants. Most involve horses, racing cars or sports where either the equipment or the game itself are potentially dangerous to spectators.[56] At golf tournaments that are telecast, television viewers regularly see spectators in the on-course gallery hit by golf balls. Depending on all the facts, this situation could see a golfer sued for negligence; or the organisers might be liable in negligence for poor crowd control, again depending on the circumstances. On the other hand, the court might find that neither had been negligent because the spectator had accepted this normal risk when entering the gallery and following golfers around the course.

Injury to others caused by participants

A 'stranger' is a person who is neither a player nor a spectator, but who happens to be in the vicinity. There is no doubt that a 'stranger' injured by a participant engaged in a sporting activity may recover damages in some circumstances. Actions involving golf balls have been successfully fought; other cases have involved the game of cricket. Whether damages can be won in a case of this type will depend on the circumstances. It has to be shown that the participant has been negligent in all the circumstances, on the tests discussed above.

A person who passes a sporting field and is hit by a flying javelin or other piece of sporting equipment might come into this category.

Liability of the manager or coach

Situations may arise in which club officials, coaches and managers or organisers of sporting occasions incur liability to participants.

This might come as a surprise to those officials and coaches who give their time to a chosen sport in a voluntary capacity. Most people who become voluntarily involved in a sporting activity do so with the best of motives, intending to foster and develop a sport or game that they have enjoyed in the past, or that is played by their children. In most states civil liability legislation now provides some protection for negligent volunteers – this is discussed below.

At the other end of the spectrum, the coaches of elite athletes need to ensure the safety of their athletes while forging champions. In that situation, where does society draw the line between forging a champion and committing a tort?[57] The coach or manager of a team or individual player might be liable for injury to either their own team or player, or the opposing team or players.

In the much publicised Watson case,[58] Stephen Watson, a schoolboy who became a quadriplegic after being injured in a school football match, sued the Department of Education and the teachers who had coached his football team. There was evidence to show that a person of Stephen's stature – tall and thin with a long thin neck – should not play in the front row of a scrum. Stephen was playing in such a position. The Minister for Education had been informed of the great dangers of this by a renowned spinal specialist, and had been offered copies of videos aimed at educating teachers and students about neck injuries by a committee of specialists in the area. The videos clearly told of the dangers for people of Stephen's build. The Education Department had failed to effectively distribute the videos to schools.

The coaches were sued in their own capacity because they had allowed Watson to play in the position. The Education Department was sued in its capacity as their employer (by way of vicarious liability, discussed later). It was also sued in its own capacity on the ground that it owed all students a duty of care and that the duty had not been discharged in this case because teachers and students had not been made aware of the dangers of neck injuries.

The teachers were exonerated completely. It was stated that

> The two teachers at the school who were concerned with the plaintiff's football that season in fact did everything that reasonably could have been expected of them. They did not [know] and it could not reasonably be expected that they should have known that the plaintiff's particular physique was such that it was unsafe to select and play him as hooker in that match.[59]

The court found for the boy on the basis that the Department of Education had breached the duty of care that it owed him, relying on an earlier High Court case that established the duty.[60] The court emphasised the failure of the department to draw the attention of those involved with football in schools to the dangers of neck injury, particularly when a video was readily available. There was clear evidence that the department did not implement its own systems successfully.

The judge was quite adamant that the case did nothing to extend the existing law, and because of the basis on which liability was found, the court did not have to decide whether the coaches owed a duty of care to their players. The case is particularly interesting because it shows the limitations of the law of negligence – the fact that the student was injured did not automatically mean that the coaches were liable. As the body responsible for providing the teachers with relevant safety information, the Department of Education clearly did not carry out its duties. Had the department not been involved, the result might have been different.

It is clear that if unfortunate accidents occur at junior levels, the governing bodies of the sports involved will be better protected in any ensuing legal battle if they have formulated some systematic approach to the selection and vetting of junior coaches.

In terms of standard of care, coaches are presumed to be reasonably competent according to their situation. A soccer team of six-year-olds, for example, might be expected to have a coach who makes sure that the children do not wander off or onto nearby roadways, and teaches them some skills.[61] A person coaching young men in football may be expected to see that they develop a degree of physical fitness appropriate to the playing of a 'physically demanding contact sport'.[62] The coach of an Olympic gymnast might be expected to have a working knowledge of anatomy and of injuries common in that type of activity, and to know when to call in a specialist if an injury is beyond the scope of the coach's knowledge.

Coaches must also ensure a reasonable level of supervision of all athletes during participation and training. In *Foscolos v Footscray Youth Club*[63] a wrestling coach was negligent because he did not act to stop a dangerous move called a suplex throw by one of his participants on the injured participant, who was made quadriplegic as a result.[64]

A former champion gymnast was reported in 1995 to be suing her coach and the ASC, claiming that training there had left her with severe health problems including the eating disorder anorexia.[65]

Dangerous techniques

A coach who intentionally employs a method or technique which is dangerous may cause injury to players. There were press reports at one stage concerning a rugby union player suing his coach and college over his participation in a move called a 'flying wedge', which left him a quadriplegic. Extreme and ill-advised training methods might be another example; for instance, if a swimming coach required his protégés to swim double the normal distances in training and a swimmer developed heart trouble or stress fractures as a result.

Removing injured players

Encouraging an injured player to play on when it is quite clear that the player should not do so raises the question of whether the coach has a duty to the player or to victory. The injured star player who begs to remain on the field in an important match creates a dilemma for the coach. In the case of a junior, one might argue that the player is unable to make an informed decision and that it is up to the coach to remove that person from the competition if there is danger of aggravating an injury. The coach may also have a duty to remove an adult player from the game in such circumstances. In this case, however, the issue is less clear-cut.

Encouraging aggression

Encouraging aggression that leads to injury of either the player or an opposing player might also expose the coach or manager to liability.

Drugs, legal and illegal

Coaches or officials who supply players with substances that could injure them, or who encourage the use of such substances, might be liable for subsequent injury. Indiscriminate use of pain-killing injections that facilitate further injury might also be relevant. Information about the long-term consequences of using particular pain-killing drugs may need to be supplied to players.[66]

Where children are involved

Those who supervise or coach children must take particular care; a normal duty of care is increased if children are involved. Children are assumed to be less capable than adults of taking care of themselves, and anyone in a position of responsibility where children are concerned should make their safety and well-being the primary concern. If a duty of care can be established in relation to a child, the younger the child, the greater the likelihood that negligence will be found.[67]

If the sporting situation involves a school, the school itself may be liable for negligence, as it was in the case of schoolboy quadriplegic Stephen Watson. It may also be vicariously liable as the employer of a teacher found to be negligent.

Liability to spectators and to strangers

Situations where an official might be liable to a spectator or stranger are not totally inconceivable.

Inadequate distance between the field of play and a rope barrier erected by officials might be the cause of spectator or 'stranger' injury in car racing, or in a golf or football game. A golf spectator following tournament players would accept some, but not all, risks.

Liability to disabled athletes

The integration of disabled athletes into competition with the non-disabled, and the increasing numbers of sporting competitions held for disabled athletes, raise issues of whether they are owed a greater duty of care.

The English case of *Morrell v Owen*[68] involved a disabled archer who was injured during a training session when archers and discus throwers were training together. While a safety net was in place, a stray discus struck the plaintiff in the head, causing permanent brain damage. During the case, the judge stated that coaches acting for the disabled sporting association owed a greater duty of care to their athletes than would be owed to able-bodied participants.

Pregnancy and participation

Sporting organisations sometimes face a dilemma in dealing with pregnant participants. Several issues arise in this context, such as:

- Is there any possibility that a sporting organisation could be liable at law for allowing a pregnant woman to continue to participate?
- Does the participation of a pregnant woman increase the legal risk to other competitors?
- Can a sporting organisation require pregnant women to sign an exclusion or waiver in an attempt to limit its liability?
- What part do the discrimination laws of the Commonwealth and states play in this situation?

Australian Netball was criticised in 2001 for imposing a ban on pregnant participants. This led to discussion of the issue by doctors and lawyers, culminating in a useful guideline paper issued by the ASC and the sports law association ANZSLA.[69]

In summary the position is that the potential liability of a sporting organisation varies depending on the degree of control it exercises over athletes. The guideline suggests that, put at its highest, the duty of a sports administrator or sporting organisation is to advise pregnant women (preferably in writing, such as on a registration form) that continued participation could present health risks and to seek advice from an appropriately qualified medical practitioner. Advice on health risks should be left to health professionals. Employers may be under a more onerous obligation. As to other participants, they owe the same duty to a pregnant participant and her child as to any other participant, and will only be liable for conduct outside the rules of the game (injury caused to a pregnant woman, however, may be greater than to another participant in the same circumstances).

A woman cannot agree on behalf of her unborn child not to sue, and owes it a duty to take and follow appropriate advice.

The guideline suggests that an additional duty may exist where an administrator knows that a participant has not obtained advice or continues to participate despite advice to the contrary. Additional advice and possibly counselling the woman to cease competing are suggested in these circumstances.[70]

Sex discrimination laws prohibit discrimination on the basis of pregnancy or potential pregnancy.[71] Limited exceptions apply under some state legislation where the health of the woman or the unborn child is involved.[72] In most cases a ban on participation would contravene sex discrimination laws.[73]

Liability of sporting bodies

The Stephen Watson case mentioned above raises interesting questions for the governing bodies of sports. If the governing body of a sport has information about serious injury, does it have a duty to inform coaches? This is a particularly important issue when the number of voluntary 'coaches' in most sports, particularly at junior levels, is considered. In many cases, the only qualification of these coaches is their own enthusiasm and experience as players. Does the duty of the governing body go beyond encouraging the attainment of some formal coaching accreditation by all coaches? Should a governing body allow those with no training or accreditation to coach?[74]

The extent to which sporting bodies owe a duty of care to amend a sport's rules to reduce the risk of harm to participants was considered in *Agar v Hyde*.[75] A complicated claim was made by two rugby players who had become quadriplegics following scrum collapses. The High Court rejected the claims despite the fact that the governing body, the International Rugby Football Board, may have had special knowledge of the particular risk they faced. The court emphasised that the participants had consented to the inherent risks of the game. It stated that common law does not ordinarily impose a duty on a person to take action where no positive act has created the risk of injury. The fact that the International Rugby Football Board was not an incorporated body meant that it lacked the control necessary to attract a duty of care.

Liability of referees

Over a number of years it has been argued that a referee might be liable for injury caused to participants through failure to enforce the rules. In *Smolden v Whitworth*[76] an injured rugby referee was found liable in negligence for his failure to control the setting of rugby scrums in a junior match. Special rules of scrum safety applied in the match; the referee had allowed a number of dangerous scrums to form, and another hooker had already been injured. Linesmen had warned of potential injury. In the particular circumstances it was found that the referee had not acted in the manner of a reasonably competent referee.

Liability of organisers

The organisers of a sporting event may be liable either as organisers, or as occupiers of the place where the injury takes place. The role of the occupier at law is discussed a little later.

The organiser of an event should ensure that it is well planned. Organising a major event, for example, without providing for a doctor or other medical personnel to be on hand would not be advisable.

What constitutes a 'well-planned' event will of course be determined by the nature of the event and the sport concerned. The organisers of a triathlon or a marathon, for example, would be expected to provide sufficient drink stations for competitors along the route of the event. It may even be expected that the organisers of a marathon event, particularly one where members of the public as opposed to athletic club members were taking part, would consider climatic conditions carefully in their planning. Running a marathon at 12 noon on the hottest day of the year would obviously be inadvisable.

Crowd control for the protection of athletes or players might also come within the responsibilities of the organiser.

In a recent case involving indoor cricket that went to the High Court, an injured participant argued that the organiser of the game, who was also the occupier of the facility at which the game was played, had breached its duty of care to him. He had been hit in the eye by an indoor cricket ball, which was softer than a normal cricket ball and more likely to cause damage to the eye itself. He lost the eye. The player claimed that the organiser had failed to provide safety equipment to prevent the injury and failed to warn of the risk of eye injury. Evidence was presented that no helmets were really suitable for indoor cricket, and that they were discouraged by the industry. The risk of being struck was obvious and, according to Gleeson CJ and Hayne J, did not require a warning.[77]

The organiser and the spectator

When a spectator pays for admission to a venue, a contract exists whether a ticket is given or not. The contract contains implied terms that the organiser will make the premises reasonably safe for spectators, and that the spectator will behave in a reasonable fashion according to the occasion. A spectator who misbehaves is in breach of this contract with the organiser, and could be asked to leave. In fact, the duty the organiser owes to others in the area may mean that the organiser must remove unruly or otherwise dangerous spectators.

Organisers will be liable for crowd violence that was reasonably foreseeable if inadequate crowd control measures could be shown. The Hillsborough Stadium Soccer tragedy, when 93 football supporters were crushed to death during an FA Cup semi-final between Nottingham Forest and Liverpool, highlights the potential danger for organisers even in non-violent situations. New safety measures were introduced following a public inquiry, and in 2002 two senior police officers in charge of ground security were charged in connection with the disaster.[78]

Obligations of the occupier

Liability for the safety of premises often rests with the 'occupier' – who is not necessarily the owner. The occupier in law may be the lessee of the field, ground or facility for the season. The occupier is likely to be a sporting body, a local council, an event organiser, or a person who rents out a venue to those organising an event.

The liability of occupiers of premises was clearly and tragically set out in the case of the Bradford football disaster in Britain. There a wooden football stand 'packed to capacity' with more than 2000 spectators was set alight accidentally, causing the deaths of 56 spectators and serious injury to many others.[79] The owner of the ground, the football club, was found to be liable for damages.

Traditionally, the question of responsibility revolved around the issue of 'control' of the property in question, and the status of the person who was injured. The status of the entrant involved issues such as whether that person was there as of right, had paid, or was a trespasser.[80] There were problems with this technical area of the law, as it often created confused and unjust situations. Some states attempted to remedy the situation by enacting statutes.[81]

As a result of three Australian decisions, however, the special duties that existed under the old law of 'occupier's liability' have been combined with the general law of negligence.[82] In the last of these cases, the High Court adopted an earlier statement by Deane J that

> in all the relevant circumstances including the fact of the defendant's occupation of the premises and the manner of the plaintiff's entry upon them, the defendant owed a duty of care under the ordinary principles of negligence to the plaintiff.[83]

The occupier may be liable to participants. A rugby league player recovered against a local council for injury suffered when he fell on a sprinkler placed in the middle of a ground.[84] The occupier must also provide protection against reasonably foreseeable risks to spectators. Most decided cases involving injury fall within this category. Spectators have been compensated for various injuries including those caused by cars leaving the track at speedway meets and flying pucks at hockey games.

The Bradford football fire, mentioned above, is a shocking example of what can happen if those in control of facilities fail to fulfil their obligations to spectators. It was found in that case that the cause of the fire was the club's failure to remove rubbish that had built up under the stand because the kick boards between the steps had not been repaired. Once lit, the fire spread through the stand within two minutes. In addition, turnstiles were chained up and a number of exit gates were boarded up. The club had no emergency evacuation system, no stewards were trained in evacuation techniques, and no-one was manning the usable exit doors, the keys to which were not readily available. The fact that the club could not afford to dismantle the stand to clear rubbish was not relevant. If it could not do so, entry to the stand should have been restricted or the stand closed altogether.[85]

Cases involving players who score tries and knock down goal posts, or shoot baskets that collapse on spectators, might fall within this area.

In a more unusual example, a cricket player who hit a sightscreen while fielding and broke his nose sued the occupier, a municipal council, alleging negligence in constructing a sightscreen inside the boundary ropes. The council was found to be in breach of its duty of care, and the player was awarded damages of $38 390.[86]

The distinction between a closed venue such as a stadium and an open public space road or parkland creates different problems for the occupier and organiser. The proprietor of a stadium has control over entry, consumption of alcohol and the safety characteristics of the venue. The organiser in an open space must consider not only spectators but passers by, and may need to ensure the safety of competitors in relation to such hazzards as traffic.

Liability to strangers

The classic case that considered liability in this area involved the game of cricket. In *Bolton v Stone*[87] a woman was hit by a cricket ball while standing outside her house. She sued the local cricket club, the occupier of the nearby oval. Evidence showed that only six balls had been hit from the ground in 30 years. It was found that the risk of injury was so slight that it was not a real risk needing precautions, although it was foreseeable. There have been numerous similar Australian cases involving errant golf balls. Some have been successful.

A more commonplace situation was examined by the courts in Queensland. A father took his young son to soccer training one evening. The ground was 'occupied' by a football club at the time, and a large portable automatic sprinkler with horizontal revolving arms, owned by the club, was operating. Although the ground was in semi-darkness, there was sufficient light to train. The ball was kicked and landed near the sprinkler and two boys, including the plaintiff's son, ran toward it. The plaintiff called to the boys to slow down. One stopped, but the other kept going. The father jumped a fence and raced to stop the boy. He pushed him out of the way of the sprinkler but suffered a compound fracture of the leg himself. He brought an action for damages against the football club on the basis of occupier's liability and of a general duty of care. On an appeal on a procedural point, the court found that it was foreseeable that the ball used for training might land in the vicinity of the sprinkler and that a boy might pursue it. It was also foreseeable that parents of the boys training might attempt to stop a child running into a hazardous situation. The probability of injury occurring was enhanced by the fact that small boys were training in the half-light.[88]

The over-zealous fan

The position of the spectator as a potential defendant in legal proceedings should not be overlooked.

A person who buys a ticket to a sporting event is expected to behave in a reasonable manner. What is reasonable behaviour depends on all the circumstances. Different behaviour is tolerated from spectators at a football or boxing match from that which would be acceptable at a snooker tournament. If the entrant does not behave reasonably, the authorities have the right to use reasonable force to remove that person.[89] The fan who causes injury to a fellow spectator would obviously be treated in the same way as a defendant in any other proceedings. The deaths of 39 people following rioting by supporters of the Liverpool and Turin clubs at the 1985 European Cup Final in Brussels show that such situations do unfortunately occur. In this type of situation, the person actually causing the injury would be liable for damages (and might also be criminally liable). If it could be shown that the organiser of the game, or whoever was liable for ground or course security, had been negligent or unrealistic in preparing for the event, that person or body might also be liable.

Crowd control is an important part of ensuring that spectators are not injured. Enough barriers, enough police or security guards, realistic rules governing the supply of alcohol to spectators, and other mechanisms for the control of rowdy spectators once they actually begin to cause problems are all relevant here. There is always potential for a fan to cause injury to participants, and in that respect the organisers have a duty to the participants to take reasonable care of them. The case in which tennis player Monica Seles was stabbed by a spectator provided a warning in this respect. Crowds surging onto cricket pitches to congratulate players could potentially cause them unintended injury. Crowds hurling missiles at opposition teams or the referee are other examples relevant to control.

The various mechanisms in the UK by police and other authorities to prevent soccer hooliganism, such as segregation of rival fans, show the lengths to which crowd control must sometimes be taken to protect the majority of fans.

Liability of volunteers

Volunteers are essential to the functioning of sport at all levels and the operation of most sporting organisations. Many people give up their time on a regular basis to assist sports. There has been a growing sense of apprehension in the sporting community about the potential for liability of volunteers.

Under civil liability legislation all jurisdictions have made provision to protect volunteers. The NSW law, for example, provides that personal civil liability of a volunteer engaged in community work will be borne by the community organisation itself if the act or omission causing the injury by the volunteer was in good faith and was within the scope of that person's designated activities or instructions, or done by an office holder.

'Community work' is broadly defined, but includes work done for a sporting purpose.

A volunteer is not excluded from this protection through receiving reasonable expenses, but will be excluded if the conduct causing the injury involves a criminal act, intoxication or use of drugs, motor accidents, or liability for which the state requires insurance. Where the volunteer is protected the organisation may be liable; its liability is similar to vicarious liability, discussed below.[90]

Good Samaritans

The civil liability legislation in each state provides protection for good Samaritans who go to the aid of someone who is injured where the person acts in good faith and without expectation of payment, as long as they are not under the influence of drugs or alcohol.

Vicarious liability

Where a contract of employment exists (see chapter 4), employers are 'vicariously liable' for the torts of their employees. This means that the employer is legally liable for the conduct, although not personally to blame for it. It is often important, therefore, to distinguish between the relationship of employer and employee, and that of employee and independent contractor or agent.

The employer is not liable for all the employee's conduct, just for that which takes place in the course of the employment contract. This covers some, but not all, unauthorised acts of the employee.

The employer was sued in this way in *Watson v Haines*, mentioned above. The Department of Education was sued both in its own capacity, and as the employer of the teachers who coached Stephen Watson. The court found that the department was only liable for its own behaviour, as the teachers had not been negligent.

Vicarious liability arises either because the illegal act is authorised by the employer, or because, if not authorised, it is within the scope of employment. In *Rogers v Bugden*[91] it was found that the act of tackling was within the scope of the player's employment, even though it had been argued that the player was not authorised to engage in conduct such as a tackle outside the rules of the game. In the course of his decision Mahoney J made some comments that should be of great interest to sporting employers; he stated that in the context of rugby league as a professional game:

> [there] was ... a clear risk that a player who was 'revved up' might yield to the temptation to 'stop' Mr Rogers by whatever means could be employed ... [these things] are relevant in determining the responsibility of the Club ... It may be that, in professionalised sport, winning, and not playing, is the object. But motivating to win carries with it consequences. The risk that motivation will, in some, lead to illegitimate means of winning is, I believe, plain ... If an employer encourages action close to the line he may, in some circumstances, have to bear the consequences of action over the line.[92]

Transmission of infectious diseases in sport

The admission by high-profile athletes such as basketballer 'Magic' Johnson and diver Greg Louganis of their infection with HIV has underlined the need for, and the difficulties of sporting administrators when dealing with, infection control policies. While transmission of HIV during participation in sport is unlikely, hepatitis presents 'a far more serious picture'[93] due to the greater number of people in the community who are known to be carriers of various strains of this disease, and to the relative ease of its transmission.

The Australian Sports Medicine Federation (ASMF) has an infectious diseases policy that emphasises the importance of infection control procedures such as the removal of bleeding players to a 'blood bin', the removal of contaminated clothing, vaccination against hepatitis B and prohibitions on sharing equipment. In many sports referees have the power to remove bleeding players from the field. None of the guidelines recommend that those carrying the specified diseases cease playing altogether, although some guidelines issued by the Australian National Council on AIDS and the ASMF to assist HIV positive people in making a decision about continuing their participation in sport strongly recommend that such people do not participate in boxing or wrestling due to the greater risk of HIV transmission.[94]

Suggestions such as compulsory HIV testing for participants raise discrimination issues, as does exclusion, unless it can be shown that the measure is reasonably necessary to protect public health.

The liability of a carrier athlete for the transmission of HIV or hepatitis involves the ordinary principles of negligence, as does the potential liability of sporting organisations. Complying with the ASMF Infectious Diseases Policy would assist an organisation to defend a claim. A sporting organisation which was the employer of an infecting participant may be vicariously liable. Occupational health and safety issues might also arise.

Compensation legislation

Where an injured professional player or official is an employee of someone like the organiser or occupier, there is the possibility that the injured person could be covered by the workers' compensation legislation of a state. All employers are required to insure in respect of their liability for workers' compensation. The application of the legislation to workers varies according to the Act in force in the relevant state.[95] A press report in 1994 stated that a weekend football umpire who had contracted terminal skin cancer lodged a workers' compensation action in the Northern Territory.[96] Previous reports of a similar nature have involved beach inspectors in and around Sydney.

A second possible application of workers' compensation legislation is the situation where an employee plays a sport such as netball, football or soccer at lunch time in an organised competition for employees of similar businesses or occupations. Competitions of this kind are often organised for the employees of banks and insurance companies, and in the public service. It has been held that these participants are covered by workers' compensation, as they play the sport in the course of their employment.[97] Employer sanction of the competition is important here. A squash game between fellow employees, for example, would not fall into this category. The entry of a corporate team in a weekend 'fun run' would probably be too remote from the employment to be covered by workers' compensation.

Another potential application of workers' compensation provisions to sport is in occupations where physical fitness is at a premium. Firemen, for example, are required to undertake constant physical training during working hours, and injury during this time would be covered by workers' compensation-type legislation. This situation would probably be distinguishable from that of police officers, who are required to undertake fitness training in their own time in order to be fit for their work. The applicability of the legislation to situations of this type will depend on the actual wording of the statute involved. Once again, official sanction will be important.

Workers' compensation proceedings are different from an action in tort because it is not necessary under workers' compensation to prove that the employer was at fault in causing the injury. It is generally enough that the injury took place in work hours, or on the trip to or from the place of employment.

The amounts of damages awarded under workers' compensation legislation are also significantly lower than those that would be available at common law. Payments are generally made as weekly amounts while the person concerned is actually unable to perform normal duties. There is usually also provision for medical and other actual expenses and payment of a lump sum for specific loss of function. If a person lost all movement in a finger, for example, there would be a set amount of compensation for the injury.

The right to sue the employer at common law is removed or limited by some workers' compensation laws.[98] Where the right remains, if an action at common law is successful, the amount paid in workers' compensation must be repaid.

The NSW Sporting Injuries Insurance Scheme

The NSW Sporting Injuries Insurance Scheme[99] was set up to provide no-fault compensation to those injured while participating in sporting activity. The scheme is unique to NSW. It covers participants in all sports that apply to be included. Premiums vary according to the 'risk factor' of the sport involved. Contact sports and inherently dangerous sports such as hang-gliding and parachuting have a high risk factor when compared to sports like croquet or lawn bowls.

A supplementary scheme was introduced by amendment in 1984. Athletes competing in organised school sport and enrolled participants of the Department of Sport and Recreation are covered by the supplementary scheme.

Benefits are payable for listed injuries in relation to both schemes. Provision is made for extra payments where paraplegia or quadriplegia are involved. Some benefits are payable in the event of death.

As with workers' compensation, if common law damages are obtained the amount obtained under the scheme must be refunded.[100]

Faulty equipment

Injuries caused by defective equipment raise questions of product liability. Various state and Commonwealth statutes are aimed at excluding unsafe products from the marketplace – these are outlined briefly below. The occupational health and safety legislation of the Commonwealth and the states, the law of negligence and the law of contract may also be relevant.

One Australian example involved a scuba diving instructor who was liable in negligence when a novice diver died of saltwater asphyxiation after being provided with equipment that was defective in various respects. The mouthpiece was loose, there was a hole in a rubber mouth grip, and the air pressure delivered by a regulator was well below the recommended minimum pressure. The court held that a reasonable instructor would have checked all the equipment thoroughly before use and rectified any defects.[101]

While there have been few Australian cases relating to defective sporting equipment, it has been suggested that the American football player is an endangered species, judging by the number of claims made against the manufacturers of football helmets:

> Helmet manufacturers, saddled with huge and numerous products liability judgments, will pass on these costs to the consumers. We may reach the point where football is simply too expensive to play.[102]

The same author cites US cases dealing with 'baseball glasses, shotgun shells, ski boats, swimming pools, golf carts, snowmobiles, motorcycles, pool tables, bicycles, and elastic exercisers'. Astro turf and other artificial turf surfaces are also mentioned as sources of litigation.[103]

Laws covering defective equipment

Some laws, both state and Commonwealth, which are aimed at protecting purchasers (including the *Trade Practices Act* and the sale of goods legislation of the various states) contain sections that imply terms into all contracts for the purchase of consumer goods. If goods are not safe they will generally be 'not of merchantable quality' or not fit for the purpose for which they were sold, which will probably infringe one of the implied conditions.

The person who buys the goods, or a person who buys from the original purchaser, will have an action against the seller if it can be proved that damage resulted from a problem with the goods. This means that if I buy a life jacket that does not float and I almost drown, I would probably be able to recover damages from the seller.[104] There are problems with these provisions, however, because although the implied terms cannot be excluded, their protection only extends to the person who actually bought the goods or one who obtains title through that person. This means that if I buy the life jacket and my son uses it and is injured, he probably cannot recover damages.

The provisions are also limited to 'consumer' transactions, as defined in the particular law, and this might take some sporting equipment purchases out of the ambit of the Acts. Part VA of the *Trade Practices Act*, however, catches a broader range of persons.

Amendments to the *Trade Practices Act* in 2004 impose limits similar to those imposed by the state civil liability legislation on actions taken under that Act in relation to personal injuries and death.[105] Other amendments introduce the concepts of 'proportionate liability' and 'contributory negligence' into Commonwealth legislation, including the *Trade Practices Act*.[106]

Product safety standards

Product standards have been set for particular products under the *Trade Practices Act* and some state Fair Trading Acts.[107] The products in question have usually been the subject of several complaints or have resulted in a death. As well as banning the sale of these goods, the laws set standards for the production of others. Where goods are supplied contrary to a standard and damage is suffered, it will be assumed in any legal action that the goods have caused it. Some laws include compulsory recall of goods likely to cause injury. While the use of the standards in relation to sporting equipment has not been widespread, a standard for pedal bicycles has been in operation since 1980.[108] There are also standards for children's flotation devices and for motor cycle helmets.[109]

Effect of the civil liability legislation

The civil liability legislation has been enacted to change and clarify areas of tort law. The changes involved are monumental, and organisations and individuals should seek specific advice on their positions. They should also should look carefully at their risks, and take advantage of the opportunities provided by the relevant state legislation to reduce their potential liability. Documentation including signs may need to be changed and updated to maximise this opportunity. Organisations should closely monitor the behaviour of their volunteers. Sporting participants should be aware of the new limitations on their rights to take action if they are injured.

Over time the law will continue to develop, and all those involved should keep track of these developments.

Chapter 8

Insurance and risk management

This chapter provides information about risk management programs and the types of insurance available for the risks to organisations and individuals that cannot be totally eliminated.

The insurance crisis and responses

The causes of the insurance 'crisis' referred to in chapter 7 in the context of civil liability legislation have been summarised as follows:

> Arguably, the current 'insurance crisis' is due to a multitude of factors: the collapse of HIH in March 2001; the losses borne by the insurance industry globally following the terrorist attacks of September 11 2001; an increased propensity for individuals to bring claims; and the poor performance of public liability insurance generally.[1]

In response to the 'crisis', from 2001 governments and agencies commissioned a number of reviews on the laws of negligence and insurance.[2] Comprehensive civil liability legislation was implemented. The framework for reform by governments included an expectation that the insurance industry would deliver affordable public liability products to the community. To ensure that the benefits of the legislation were passed on to consumers the Australian Competition and Consumer Commission was asked to perform an ongoing role monitoring the insurance market on a six monthly basis for two years.[3]

As part of the process governments undertook to amend certain insurance practices, and several governments established or funded group liability schemes for non-profit organisations.[4]

A common conclusion among the reports on insurance was that 'sporting organisations are generally poorly informed as to their insurance cover and what activities and events are excluded.'[5]

Risk management is essential

With increased insurance costs, the importance of the traditional areas of risk management – risk assessment, risk minimisation and risk reduction – has become even more critical. Organisations must take more active responsibility for both their insurance coverage and their risk management procedures to reduce the prospect of incidents. Insurers often require evidence that these key steps are being undertaken as a condition of insurance.

Risk standards

In days gone by a sporting organisation's risk management process would have been a very haphazard affair determined by the common sense of the administrator running the organisation.

The Australia/New Zealand Standard on Risk Management[6] is a generic framework developed by Standards Australia for establishing the context, identification, analysis, evaluation, treatment, monitoring and communication of risk.[7] It is not intended to create uniform risk management systems – systems should be developed according to the needs, objectives and business of an organisation. Risk management has become an important and a much more formal process.

The standard has been adapted for the ASC in the document *Risk Management for Directors and Board Members of a National Sporting Organisation*.[8] The document emphasises risk management as a part of effective governance, and notes the essential involvement of both individuals and the organisation as a whole. It sets out in detail practical information on processes aimed at developing a 'whole of sport' risk management policy for an organisation and integrating the risk management process into normal organisational practice. Many of the areas it covers are also relevant to state and other sporting organisations. Both the ASC document and the standard emphasise that risk management is an on-going process.

What is risk?

The Standard on Risk Management defines risk as 'the chance of something happening that will have an impact on objectives.'

Risk of injury

While potential areas of legal liability for organisations and individuals involved in sport are considered throughout this book, clearly the tort law issues raised in chapter 7 have particular personal injury and public liability implications. The nature of sport means that people are regularly injured. If an injury has been caused by someone else, or is due to someone else's failure to take care, insurance may provide a remedy. From the opposite point of view it protects the person who has caused the injury or allowed it to occur.

Following the introduction of the civil liability legislation, sporting organisations and individuals have greater opportunities to reduce their exposure to risk by using warnings, indemnities and waivers. Particular care should be taken in the drafting of documents for this purpose. The legislation means that existing documentation should be revisited to ensure that it takes full advantage of the opportunities offered in a particular state for risk minimisation. Compliance by an organisation with any applicable industry standards or codes will prove useful in arguing against negligence, should an incident occur.

Other business risks

Other areas of potential risk for an organisation involve the whole way in which the organisation itself operates and the relationships it has with its participants, its staff and third parties. All the areas of law discussed in this book have potential relevance as risks. For example, is the organisation's standard documentation in relation to subleasing its premises clear and up to date? Does the organisation have policies to deal with harassment and discrimination in relation to its employees? What about an appropriate employment agreement? How secure are its banking practices? Are its accounts prepared in a timely and appropriate manner? Has anyone audited its insurance policies to ensure that they meet its requirements? Are there systems in place to ensure that the requirements of the *Corporations Act* and the constitution are complied with? Is the organisation taking necessary steps to protect its name, image and reputation? How does the organisation handle conflicts? What is its policy on the timing of briefing lawyers? Is there an asset register, and is it maintained?

These random questions give an indication of the areas that might expose the organisation to the risk of legal disputation, and cost.

Concepts of risk management

'Risk management' means the reduction of loss by identifying risks that will impact on the objectives of an organisation, assessing their level and the likelihood of loss, and formulating mechanisms to avoid, reduce or eliminate the loss.

Risk identification

Most organisations are aware of their obvious injury risks because people are routinely injured in a particular way due to the requirements of the sport, the nature of the premises and so on. It is important, however, for them to regularly assess the way they operate, the nature of their equipment and premises, and the way in which accidents or injuries or other losses might occur and have occurred if they honestly wish to limit their potential liability for injury.

In any organisation, both records and the experience of managers and long-serving officials will provide evidence of areas that involve risk. The experiences of similar organisations will also provide information. Some previous accidents may have been unlikely or unusual, but generally records give a good guide to the areas of greatest risk. On the other hand, some likely accidents may not have occurred yet due to good luck rather than good management. Special care should be taken to identify situations that might be classified in this way.

The ASC document mentioned on page 123 argues that the best way of identifying risks is brainstorming in a group workshop, as checklists 'precondition the expectations of those involved and block the identification of risks that go beyond those on the list.'[9] People from outside the organisation can provide invaluable assistance.

Risk assessment

After assessing potential areas of risk, the danger of a particular incident occurring must be assessed by analysis and evaluation. At this stage risks should be assembled in priority order – that is, starting with the greatest risk and working down – and attacked on that basis. This step prioritises risks compared to other risks. An organisation should then work through a plan setting out all the areas of risk.

Risk treatment

Once risks have been identified and assessed, organisations and individuals must implement a planned risk treatment campaign. Planning at this stage should aim to address risks in a concerted way, and should set out achievable goals in respect of the most serious risks. Some risks can be avoided, some can be reduced and others can be transferred to another body. The implementation of well designed treatment responses can decrease the number and likelihood of risks materialising, and may help maintain or even reduce insurance premiums. For example, a policy of postponing events in dangerous conditions may enable an organisation to completely avoid some risks of injury.

Even the best risk management programs, however, will generally not completely prevent accidents and incidents from occurring. Insurance is always a part of the risk equation and in itself helps to minimise risk to the organisation – it is itself a transfer of risk.

Monitoring and review

Risk management should be linked to a body's other processes. It should be continually monitored, and backed by continuous improvement. An organisation is in a good position to learn from its past.

The role of insurance

An insurance policy is an agreement by an insurer, in return for payment of a premium, to indemnify the insured against the occurrence of a specified event that gives rise to loss.

Insurance companies categorise their policies in relation to particular risks. Be aware, however, that insurance policies sold by two different companies under the same or similar names may be very different. It is always best to compare the terms of the policies (the actual wording) in making comparisons of premium rates; the cheaper policy may be very different in its cover from the more expensive policy. Policies should also be considered for their suitability. If the cheaper policy is adequate for the organisation's purposes, well and good. It is quite useless, however, to buy insurance that does not cover your major area of risk or other foreseeable risk areas.

The limit of indemnity and the amount of the excess on different policies may also vary. The *limit of indemnity* may be described in the policy as a total amount or as an amount for each occurrence – that is, each injury or other incident – that needs to be compensated. The *excess* is the amount that the organisation must contribute in respect of a particular occurrence before the policy kicks in. Organisations may decide to have a high excess and self insure to that point, or they may take a lower excess, in which case the policy is likely to cost more.

The main policies that an organisation should hold are briefly described below. Not all will be relevant to every organisation or individual, and there are others that might also be considered in particular circumstances.

Public liability

Public liability insurance provides indemnity in respect of bodily injury or property damage caused by an accident. The accident must have occurred during the period for which the policy was operative. If a claim is made against the insured person and that person is liable to pay damages, the insurer will either pay the amount claimed or dispute the coverage of the policy in the circumstances.

Members of a sporting club are not generally covered under a public liability policy for injury inflicted on them or fellow participants. Generally only members of the public may be compensated. Some public liability policies, however, may be extended on request to cover club members and other participants.

A public liability policy may or may not cover volunteers who are not members and volunteers who are members. Coaches who are volunteers and are not accredited may need to be covered under a public liability policy rather than a professional liability policy (see page 128). Those who volunteer to perform services on behalf of an organisation such as coaching, officiating, staffing canteens, supervising children or the many other volunteer capacities that enable sports to survive are likely to assume that they are covered in some way. It is usually possible to cover your own members and other volunteers by an extension to your policy if they are not already covered.[10]

Product liability

Product liability cover, or cover for injuries resulting from products sold which, for example, cause food poisoning, may be sensible if a sporting organisation sells food and drink at sporting events. Sports sometimes sell or provide equipment and clothing to members and others; this potential source of liability should also be considered.

Product liability policies are generally 'events occurring' policies. This means that if the organisation or individual against whom a claim is made is insured at the time of the event that causes the injury, the policy will potentially cover the incident. This is in contrast to a 'claims made' policy, in which the organisation or individual needs to be insured at the time of the making of a claim.

Player accident insurance

Even if players are covered under an extension to a public liability insurance policy, they will not necessarily be covered for all injuries suffered while participating in a sport.

A public liability policy will cover those accidents for which the organisation or someone else covered under the policy might be liable at law. The nature of sport, however, is such that in many cases participants are injured and no-one is at fault. In these circumstances, player accident insurance would cover the injured player. Player accident insurance may include a tragedy benefit to compensate for death, as well as compensation for the loss of various bodily functions, loss of income and other losses. Under a player accident policy these benefits are set at a fixed sum regardless of the loss the person actually suffers.

An injured player covered by player accident insurance may still claim under a public liability policy against the organisation or person causing the injury. Any payments made under the accident policy, however, will be taken into account in assessment of damages at law.[11]

Player accident insurance may reduce the likelihood of claims for negligence by compensating victims quickly for their immediate costs.

Defamation insurance

Insurance against being sued for defamation is particularly important in a sporting context. Defamation is not generally covered under public or professional liability insurance, but an insurer can be approached to provide the additional cover. It is important that organisations do not overlook defamation when organising insurance for board members and staff, as the nature of sport means that defamation is not unlikely.

Professional indemnity insurance

Professionals are generally those who have a qualification that enables them to provide services by way of giving specialist advice. Professional indemnity insurance indemnifies the insured against claims for personal injury, property damage or loss covered by an act, error or omission in breach of a person's professional duty. The type of incident covered by a professional liability policy in a sporting context is generally injury suffered as a result of some instruction or advice from a coach or trainer.

The type of qualification required for the various types of professional liability policy for coaches is generally accreditation under the National Coaching Accreditation Scheme, although some policies list and cover specific persons with special experience in a particular sport.

In contrast to the public liability policies discussed above, which are 'events occurring' policies, professional indemnity policies are generally 'claims made' policies; that is, a coach needs to be insured at the time a claim is made. As a claim can be brought up to three years from the date of an accident, it is generally accepted that coaches need insurance cover for several years after they cease to coach. Most insurers will provide 'run down' cover at a lower cost to ensure that a coach still has cover even after ceasing to coach.

Directors' and officers' policies

The directors and officers of an organisation which is a company or an incorporated association may be sued by the organisation or by another person for breaches of their duties as directors or officers.

While earlier laws provided that a company could not take out insurance on behalf of its directors, this prohibition has now been removed. A company may now, in its rules, indemnify its directors and officers and insure them against liability to a third person, provided that the liability does not involve a lack of good faith. A company may not indemnify a director or officer for negligence, default or breach of duty, and directors and officers cannot insure for liability of this kind. A company may pay for insurance covering the costs and expenses of defending an action in these areas, provided that the director or officer is successful in defending the action.

Corporate directors' and officers' policies cover the company itself and its directors and officers against those legal costs, expenses and civil claims that may be insured at law. Personal directors' and officers' policies may be taken out individually by a director or officer to cover costs and allowable civil damages in respect of a nominated company. Directors' legal expenses policies cover those costs in relation to an individual director.

These policies are 'claims made' policies (see Professional indemnity insurance on page 128).

Association liability insurance

Association liability insurance provides cover for associations for a combination of the liabilities covered by directors and officers and professional indemnity policies.

Workers' compensation insurance

The laws of the various states provide that workers must be insured by their employers against injury in the course of employment.

Legal expense insurance

Legal expense insurance provides indemnity against legal expenses associated with court proceedings.

Property insurance

All organisations should take out insurance to cover their assets.

General rules for persons insuring

Read the policy

While it may be difficult and time-consuming, there is no substitute for knowing what the policy covers and how it operates. If you cannot understand exactly what your policy means, write to your broker or insurer setting out your queries. If they explain the issue properly, you may realise that your cover is inadequate or inappropriate. If they do not explain it properly, you may be able to take legal action against either of them if you suffer damage because the policy fails to cover some situation that you believed it to cover. Critical questions include coverage as to persons, area and timing; exclusions; and whether there are any conditions for claims.

Notification under the policy

The policy may require you to notify the insurer of changes to your organisation, or any possible claims, as soon as you become aware of them. If you do not do what the policy requires in this regard, you may forfeit your right to make a claim.

Do not admit liability

Your policy will often prevent you from admitting liability before discussing the issue with the insurer.

Eliminate the possibility of gaps

It is important for an organisation to have insurances that cover all those who might conceivably be sued, and in respect of all those who might conceivably be injured or suffer damage. For this reason it is often better to insure with one insurer or through one broker lest valuable time and resources be expended on determining which, if any, of several insurance companies must indemnify in respect of a particular injury or damage.

Limits of indemnity

It is important for organisations to know how much cover they have. Verdicts in relation to very serious injury are rising rapidly, and cover should be appropriate for a verdict in several years time rather than today. Proceedings need not be instituted for three years, and with court delays a significant time may elapse before a matter is heard.

It is also important to know whether the indemnity limit on your policy is an aggregate limit, or a limit for each occurrence. If there is an aggregate limit and two serious accidents occur in one year, the policy may be insufficient to cover the organisation's liability.

Alternative insurance arrangements

In a number of sports there are pooling arrangements that involve group purchases of insurance to obtain the benefits of greater buying power. There may be administrative efficiencies from the point of view of both the insurer and the insureds. Pooling with the larger groups of one sport has advantages in that the risks are likely to be similar, well known, and able to be factored into risk management programs.

Where low risk sports are linked to higher risk sports costings in the policy will often be determined at different levels to reflect the different risks.[12]

Chapter 9

Criminal liability

The question of criminal liability for action on the sporting field is highly topical in a society that is increasingly focusing on violence.

It has already been emphasised that those in sport should not assume that they are immune from prosecution just because a particular incident takes place in a 'game'. This chapter focuses on broad categories of crimes that may be committed by players in the course of their activity, and includes some comment on crowd violence. The complexity of the criminal law in Australia makes more detailed discussion unproductive.

Many areas of criminal law that are not considered in what follows might arise in sport: examples are 'fixing' or rigging of matches, illegal gambling carried on at some sporting venues in relation to the outcome of a match, horse doping or failure to allow a horse to run on its merits, appropriation of funds of a sporting club by its officials, theft of equipment, and illegal use of drugs by athletes. Most of these situations attract the normal application of the law or are relevant to only one or two sports, and so are not discussed here. Allegations of impropriety and 'fixing' of events in several sports have underlined the view that sport is similar to other areas in the potential for corruption that it offers.

Standard of proof

Standard of proof is the extent or degree to which a charge must be proven before a person can be convicted in court. The standard required in criminal law is 'beyond reasonable doubt'.[1] This means that the jury or judge must be satisfied that the charge against the accused person has been proven to this extent before a conviction can occur.

To prove most crimes it is necessary to show that the accused person intended to do the act that constitutes the crime. In some cases, however, it is enough if the person charged was 'recklessly indifferent' about the consequences of their actions.

Criminal law

The criminal law is administered by the states. This means there is no single piece of legislation that contains all the laws relating to crime. There is a Commonwealth *Crimes Act*, but this only deals with crime in areas that the Commonwealth administers under the Australian Constitution. Other Commonwealth Acts also create criminal offences. The *Corporations Act*, for example, sets out various offences that may be committed by company officers

Each state has a major piece of legislation dealing with crime. Queensland, Western Australia and Tasmania have enacted laws that aim to remove all operation of the common law in relation to crime in their states. This is called 'codifying' the law, and these Acts are called criminal codes.[2] All the other states have a major piece of legislation dealing with crime, but the legislation does not attempt to cover the whole area to the exclusion of the common law. Murder and manslaughter, for example, are dealt with under the common law in South Australia and Victoria. The NSW *Crimes Act 1900* contains a section dealing with murder that differs in some respects from the common law.[3] State laws other than criminal codes or Crimes Acts may also create criminal offences punishable by the courts.

The areas of crime discussed here are those involving physical harm to participants or others involved in sport, including the major categories of assault, murder and manslaughter.[4]

Assault

As discussed in chapter 7, a person who suffers harm due to an assault may have a common law action in tort.[5] Assault is also a crime. The distinction between tort and crime means that as well as the victim having the right to sue to recover damages, the police may charge someone, resulting in a jail term or a fine. The burden of proof in the two situations is different; a higher standard applies to the criminal proceedings, and the issue of intent must also be considered.

Criminal assault is 'a term used to describe a range of activities constituting an interference, actual or apprehended, with the person of another'.[6] Behaviour that injures another may be an assault. In theory, behaviour that threatens another may also involve an assault.

Offences involving assault are generally categorised according to the severity of their result. Intention or recklessness are necessary to prove an offence. How does this fit in with the idea of contact sport, be it soccer, hockey, touch football, rugby or water polo? Where should the line be drawn between 'rough play' and assault?

In 1995 the NSW Court of Criminal Appeal imposed a sentence of three months' jail on a football player who raised his arm and struck the head of an opposing player. Of interest were these comments:

> The policy of the law will not permit the mere occasion of a rugby league match to render innocent or otherwise excuse conduct which can discretely be found, beyond reasonable doubt, to constitute a criminal offence.[7]

In a similar case, an English rugby union player was jailed for 28 days after a punch that left his opponent requiring facial reconstruction.[8]

The question of implied consent to assault by other players is the major issue in any consideration of assault in sport. It is only fair to acknowledge that those taking the field may expect and agree to some degree of violence. The extent to which this consent provides a defence to a criminal charge has been considered by the courts.

In an old English case involving an illegal prize fight, all the judges found that the consent of the 'victim' is irrelevant where a criminal charge is involved. The idea that it is against the public interest to recognise such consent was an important consideration.[9] The fact that the fight in question was illegal is relevant to that particular decision.

In a non-sporting situation, consent to an act that is unlawful in itself is irrelevant.[10] Duelling, for example, is unlawful and the consent of the injured party is irrelevant to any subsequent legal proceedings.

In the area of sport, there is authority suggesting that ordinary and reasonable violence that is incidental to the sport in question has the implied consent of participants, which would preclude assault.

It seems, however, that a person cannot consent to the infliction of grievous (serious) bodily harm. In a case where a rugby scrum half punched an opponent and was charged with inflicting grievous bodily harm, the defence of consent was raised. The defendant was found guilty. The extent of the force used was the deciding factor in this case.[12] It has been stated that the issue boils down to 'the intention of the parties and the mode and conditions of the particular encounter'.[13] So anger or hostility and a predominant intention to inflict substantial bodily harm may transform a sporting performance into a criminal activity.

In Australia, a celebrated case involved a finding of assault against Leigh Matthews, an Australian football player of great fame and experience (and later a high profile coach).[14] Matthews was charged with assault occasioning actual bodily harm, and with unlawfully and maliciously inflicting grievous bodily harm, following an onfield brawl. At the hearing, Matthews pleaded guilty to the first charge, and was fined $1000 and bound over for two years. An appeal against the fine was upheld owing to the defendant's previous good character.

Where the injury is not so great and the defendant is not a figure in the public eye, it could be that Australian courts see the disciplinary tribunal of the sport as the appropriate body to deal with an assault.

In a South Australian case, a player found guilty of assault had his conviction set aside on appeal. The player had broken an opponent's nose during an Australian football match. An umpire had reported the matter to the relevant association, which had dismissed it for technical reasons. The appeal court confirmed the magistrate's finding of guilt, but exercised its discretion to dismiss the charge without recording a conviction. In so doing, Johnston J stated that it would be

> turning a blind eye to reality to overlook that such matters were dealt with week by week in the various football associations in this State and other States by other tribunals that are set up within the framework of the game to hear such reports.[15]

This finding indicates that the courts may not be prepared to deal with 'everyday' sporting violence that is part of the game involved. Violence that is out of the ordinary would presumably be appropriately handled by the criminal courts.

Murder and manslaughter

A number of offences that involve the killing of a human being come into the category of homicide. Offences involving unlawful death fall into two broad categories: murder and manslaughter. The two may be distinguished by the mental element involved.

Murder generally requires 'malice aforethought',[16] which means the act causing death must be done with the intention of causing death or grievous bodily harm. Murder may also involve an act causing death accompanied by 'reckless indifference' as to its outcome, where the probability of death or grievous bodily harm was foreseen by the person doing the act, but was not necessarily an intended outcome.

There appear to be no reported cases involving murder by sporting participants. One reason for this is that the intention element in such a crime is particularly difficult to prove in a sporting situation. A situation where a player pulls out a knife and fatally stabs an opponent would potentially involve murder; but this rarely, if ever, occurs.

Sporting situations would generally involve a less direct form of killing. A case where, for example, a racing driver deliberately and dangerously went out of his way to force an opponent off a track might involve a premeditated act.

The pace of sporting competition and the partisan attitude of almost all those present make the collection of evidence in relation to offences difficult. Some sports involve the automatic video recording of games for television or other purposes, and this solves the evidence difficulty to some extent. Even so, the camera may not be focusing at the time on the particular event causing injury. Other sporting events, the majority of them, are not recorded. This means that clear evidence of what has occurred may be difficult to produce, and evidence indicating actual intention more difficult still.

Manslaughter is generally an unlawful killing that does not involve the element of intention required by murder. It may involve death caused by a culpably negligent act, or accidentally by an unlawful act. Provocation or other mitigating circumstances may also be involved.

In an English case, manslaughter was proven where a deliberate and reckless soccer tackle outside the laws of the game resulted in death.[17] Death from a 'niggling' blow during another soccer match resulted in a charge for the same crime.[18] Murder charges were reduced to a finding of manslaughter in both these cases because the required element of intention was not proven.

The Heke case in Brisbane received huge publicity throughout the country in 1991. It involved a charge of manslaughter following the death of a rugby league player who had been tackled high while running with the ball. Heke was acquitted after ten hours of consideration by the jury.

Fortunately, deaths in sport are more likely to result from mere accident than from intentional or reckless conduct; but a suspicion of murder or manslaughter cannot be ruled out in some circumstances. The situation in relation to criminal liability for sporting activity has been summarised as follows:

> If a man is playing according to the rules and practice of the game and is not going beyond it, it may be reasonable to infer that he is not actuated by any malicious motive or intention, and that he is not acting in a manner which he knows will be likely to be productive of death or injury. But, independent of the rules, if the prisoner intended to cause serious hurt to the deceased, or if he knew that, in charging as he did, he might produce serious injury and was indifferent and reckless as to whether he would produce serious injury or

not, then the act would be unlawful. In either case he would be guilty of a criminal act and you must find him guilty; if you are of a contrary opinion you will acquit him.[19]

There is always the possibility that a coach, manager or other person involved in one of these offences might be open to a charge of being an accessory to the crime. The encouragement of violent behaviour by team members might be an example of this kind.

Criminal negligence

Criminal liability may apply to grossly negligent conduct. When a grandstand collapsed killing 15 spectators in 1992 at the French FA final in Corsica, the president of the French Soccer Federation (the organisers) was charged with manslaughter.[20]

Policy issues

While an injured player may derive little benefit from laying criminal charges in relation to a violent sporting incident, proceedings may be initiated on behalf of the community by police or other law enforcement authorities. In some circumstances the victim of the crime may be entitled to compensation for any injuries (see Compensation on page 139).Given the high profile that sport enjoys in our community, criminal punishment may be an extremely symbolic form of deterrent against unacceptable behaviour. A criminal record is not generally an attractive proposition to an otherwise law-abiding citizen.

The issue of public interest in prosecuting criminal acts in sport was recognised as far back as the nineteenth century. In a case involving an illegal prize fight, the judge noted that not only the victim but also the public had been injured by the act in question.[21]

Whether a person is charged with a criminal offence will depend on a variety of factors. A charge may originate with the police or other law enforcement authorities; or, less commonly, an individual may lay a complaint.

The police have traditionally refrained from involvement in sporting violence, leaving the hierarchy of the particular sport to deal with it. It is clear, however, that the approach of the sporting body to violent behaviour in its code may influence whether or not police action ensues. In Victoria, for example, following a spate of onfield violence, the Victorian police laid charges in the Leigh Matthews case. The VFL had taken no immediate action in that case because the player in question was not reported by the umpires. The Victorian police minister suggested that police action might be necessary; the VFL then handed down a four-week suspension. Police charges were laid almost at once,[22] even though more commonplace occurrences may be considered more properly handled by the sport's administration.[23]

This suggests that despite their general reluctance to interfere in sporting matters, law enforcement authorities will involve themselves in extreme circumstances, particularly where the governing body of the sport is not seen to be acting decisively to eliminate violence. Whether these trends will extend to other sports and states is yet to be seen, but those involved in sport should be aware that criminal action is not out of the question.

In relation to the duties of sporting associations to control and sanction violent play, a report has suggested that they consider the establishment of a policy

> whereby, in addition, to action by their Judiciary/Tribunal, details of violent behaviour on the field of play on the part of their members which in the opinion of the sporting associations constitutes a criminal act are referred to law enforcement agencies for the appropriate action.[24]

Violence in sport

An Australian study on violence in sport prepared by the Sport and Recreation Ministers' Council[25] makes the following comments on the current position:

> Research has indicated that very little statistical data has been collected and is available to support the hypothesis that the intensity and incidence of violence in sport has actually increased over the past 5–10 years in Australia.
>
> The general perception by most sporting organisations and the media is that the incidence and intensity of violence in sport, both on and off the field, has at the best decreased and at the worst remained static.
>
> It is also the collective view of many sports administrators, coaches and referees, that there has been no increase of violence in sport at senior levels, but that at junior level a problem may exist.
>
> Nevertheless increasing community attention is being directed towards violent sports behaviour and the Task Force believes that no matter what the current level of violence in sport, the important thing is to ensure that overseas trends and experiences do not occur in Australia.

Whether these perceptions owe anything to administrative failure to admit that there is an increase in violence in their own sport is unclear.

Whether sport is actually becoming more violent is not as important, however, as whether the community in general is prepared to tolerate even the existing levels of violence. It might be argued that even static levels of violence have taken on a new dimension over the past few years with advancing television technology and increased public access to sports programs.

The strategies adopted by the Ministers' Council as a result of the report focused on junior players. The council favoured the develop-ment of codes of ethical behaviour in all sports for players, parents, spectators, referees and officials. Various states have developed mater-ials on dealing with 'sports rage'.

In relation to media influence in the area of sports violence, the council stated:

> The mass media is a very powerful agent in the formulation of an individual's attitudes, and can induce positive or negative behaviour … The Task Force is of the opinion that in as much as the media reports on/off field violence, it has an obligation to do so responsibly and that any developed strategy should address the de-emphasising of reporting and highlighting on/off field violence in sport and reflect the positive attributes of individual/team effort, skill, competition, fair play and excellence.[26]

Approaches to various media groups for assistance in reducing the number of undesirable incidents have been made on that basis.[27]

The sporting crowd

Crowd violence has become an important issue. Soccer gang warfare in the UK shows the repercussions of uncontrolled crowd activity. Both organisers and police have a duty to provide adequate protection for members of the general public attending sporting matches.

The question of crowd control and the impact of alcohol was another issue considered by the Ministers' Council, which suggested that state and territory ministers recommend to sporting organisations that where alcohol is seen to be a problem, alcohol consumption at a particular event should be restricted to sale in appropriate containers in designated areas. Many sporting organisations have heeded that recommendation.

Compensation

All the states have statutory schemes that provide compensation for those injured during the commission of a crime.[28] This is necessary because any fine paid by a convicted criminal does not go to the victim. The victim may sue for damages, but this may be a long and costly process, and the offender may not have assets to pay any damages awarded. In many situations, therefore, statutory compensation is essential to the victim.

When claiming compensation, a victim is not required to prove beyond reasonable doubt that an offence occurred, and it is not necessary that the offender has been convicted. The civil law standard of the balance of probabilities is all that is required.

Chapter 10

Discrimination and other issues

Sport reflects the society in which it occurs. Different sports have traditionally been played by members of various social classes. Polo, for example, has never been truly accessible to the general community because of the prohibitive cost of keeping the number of ponies required for a game. In contrast, swimming in Australia has been a relatively classless sport because of the availability of facilities for training and so on. Other sports such as tennis and golf have been reasonably accessible in this country, while in some other countries where space is at a premium they are played only by the wealthy.

Access to some sports clubs and venues has traditionally been closed to people from certain socioeconomic, racial or religious backgrounds. Women have also been excluded from some sports and sporting clubs. Disabled athletes have been penalised for failure to perform simple tasks rendered impossible by their disability after competing with distinction in the contest itself. Indigenous Australians have been the victims of 'exclusion from competition, discrimination within it, and at times gross inequality of chances, choices and facilities'. It has been said that they are denied competition in two ways: structurally, because of their place in the 'political, legal, economic and social system', and institutionally, because 'within their domain facilities do not exist.'[1]

What is discrimination at law?

The word 'discriminate' generally means to treat one person differently from, or less favourably than, another.

Two types of discrimination are generally recognised by the law. Discrimination may occur directly, as in a situation where a woman is refused a job because of her sex. Sex stereotypes may be important in direct discrimination. An employer may refuse to give a married

woman a particular job, for example, because married women sup-
posedly dislike travelling in their jobs, or because the employer
believes that women are not career-motivated.

Indirect discrimination involves the situation where a class of
people is excluded because of a particular requirement that is not of
fundamental relevance. A height requirement for a job, for example,
may exclude most women and many people from certain ethnic
groups. It may also unreasonably exclude the disabled.[2]

Laws against discrimination

Laws exist to help people who encounter discrimination, and as means
of showing the community that discriminatory practices are not
accepted. The laws dealing with discrimination are not aimed at discrimination at large, but at discrimination against particular categories of person, and in particular circumstances. In Australia, there are
anti-discrimination laws at both the Commonwealth and the state
level. The legislation is outlined briefly below, with some discussion of
its possible application to sports.[3]

This section does not set out to thoroughly cover the various laws
aimed at discrimination. It is included to inform readers of broad areas
where the law may apply, and to show some of the problems associated with discrimination laws in sport.

Racial discrimination

One of the first laws aimed at discrimination in Australia was the
Commonwealth *Racial Discrimination Act 1975*.[4] It prohibits discrimination on the basis of race, colour, descent, and national or ethnic
origin, in relation to access to places or facilities, housing and accommodation, the provision of goods and services, employment and the
right to join unions.

The basic question is whether the racial distinction is a material
factor in making a decision or performing an act. For example, the
naming of and the failure to change the name of the 'ES Nigger Brown
Stand' at the Athletic Oval in Toowoomba was found not to be discriminatory against indigenous Australians, as racial distinction was
not a factor in the decisions.[5]

Racial vilification

Racial vilification is offensive behaviour based on racism, and is prohibited.[6] Most professional sports have codes to deal with racial vilification.[7]

Sex discrimination

Sex discrimination in sport has existed in various forms since the development in Britain of the amateur 'gentleman' sportsman who was described in chapter 1. There is no doubt that in many ways women are treated less favourably than men in a sporting context. Consider, for example, the greater number of Olympic sports available to men. The marathon for women was first introduced only at the Los Angeles Olympics in 1984. Women competitors generally receive less prize money than men. While some argue that this difference is quite justified because in sports such as tennis, women are less skilled and offer less of a drawcard than men, this is not generally borne out by attendances at women's tournaments.

The Commonwealth government enacted the *Sex Discrimination Act* in 1984. That Act makes it unlawful to discriminate against a person on the grounds of sex, marital status or pregnancy, or stereotyped views about those areas. It relies as one of its main constitutional bases on the United Nations Convention on the Elimination of All forms of Discrimination against Women, a document that resulted from various international forums held during the International Decade of Women.

The *Sex Discrimination Act* prohibits sex discrimination in employment, education, the provision of goods, services and facilities, accommodation and clubs. Both direct and indirect discrimination are covered. There are some exceptions to its operation, and there is a general consideration of 'reasonableness' in relation to pregnancy.

Under the Act, written complaints of discrimination are made to the Human Rights and Equal Opportunity Commission (HREOC), which undertakes a process of investigation and conciliation. Relief can be sought at the same time to maintain the status quo until the complaint can be dealt with. If the conciliation process is unsuccessful, the person complaining has the right to take the matter to the Federal Court. If the court finds the complaint proven, it can make various orders; for example, it can order the offender to stop the behaviour, and make good any loss or damage caused by it, or make orders for employment or reemployment.

In *Gardiner v AANA Ltd*[8] it was found that the netball organisation discriminated against Gardiner by preventing her from playing in elite netball matches because she was pregnant. An exemption relating to membership of a voluntary body was not applicable because she was not a member of that body. The netball organisation was ordered to pay her $6750 in damages.

Disability discrimination

The Commonwealth *Disability Discrimination Act 1992* makes discrimination on the grounds of disability unlawful in the areas covered in other discrimination legislation and discussed below.[9] Where the Act differs from other discrimination legislation covering disability is in the definition of 'disability', which is extremely broad.[10] The disabilities covered by the legislation include physical and intellectual disabilities as well as those caused by disease or illness. Infection with HIV, for example, is a disability for the purposes of the Act.

The Act contains some exceptions; for example, where a disability means that a person would not be able to carry out the inherent requirements of a job, or could only carry them out at the cost of 'unjustifiable hardship' to the employer. Other exceptions relate to insurance and superannuation. HREOC has the power to grant exemptions from its provisions in other circumstances on application.

An important US sporting case in relation to disability concerned Casey Martin, a talented golfer with a degenerative circulatory disease that made walking difficult. His disability fell within the *Americans with Disabilities Act* of 1990. He sought permission from the PGA Tour to use a golf cart in the third stage of the PGA Tour School. He was supported by medical records. The rules of golf did not prohibit the use of carts, but the PGA Tour rules did not allow them during the third stage of the Tour School. When the PGA Tour refused he took the matter to court. The legislation required entities operating 'public accommodations' to make 'reasonable modifications' in policies to accommodate people with disabilities unless making them would 'fundamentally alter the nature of ... such accommodations'. The Supreme Court found that the PGA Tour School was a public accommodation, and that Martin clearly fell within the protection of the provision. Allowing him to use a golf cart was not a modification that would fundamentally alter the character of the competition. The essence of golf had always been shot-making – the walking rule was neither an essential attribute of the game itself or of tournament golf, and in any case Martin endured greater fatigue with a cart than an able bodied competitor did when walking.[11]

In *De Alwis v Hair*[12] a cricket fan lodged a complaint that bowler Muttiah Muralitheran had been discriminated against by umpire Hair because he had a disability. The bowler had a 'flexion deformity' of one arm, and was called for many 'no balls' by the referee. The action was dismissed at first instance on the grounds that the complaint lacked substance and that it had not been lodged by the aggrieved person as the Act required. The application for review by the Federal Court was found to be misconceived.

Maguire v SOCOG[13] involved a claim of a failure to supply certain services for the blind during the Sydney Olympics.

Hall v Victorian Amateur Football Association involved a refusal to allow an HIV positive athlete to participate in a football competition. The discrimination was not covered by a general exception that allowed discrimination where it was reasonably necessary to protect the health and safety of any person.[14]

State legislation

All the states and territories have laws aimed at discrimination of one type or another.[15] The state Acts cover similar ground to that covered by the Commonwealth *Sex Discrimination* and *Racial Discrimination Acts*. The state Acts operate side by side with the Commonwealth legislation, but if there is any inconsistency between the two Commonwealth law will prevail.

Some behaviour that would fall within one law is not prohibited by the other, so careful consideration is needed to determine which law to use in a given situation.

Women and sport

Although some of the most famous Australian sports achievers have been women, the general level of female participation in sport has not been as high as that of males. Biological evidence suggests that the abilities of women are closer to those of men than is shown by current standards.

The situation of women's sport has been summarised in this way:

Women's sport, it seems, is caught in a curious and frustrating paradox between the twin and opposite conditions of moments of brilliant achievement and persistent neglect and discrimination. Consider the example of the winner of the women's 800 metres final in the 1928 Amsterdam Olympics. Having won the race and set a new world record, she and some of the other runners collapsed on the track from the exertion. The male administrators were so upset by this sight that the 800 metres, one of only 5 track and field events for women, was removed from the Olympic program. The fact that men regularly collapsed after major competitions did not seem to have the same effect in any of their events. The women's event did not reappear until 1960.[16]

Although laws aimed at discrimination attempt to provide equal access and opportunities for men and women, exceptions are provided for some types of sporting activity. The *Sex Discrimination Act*, for example, allows discrimination that excludes one sex 'from participating in any competitive sporting activity in which the strength, stamina or physique of competitors is relevant'.[17] This exception does not apply to those participating as coaches, umpires, referees, administrators or in any 'prescribed' sporting activity. It does not apply to the sporting activities of those aged 12 and under. This sex-based sports exception is repeated in differing forms in the state Acts.

Discrimination in employment

In employment situations, the various discrimination laws cover recruitment, standard terms and conditions of employment, dismissal, retirement and enterprise agreements.

Complaints about discrimination in employment are probably the most common complaints under discrimination legislation.

The Commonwealth Act provides many exclusions where there is a genuine occupational qualification that a person be of a particular sex: for example, that the duties of a position can only be performed by a person with particular physical attributes not possessed by a person of the other sex; that the duties must be performed by a person of a particular sex to preserve decency or privacy because they involve fitting clothing for persons of a particular sex; or that the position involves searches of the clothing or bodies of persons of a particular sex. Similar exclusions apply under several state Acts.

Discrimination in a sporting context

An important case involving discrimination in a sporting context involved well-known Sydney racing identity Gai Waterhouse. Action was taken under the NSW legislation. Waterhouse claimed that she had been discriminated against by the refusal of the Australian Jockey Club to grant her a trainer's licence. She claimed that the refusal was on the basis that her husband had been warned off racecourses following his part in a racehorse ring-in scandal and that it contravened the legislation. The case turned on the meaning of the words 'marital status' under the Act, and whether marital status could extend to the identity of the person to whom one was married. The Equal Opportunity Tribunal dismissed the claim initially, finding that it did not. On appeal, the Court of Appeal found that this was a case of indirect dis-

crimination, the assumption of the Jockey Club being that all wives
were susceptible of corruption by their husbands.[18]

In a case under the Commonwealth *Racial Discrimination Act*
involving employment in a professional sporting context, a naturalised Australian complained about the rules of the National Basketball
League (NBL) in relation to overseas players. A combination of the
rules of the Australian Basketball Federation (the governing body of
the sport in Australia) and NBL Management (the body conducting
the NBL), and the regulations of the International Basketball Federation, meant that the complainant, although a naturalised Australian,
was required to complete a three-year period of continuous domicile
in Australia after his application before he could be registered as a
non-restricted player with an NBL club. The rules formed part of a
code for determining the 'basketball nationality' of the player concerned. There was no such requirement for a player born in Australia
or registered there at an early age. The complainant, Henderson,
claimed discrimination on the basis of place of birth or 'national
origin'.

It was found that the requirement was imposed upon Henderson
not because of his country or origin but simply because he had
changed his legal nationality, and it applied regardless of the origin of
a player wishing to change his basketball nationality. The claim of discrimination was dismissed.[19]

Use of facilities

Most of the laws under consideration prohibit sex discrimination in
relation to the provision of goods and services. In an interesting
decision under the Commonwealth legislation, damages of $7300
were awarded against the NSW attorney general and the Sydney City
Council in relation to the cancellation of a women's kick boxing competition. Men had been permitted to compete in a similar tournament.
Following the advertisement of the women's tournament, the attorney
general gazetted a notice prohibiting it; as a result the council refused
to allow Sydney Town Hall to be used for the event. It was found that
the conduct of the attorney general and the council were in breach of
the Act.[20]

In a case under the Victorian legislation a man complained of discrimination in relation to refusal of access to a 25 metre pool and male
sauna at the Moe Recreation Centre on Monday nights. Monday night
had been designated 'women's night', when women could attend

aerobic classes and swim in the pool, which was closed to men for two hours. The judge found that while the exclusion of a person of one sex from a single sex sport was permissible under the Act, the exclusion by reason of sex from a place that was being used, but not wholly or exclusively, by members of the opposite sex was not. The circumstances at hand fell within the latter category and the discrimination was proved.[21]

Provision of services

In another case under the Victorian legislation, the setting aside of a light weight and rehabilitation room at the Sports Union in the University of Melbourne for 'women only' at certain times was found to constitute the less favourable treatment of men in the provision of services by the university.[22]

An application by the City of Brunswick to the Victorian Equal Opportunity Board for an exemption from the legislation to open Brunswick Baths to women only for a total of four hours per week was refused in 1992; the board was not satisfied that an exemption for a trial period was the most appropriate way to assess the relevant need or would provide the relevant information to assess such a need.[23]

Discrimination and sporting clubs

Discrimination against women has been particularly marked in Australian sporting clubs. The traditional situation was that women only wished to participate in sporting clubs during the week while their husbands were at work. The growth in the number of working women has brought different demands.

Many clubs, particularly in NSW (which has the largest number of registered clubs in Australia), restricted full membership rights to men and admitted women as 'associate' members only.[24] Club membership is now covered by sex discrimination laws. The categories of club covered by the legislation differ from Act to Act. Some cover voluntary associations, other do not. The NSW Act, for example, covers only 'registered clubs'. This means that it is important for administrators to establish whether or not a club falls within the ambit of the relevant law and whether it complies with the requirements of that law.

Sex discrimination in relation to clubs will generally involve both membership and its terms and conditions, and limitations on access to club benefits.

Exceptions to the basic prohibition are found in each of the relevant Acts. Under the Commonwealth legislation, for example, discrimination is not unlawful if membership of a club is available to persons of one sex only, but it is unlawful to offer different kinds of membership on the basis of sex. Also under that Act, where it is not practicable for both men and women to use a facility simultaneously, and similar facilities are available for use separately or for a reasonable proportion of time, prohibitions on the use or provision of benefits will not infringe the Act. Factors such as the purposes for which the club was established must be taken into account when considering these exceptions.

These exceptions were considered in a case involving a Queensland golf club which had severely restricted the right of female members to hit off on Saturdays. It was found that the women's access to a club benefit had been limited in a way that breached the Act.[25]

Questions concerning the membership categories open to women and the rights that accrue to them have also come under consideration by the bodies administering the Acts.

Penalty in disciplinary proceedings

A claim of racial discrimination was laid against a football league tribunal in a case involving the rehearing of a charge which resulted in a higher penalty being imposed on a player who had struck a fellow participant during the course of a game. The rehearing had been requested by the president of the player's club due to the severity of the original penalty. The president of HREOC found that, although the circumstances surrounding the rehearing were clearly unfair, there was no evidence that there had been any racial discrimination. In effect, the president found that the tribunal was equally unfair to indigenous and non-indigenous Australians.[26]

Licensing

The failure of a sporting organisation to license a paraplegic for general competition may not infringe the *Victorian Equal Opportunity Act 1984* if there are reasonable grounds for believing that the person is not adequately capable of performing the actions required of them in respect of that sporting activity. In *McInnes v Confederation of Australian Motor Sport*, a paraplegic holder of a car licence, using hand controls rather than foot controls, was refused a licence

by the confederation on the basis that he did not comply with international requirements for at least 50 per cent free movement of
limbs. McInnes complained. Ultimately it was found that, in the circumstances, the confederation's act in refusing the licence was not an
act of discrimination in terms of the legislation.[27]

Single sex sport

The sex discrimination legislation makes it unlawful for an educational authority to discriminate against a pupil on the basis of sex.
Sporting opportunities in schools fall within the provisions of the Act.

It is not, however, unlawful to exclude a person of a particular sex
from participating in a competitive sporting activity where the
strength, stamina or physique of competitors is relevant. This exception does not extend to coaches or referees, to any prescribed sporting
activity or to the sporting activities of children under 12 years old.[28]
This means that single sex sport in schools is not necessarily prohibited
by the Act, except for the under 12s.

At one stage in NSW the policy of education authorities was to
provide for 'mixed' and 'girls' sporting categories to encourage better
performance by girls. This policy was reportedly discontinued on the
basis of advice that the system breached the *Commonwealth Sex Discrimination Act*.

In a recent case, Victorian girls aged 14 and 15 challenged a ban
on girls playing football alongside boys. Under the Victorian law,
participants aged 12 and over can be excluded from sports where the
strength, stamina or physique of competitors is relevant. The judge
considered the disparity between boys and girls of various ages in
these areas and decided that any disparity was not significant enough
in the under 14 age group to justify a ban. The disparities were considered significant enough to justify a ban for the under 15 age
group.[29]

Determining the sex of competitors

Press reports over the last few years have chronicled the difficulties of
various athletic bodies in determining the sex of competitors. The
determination of the correct gender classification of male to female
transgender persons has caused particular problems, and statistics
suggest that this difficulty will continue. It has been suggested that in
Australia fifty men per year undergo such a process.[30] In relation to
sport, perhaps the most celebrated case was that of tennis player

Renee Richards, a male to female transsexual who went to court to secure the right to play in the US Open. Medical opinion in the case indicated that Richards would have no unfair advantage in competing against women, and the court found that there was 'overwhelming medical evidence' that Richards was now female.[31]

Discrepancies in the results of chromosomal testing up to 1991 caused the IOC to abandon that method and adopt a method whereby the National Federations would determine sex after a physical examination. Physical examination raised questions such as:

- could sex be objectively determined?
- would gender reassignment be obvious?
- how would a physical examination treat those born with characteristics of both sexes?
- would National Federations accurately assess gender?

These tests were stopped before the Sydney Games. In May 2004, effective for the Athens Games, the IOC announced that athletes who have undergone sex-change surgery would be eligible to compete if their new gender was legally recognised and they had gone through a minimum two-year period of post-operative hormone therapy.[32]

The legal position of transgender people in Australia is ill-defined; various areas of law have treated them in a variety of ways.[33] It seems that this area will continue to provide headaches for sports officials and competitors.

NSW discrimination legislation provides that it is unlawful to discriminate on transgender grounds.[34] There is, however, an exception – it is not unlawful to exclude a transgender athlete from sports participation, although this exception does not apply to coaching, administration or any sporting activity prescribed by regulation.[35] The Victorian legislation also prohibits discrimination on the basis of 'gender identity'. Other state definitions of sexuality or sexual orientation mean that transgender discrimination is prohibited throughout Australia.

Chapter 11

Sport and taxation

One important consequence of the increasing availability of money in the sporting arena has been a growth in the number of professional athletes who earn money in a variety of ways because of their involvement in a sport. The growth in sponsorship and endorsement opportunities must be added to the explosion in prize money available in many areas of sporting competition. It has been estimated that some athletes may earn far more in endorsements than they do in actual prize money.

The traditional professional sports like golf, tennis and football continue to provide a good living for those who are good enough. Golf professionals augment their tournament earnings with their club professional duties. Many elite footballers in Australia are only semi-professionals. They still have other paid employment in addition to their paid football, although it is often in areas related to their sport. At the other end of the scale, there are many sports that involve no promise of payment; participants compete only for the enjoyment involved.

Times and sports, however, change. A few years ago there was no potential for payment in athletics. The best athletes are now able to receive payment in accordance with the rules of their association. The preparation time required to be competitive today means that if this were not the case, athletes would be in extreme financial difficulty.

Those involved in sport should be aware that, just as in other legal areas, the fact that money was received for playing a game or participating in a sport does not mean that taxation laws do not apply. If the money can be classified as income, it will be treated as such. It follows that expenses incurred in earning the income may be classified as deductions, and sportspeople may need to be reminded of this fact.

This chapter contains a brief outline of the issues involved in the taxation of income derived from sport. Taxation law is a specialised area, and what follows is intended merely to indicate potential tax issues.

Income tax laws have, in part, been rewritten, so two pieces of legislation are potentially relevant.[1] Differences in drafting style between them do not necessarily indicate a difference in meaning. Judicial precedent and rulings under the older (1936) Act are generally still relevant.

Income tax in Australia

People who are Australian residents and who receive income are liable to pay income tax on income from all sources in and out of Australia. Non-residents who receive income from Australian sources must pay income tax on that part of their income. The issues of residency and the question of income earned outside Australia are discussed below.

The amount of income tax payable varies, depending on the total amount of income earned in a particular year.

What is income?

Income tax is payable on amounts of money classified as 'income'. Taxable income is assessable income minus deductions. There is no comprehensive definition of 'income' in the *Income Tax Assessment Acts*; general usage and previous judicial decisions must be considered in determining what constitutes income.

Generally speaking, an amount is more likely to be income if it is earned or is related to the exploitation of assets or performance of services. Amounts received as compensation for loss of other income also constitute income. On the other hand, gifts, windfalls and amounts received as compensation for the loss of other assets are not generally classified as income.

How does this fit in with the idea of money received in sport?

In a recent case involving athlete Olympic javelin thrower Joanna Stone[2] the Full Federal Court looked at whether she was carrying on a business to determine whether payments like prize money and grants were income. Considerations were whether she conducted her activities in a businesslike and systematic way, according to commercial principles. Whether she had a profit-making purpose was more important than whether she made one. Stone had a full-time career as a police officer. She did not select competitions on the basis of likely prize money but rather gaining competition experience. The court found in the circumstances that her purpose was enjoyment of competition rather than profit. The money defrayed her considerable sporting expenses. Grants were not income as they were not made to compensate for lost income. Appearance fees were income, being a reward for a service – attendance at functions.

A consideration of some of the types of payments commonly made in sport is set out below.[3]

Salary, wages, allowances and commissions

These are generally paid to employees and are classified as income. If, for example, a full-time tennis coach is employed by a sporting complex for a fixed amount per week, the coach is probably an employee and the payments will be income. The coach may receive an equipment allowance, or commission on sales made at the equipment shop; these amounts are also income.

Fees received by umpires and other officials are income.

Prizes

Prize money is assessed in the same way as other income. Cars, trophies and trips received for winning a sporting contest will be assessed if the player is a professional or semi-professional. Random prizes may fall into the category of windfalls. Prize money won where the athlete does not carry on a business may not be income.[4]

Appearance money and match fees

These are classified in the same way as salary or wages, because they are generally derived from performance of services. The golfer who receives $100 000 appearance money and the footballer who receives $500 per winning game are earning assessable income.

Awards for sporting achievement

While pure gifts are not classified as income, where the amount involved is directly related to an employment situation it will be income. Awards made to professional sportspeople generally fall into this category. A 'best and fairest' award made to a footballer, for example, is assessable.[5] Awards of this nature in the form of television sets, videos and cars will be assessable under this principle.

If the names of all competitors in a particular sporting event are put in a draw for a prize, the prize may be classified as a windfall gain, like a lottery win, and not assessable. The Sydney City to Surf Race, for example, often conducts a draw for air tickets to compete in a similar overseas event. The prize winners are generally non-professional community members, and this type of award would not be assessable. If a professional runner competing in the event won the trip draw, however, the value would probably be assessable.

A bonus for having played well, for being selected to play for Australia and for contracting not to play outside Queensland were assessable income for a rugby league player.[6]

In the Stone case discussed above, athletic awards were not income because Stone was not carrying on a business.

Signing on fees

Signing on fees, which are commonly received by persons such as professional footballers, are assessable.[7] If the payment is classified as compensation for the loss of a capital asset, however, this may not be the case. A payment to an amateur to compensate for a loss of amateur status may not be assessable, as long as the taxpayer can show that it is made for that purpose and is not payment for services rendered.[8]

Covenants to play for one team

Amounts received for giving an undertaking to play for a particular team for a set time are generally classified as income because they relate directly to the actual employment.[9] Alternatively they may be classified as the disposal of an asset for capital gains tax purposes, and hence be assessable under that regime.

Transfer fees

This category covers payments made by one club to another on the basis that a particular player is released to play with the paying club. Where the practice is common in the sport concerned the payment would probably be classified as income because it would constitute a payment made in the course of carrying on the club business.

Sponsorship, advertising fees and appearance money

The trend for sportspeople to be in demand for advertising and sponsorship of goods or services and personal appearances was discussed in chapter 5. Payments received for this type of activity are assessable because they generally involve a performance of services.

Testimonials

Monies received from a testimonial may be assessable, but they may also constitute an eligible termination payment if the necessary relationship to termination of employment exists.

Amateur athletes trust fund payments

Money paid into the trust fund of an amateur athlete is income. Some deductions are allowable.

Money received as grants and other assistance

The Taxation Commissioner ruled in 1999 that financial assistance for high performance athletes is generally income.[10] Voluntary payments are not income, so there are no deductions. In *Stone v Commissioner of Taxation*, however, the Full Federal Court considered whether the Olympic Athlete Program, the Medal Incentive Scheme, other grants, prize money and appearance fees could be characterised as income. The basic issue for the court was whether Stone had been engaged in a business activity in receiving the money. The Full Court concluded in the circumstances that she had not been engaged in carrying on a business in relation to the grants and prize money.[11]

In particular, grants made under the AOC's Medal Incentive Scheme were not income despite the fact that they were awarded for athletic prowess in the hope of medals. The grants were to defray the costs of competing.

Income from outside Australia

A resident of Australia, as a basic rule, has to pay tax on all income even if it comes from outside Australia. An Australian resident golfer, for example, must generally pay tax here on income earned overseas.

Persons who actually live in Australia qualify as residents. A resident may also be someone who has spent more than half the income year in Australia. The question of residence is important, because if a person is a resident all money earned is potentially assessable, while if a person is not a resident, only money earned in Australia is subject to taxation in this country.

Persons resident in one country and earning income in other countries are subject to the operation of double tax agreements. Australia has such agreements with most of its major trading partners. They provide for tax credits to be given in respect of tax paid in another country, and may be important to those who earn the bulk of their money overseas, but technically 'reside' in Australia.

Exempt income

Not all amounts received as income are taxable. Some classes of income that would ordinarily be assessable are categorised as exempt by the legislation. Examples of exempt income relevant to sport are discussed below.

The income of some sporting associations, societies or clubs is exempt. Where an association, society or club is established with a main purpose of promoting an athletic game or sport in which humans are the sole participants, and it does not conduct its operations for the profit or gain of individual members, its income is exempt. If the organisation is to qualify for an exemption, the documents setting it up must specify its purposes. Societies established for the encouragement or promotion of animal races may also fall within the exemption. The provision of other 'independent social facilities' for members and guests may take a club outside the exemption, but some social activities may be permissible.[12]

Deductions

Business deductions are expenses incurred in order to produce income.[13] Everyone who conducts a business has expenses, and those involved in sport are no exception. In order to claim deductions on sporting expenses a person must be engaging in the sporting activity for reward and not just for enjoyment.

There are many examples of items that would be considered deductible for taxation purposes. Two of these are discussed below:

- *Travel* In a well-known case, a part-time professional footballer was allowed a deduction for expenses incurred in travelling from his place of full-time employment to training sessions and then home, and from his home to various matches and back. The claim was found to be justified on the ground that as he had no regular place of sporting employment his home could be regarded as his base of operations. Travelling alone in his own car was found to be necessary for reasons of concentration and practicality.[14]

- *Costs of other fitness training* In another case involving a footballer, the cost of playing squash was allowed as a deduction. The player was required under his contract to do everything necessary to keep himself fit. His coach had, in fact, requested that he play squash to improve his fitness level.[15]

It is not difficult to imagine many of the types of items that are allowable deductions for sportspeople: items of clothing and equipment such as football boots and golf clubs, taxis to and from the airport for interstate competition for cricketers, track work fees for jockeys, gymnasium fees for wrestlers.

Legal expenses (costs of legal advice) incurred by a professional footballer in procuring a clearance from the New Zealand Rugby League to play with the Newcastle Knights were found not to be deductible in a case. There the fees were characterised as payments to obtain a structural advantage of a capital nature, and not to obtain income.[16]

Items that are tax deductible may change from time to time and should be checked with the Taxation Office. It is important to note that to cut down on abuse in this area, rigorous substantiation rules apply to deductions. Any deductions over $300 must be capable of substantiation.[17]

Capital gains tax

Capital gains tax involves tax that must be paid on the disposal of a capital asset, based on the asset's appreciation in value over time. It is not a separate tax; it is dealt with in the *Income Tax Assessment Act*, which makes capital gains assessable as income. The system of capital gains tax is complex. While many sportspeople acquire investments and capital assets from the proceeds of their activities and the tax may apply to those, the mere activity of working in a sporting context will not generally result in capital gains consequences.[18]

Tax averaging provisions

A special form of tax relief applies to sportspeople and others who have incomes that may fluctuate wildly. Many sportspeople have a short sporting life during which they earn large amounts of money, only to return to an ordinary amount of income after a few years. Tax averaging provisions now prevent these people from being pushed into high rates of taxation for a few years by taxing their 'abnormal' or excess income at a concessional rate.

Fringe benefits tax

Fringe benefits tax involves a tax on the provision of a benefit to an employee by an employer (or at the employer's direction).[19] The tax is paid by the employer and not the employee. Players in professional clubs in the major football competitions in each state are employees for the purposes of the tax, and it must be paid on the value of end-of-year trips and other similar benefits provided by such clubs.[20] Trips made for the purpose of competing are, of course, assessable.

Sports clubs and associations that may be exempt from income tax are nevertheless subject to fringe benefits tax, and must lodge returns.

Provisional tax

Self-employed sportspeople may need to pay provisional tax. Provisional tax must be paid in advance, and is calculated according to the income received in the previous year. Provisional tax can sometimes prove a problem for those who forget that their first tax bill will be double – the amount for the current year and the amount for the next year as well. People who derive income from sport should be aware of this fact and seek advice so that suitable arrangements can be made.

Chapter 12

Anti-doping

This chapter provides a simple explanation of the application of anti-doping policies and the World Anti-Doping Agency Code for sportspeople and sporting organisations. The numerous decisions of CAS worldwide in relation to anti-doping are too specialised to fall within the scope of this book.

The problem

The use of drugs by sporting competitors is not new. In recent years detection of drug use has become more widespread, more scientifically based and better targeted, but drugs appear to be more difficult to detect.

The year 2004 proved a high water mark for the number and novelty of doping incidents. In the US a number of high profile champion athletes were linked to a California laboratory, BALCO, after a syringe containing a performance enhancing substance, THG, was sent to the US Anti-Doping Authority. Subsequently a steroid charge was laid against world record holder Tim Montgomery, who faces a possible life ban if the charge is proven. Former Olympic champion Marion Jones was investigated. Five athletes tested positive for THG, including the British champion Dwain Chambers. US sprinter and world 100 metres and 200 metres champion Kelli White tested positive to a stimulant. She then admitted use of THG and other banned drugs.

The Athens Olympics provided an array of new doping cases. Hungarian Robert Fazekas was stripped of his Olympic discus gold medal for refusing to provide a complete urine sample and trying to tamper with it. Irina Korzhanenko of Russia was stripped of her shot put gold medal when she tested positive to a banned substance. In anther twist two Greek athletes, Sydney Olympic 200 metres champion Kostas Kederis and his training partner, Sydney Olympic 100 metres silver medallist Ekaterini Thanou, failed to attend a scheduled drug test amid reports that they had managed to evade testers for a significant period of time prior to the Games. There were stories of injury in a motor bike accident preventing the tests, but ultimately the athletes did not compete in Athens.[1] In December 2004 it was announced that the IAAF had provisionally suspended the athletes and their coach pending disciplinary proceedings, with the prospect of a CAS appeal.[2]

Back in Australia controversy reigned in cycling. One cyclist admitted injecting a banned substance. Another was removed from the Olympic team for lying to the committee inquiring into the first incident. Other cyclists were investigated and cleared. The Australian team was nevertheless successful on the track.[3]

These examples provide solid evidence of continuing attempts by athletes to assist performances pharmaceutically.

Why athletes use drugs

Drug use in sport is not new. Athletes may use drugs to enhance performance, for medicinal purposes or for recreation. The nature of the drugs used to enhance performance depends on the sport involved. Medications may be used for treating a short-term illness or a long-term condition. Even medication taken for legitimate purposes may contain banned substances, and should be checked to avoid inadvertent doping.

The position becomes more complicated with the use of dietary supplements by athletes. It was reported in 2002 that 15 per cent of supplements tested by the IOC were spiked with enough banned steroids and hormones to cause an athlete to fail a doping test, but none was listed on the relevant product labels.[4]

Sometimes athletes use drugs that are performance enhancing inadvertently for legitimate purposes. The difficulty for authorities is that it is impossible to determine whether the use is legitimate or not; and either way the athlete may have actually obtained a performance enhancement.

A brief history of regulation

Several European nations began to enact anti-doping laws in the 1960s, and the Medical Commission of the IOC was established in 1967. The first drug tests at an Olympic Games were conducted in 1968.

The whole question of drug-taking in Australian sport was being investigated by a Senate Committee in 1989, when the first edition of this book was written. The inquiry followed events at the 1988

Olympics in Seoul where athletes were sent home after testing positive to banned substances. Australian modern pentathlon representative Alex Watson was sent home after testing positive to caffeine. Watson had excessive amounts of caffeine in his system, but maintained that he took no drugs but merely drank coffee during the competition.

The Australian Sports Drug Agency (ASDA) was set up under the *Australian Sports Drug Agency Act* in 1991[5] to collect samples from athletes and arrange testing. Its processes and policies have been developed and refined under the Act and regulations since that time. The Act gives ASDA the power to test certain athletes in accordance with specific criteria. It has been amended to conform to the WADA Code.

In the 2003–04 financial year ASDA conducted 6614 tests, 71 per cent being 'out of competition' tests. The tests resulted in 24 adverse findings from 19 athletes (one international). This included one positive test result for the drug EPO.[6]

ASDA also fulfils an educational role, and can provide advice on the use of various drugs and assistance for sporting organisations in developing doping policies.

The WADA Code

The impetus for the WADA Code was the recognition that a unified approach to anti-doping was the only effective way to reduce the use of performance enhancing drugs in sport. On the adoption of the WADA Code at the Copenhagen Conference in 2003, IOC president Jaques Rogge stated:

> The revelations of the Tour de France taught us that 30 years of parallel but uncoordinated efforts by governments and the sports movement were not successful. The sports movements have called for the help of governments within WADA and the governments have accepted.[7]

The Copenhagen Conference was attended by representatives of all International Federations, nearly 80 world governments, athletes, National Olympic Committees, national anti-doping agencies and accredited laboratories who supported the Code. The Copenhagen Declaration was signed by 51 governments, and another 27 committed to signing at a later date. All Olympic International Federations accepted the WADA Code. The AOC signed at that time.

WADA's president Dick Pound described the universal support for the code in terms of delegates putting aside 'all other considerations except what is best for the athletes and sent a powerful message to drug cheats: your days are numbered'.[8]

Implementation in Australia

The IOC required all athletes who were possible team members for the Athens Olympics to be available for out of competition testing for one year before the Olympics, in conformity with the WADA Code. Most International Federations had agreed to adopt the code, although they had not formally adopted code-compliant anti-doping policies; as a result most Australian sports had not formally done so. Olympic sports went through a process of signing up all potential team members to agree to testing, and to the retrospective application of the WADA Code once policies had been adopted.

Following the adoption of the WADA Code, both the ASC and the AOC issued templates for an anti-doping policy for sporting organisations that would comply with the code. National sports also needed to adopt a policy that complied with the requirements of their International Federation and of the IOC, if relevant. Sports also needed to ensure that their constitutions and internal policies were consistent with the code-compliant anti-doping policy adopted.

Any organisation funded by the ASC must now:

- have an anti-doping policy that complies with ASC requirements – this now means a WADA-compliant policy
- provide complete and current athlete contact details to ASDA
- facilitate timely and defensible hearings in relation to doping infractions
- educate athletes, coaches, officials, administrators and medical personnel about the sport's anti-doping policy.[9]

WADA Code prohibitions

The WADA Code prohibits an increased range of doping activities. The following are doping offences under the code:

- the presence of a prohibited substance or its markers in an athlete's bodily specimen (this means that the issue of intent is irrelevant – consumption may be inadvertent)
- use or attempted use of a prohibited substance or method
- refusal to comply with a request to supply a sample, or evading a test[10]
- failing to provide the required whereabouts information, or missing tests
- tampering with doping control
- possession of prohibited substances or methods
- trafficking
- being involved in a contravention.

The prohibited list

WADA's mandatory prohibited list came into effect on 1 January 2004.[11] Substances and methods are considered for inclusion on the WADC list where they satisfy any two of the following three criteria:

- medical or other scientific evidence, pharmacological effect or experience that the substance or method has the potential to enhance sporting performance
- medical or other scientific evidence, pharmacological effect or experience that the substance or method represents an actual or potential health risk to an athlete
- WADA's determination that the use of the substance or method violates the spirit of sport described in the introduction to the code.

Substances that mask the use of other prohibited substances or methods can be included.

Legitimate medicinal use of drugs by athletes

The WADA Code requires all sports to recognise 'therapeutic use exemptions', and to establish procedures consistent with the international standard for granting them.[12]

Doping offences in Australia

If an athlete in Australia tests positive or is otherwise in breach of the anti-doping policy of a sport, a doping offence is committed. An entry to that effect is made by ASDA on the Register of Notifiable Events set up under its Act. A competitor has a right to apply to the Administrative Appeals Tribunal for review of ASDA's decision to enter the competitor's name and particulars on the register.[13]

Penalties

Testing may be done in or out of competition. A doping offence in competition means automatic disqualification from that competition and possible provisional suspension until a final penalty hearing.

Penalties for breaches in competition or out of competition are the same. Where a person is found to have committed a doping offence, the penalty is suspension for two years for a first violation and a life ban for a second violation. Some lesser sanctions apply for substances that are more likely to be implicated in unintentional doping and less likely to be abused as doping agents.

A reduction in the period of suspension may be available where the athlete can establish that there was no fault or negligence in relation to the violation – that is, that the athlete did not know or suspect, and could not reasonably have known or suspected even with the utmost caution, that the prohibited substance or method had been used or administered.

An athlete who provides assistance to an anti-doping organisation with the result that another athlete is caught may have a penalty reduced.

Suspension generally applies from the date of the hearing. During the period of suspension the athlete is prohibited from any competition organised by any signatory or its member organisation. Funding will also be withheld by signatories, their member organisations and governments.

Hearings

The 'guilt' or 'innocence' of the athlete, and the penalty, are determined by the sporting organisation, not by ASDA. The Register of Notifiable Events contains the names of those who have committed a doping offence. When a sporting organisation is notified by ASDA that an athlete's name has been placed on the register it must hold a hearing to determine a penalty. The matter is heard by a tribunal, which may be a tribunal set up by the sport or CAS depending on the content of the anti-doping policy. All Olympic sports must have CAS as their initial tribunal.

Hearings address the question of whether or not the doping offence was committed and the consequences under the anti-doping policy. They are conducted in accordance with the principles of natural justice. Appeals must go to CAS.

Establishing a breach of anti-doping policy

To establish a case against an athlete in relation to a positive test it is necessary to prove:
- the identity of the person giving the sample
- that the sample came from that particular competitor
- that the sample contains the prohibited substance.

Testing: the practicalities

Drug testing may take place at any time anywhere. An athlete is contacted by a drug control official, and can be asked to provide both urine and blood samples.

With a urine test a chaperone accompanies the athlete to a drug control waiting room where sealed drinks are provided. A representative of the athlete may be present. The athlete selects a sealed sample collection unit. The chaperone must observe the athlete passing urine.

A blood sample is provided in the presence of a drug control official and the athlete's representative.

The urine or blood is placed in two sample containers with security seals. The athlete is responsible for controlling the sample until the containers are sealed. The drug control official records the seal and sample numbers, and the drug testing forms are checked and signed by the competitor.

Failure to attend test

If an athlete fails to comply with a request to provide a sample ASDA notifies the relevant federation, and its anti-doping policy will apply to the refusal.

Testing of samples

Initially only the first sample is tested. If the result is positive the competitor is informed and entitled to be present at the testing of the second sample. If the second sample is also positive, the name of the competitor may be entered on the register.

Australian cyclist Martin Vinnicombe commenced legal proceedings following the imposition of a two-year suspension after a positive test, on the ground that the entry of his name on the register was misleading as all procedures had not been complied with. His test had been performed by Canadian authorities in the US, and the Canadian requirements were different from those of ASDA. There was no argument that the testing itself was faulty. After his test Vinnicombe admitted on television that he had taken the banned substance. Following mediation, Vinnicombe regained his licence; other aspects of the case were later settled. The law was subsequently amended to allow positive results to stand even where there has been a departure from the ASDA procedures, unless the variation casts doubt on the results (for example, if the sample has been tampered with or not properly sealed, or the test has not been carried out in an accredited laboratory). The law was also amended to allow other anti-doping organisations to test on behalf of ASDA.

Notification

Once the entry has been made, ASDA must give written notification to the competitor, the relevant sporting organisation, and the ASC if the competitor receives funding.

Natural justice

Before any sanctions are imposed following a doping offence, an athlete must be given a chance to attend and be heard by the sporting organisation. ASDA is also charged with the responsibility of complying with the principles of natural justice in relation to a positive test on athletes. An internal review of all procedures involved in the collection of samples in relation to a positive test must be undertaken before entry of any competitor's name on the Register of Notifiable Events. As stated above, there is some right of appeal to the Administrative Appeals Tribunal from decisions of ASDA.

In a decision involving a professional cyclist,[14] the court found that the two-year penalty imposed on him for using anabolic steroids was in restraint of trade (see chapter 4). Although the two-year ban was virtually mandatory under the then Model Drug Policy of the ASC, which the professional cycling organisation had adopted, the judge stated that the restraint was not reasonable in the circumstances, as the international cycling body would only have imposed a three-month ban on the cyclist. This cast doubt on the ultimate effectiveness of a mandatory penalty, and indicated the difficulty facing sporting organisations when attempting to apply ASC policy, yet comply with the law and with the requirements of their overseas parent bodies. With the adoption of the WADA Code by most sports, these inconsistencies should disappear, leaving less room for such arguments.

Impact of the WADA Code

The WADA Code is still in its early days, but going forward it should assist both sporting organisations and government bodies to combat the use of performance enhancing drugs. The greater use of a common anti-doping policy will make testing procedures simpler and more easily understood. The imposition of common penalties will eradicate the possibility of some sports minimising penalties involving their best players, and the possibility of conflict between the rules of the tiers within a sport and administrative and funding bodies. The use of CAS will stimulate a range of decisions both in Australia and internationally which can be used as precedents in later proceedings. This should result in more consistent penalties for similar conduct.

One of the most important amendments to the obligations of athletes under the WADA Code is the formalising of the provision of athlete whereabouts information for elite or national level athletes, and the placing on athletes of the onus of ensuring that it is accurate and up-to-date. While athletes on the ASDA out of competition testing register have been required to supply information on their whereabouts for some time, this process is formalised under the WADA Code, and a failure to supply information is a code violation.

This should mean that out of competition testing of athletes cannot be avoided because they cannot be found. If they are not found they can be subject to a penalty. This is a big step forward.

Notes

Chapter 1

1   In 2000–01 almost 100 000 people were employed by organisations involved in providing sport and recreation activities. They were assisted by almost 180 000 volunteers (Australian Bureau of Statistics (ABS) Year Book 2003, *Culture, Sport and Recreation*).

2   *The Concise Oxford Dictionary* (1951) (4th edn), Oxford University Press, Oxford, p. 1219.

3   HL Nixon (1976) *Sport and the Social Organisation,* Bobbs-Merrill, Indianapolis; see H Edwards (1973) *The Sociology of Sport*, Dorsey Press, Homeward, Illinois, p. 57, for a more detailed approach to definition.

4   J Green & D Atyeo (1970) *The Book of Sports Quotes*, Omnibus Press, London, pp. 6, 7, 10.

5   Green & Atyeo, pp. 9, 14, 16.

6   K Dunstan (1973) *Sports*, Cassell, Australia, p. xiii.

7   The controversial Chappell 'underarm bowling' incident in a test match against New Zealand was seen by the cricket establishment as a breach of convention. The 'sledging' that reportedly occurs in first class cricket presents a challenge to those who value the old approach.

8   Nixon, *Sport and the Social Organisation,* p. 55, citing PC McIntosh (1971) *Sport in Society*, Watts, London.

9   Thorpe was later reinstated.

10   Nixon, p. 55, citing McIntosh, p. 171ff.

11   See D Farnsworth (2001), 'Does English Law Lack Personality?' *I.S.L.R.*210, citing the *Guardian*.

12   See N Shoebridge, 'Catch a rising star, put it in your pocket,' *Australian Financial Review* 20 September 2004, p.55.

13   See Olympic Charter in force 1 September 2004.

14   ABS, *Culture, Sport and Recreation*.

15   ABS, *Culture, Sport and Recreation*.

16   See chapter 7 for the NSW Sporting Injuries Compensation Scheme.

17   As to this see chapter 7.

18   *News Limited & Ors v South Sydney District Rugby League Football Club Limited* [2003] HCA 45 (13 August 2003).

19   See M Beloff (2001) 'The CAS Ad Hoc Division at the Sydney Olympic Games', *I.S.L.R.*105.

20   *Raguz v Sullivan* (2000) 50 NSWLR 237.

21   The CAS Code can be found on the CAS website: http://www.tas-cas.org.

22   See JR Nafziger (1988) *International Sports Law*, Transnational Publishers, p.35ff.

23   See U Naidoo & N Sarin (2001–02) 'Dispute resolution at Games time', 12 *Fordham Intell. Prop Media & Ent L. J.* 489.

24   Following his disqualification from competition for use of performance enhancing drugs, cyclist Martin Vinnicombe took action in the Federal Court against the ASC, the ASDA, the Australian Professional Cycling Council and the Australian Cycling Federation. The claims against the ASC and the cycling bodies were resolved following mediation.

25   See IOC Code of Ethics, Rule B.1.

26   A Fitness Industry Code of Practice is, for example, prescribed by the *Fair Trading Regulations 1995*(ACT) made under the *Fair Trading Act 1992* (ACT). See

Commissioner for Fair Trading v Stephen Pashalidis t/as Bodyworks Fitness Clubs [2004] (unreported, Crispin J, ACTSC, 23 April 2004) which discusses the failure of the defendant to comply with the form of agreement prescribed under the code.

27   (1979) 23 ALR 439 *Re Adamson*; Ex Parte West Australian National Football League.

28   See, for example, the groundswell of public support for the South Sydney Club when it was omitted from the NRL competition, and the unselfish behaviour of swimmer Craig Stevens when faced with the likely non-participation of Sydney Olympic champion Ian Thorpe in the 400 metres freestyle in Athens.

29   [1975] 1 NSWLR 295.

30   *Nagle v Fielden* [1966] 2 QB 689.

31   [1998] 2 VR 546 at p 549–50.

32   T Davis (2001) 'What is Sports Law ?' *Marquette Sports Law Review* 211.

Chapter 2

1   N Richardson (1994) 'Sport's great sell-out', *The Bulletin*, 11 October.

2   'Special Report on Sports Marketing', *Australian Financial Review*, 16 October 2003, p 16.

3   See generally C Chapman (1999) 'Sport in the new millenium: the global game', paper presented at the Australian and New Zealand Sports Law Association (ANZSLA) Conference, August.

4   *Broadcasting Services Act 1992* (Cth) s.115.

5   Licence condition 10(1)(e).

6   The Australian Competition and Consumer Commission (ACCC) agrees. See ACCC, *Emerging Market Structures in the Communiciations Sector,* June 2003.

7   See Australian Broadcasting Authority (ABA), *Investigation into Events on the Anti-Siphoning List*, June 2001; Productivity Commission, *Broadcasting*, April 2001.

8   S.146.

9   It was reported in November 2004, for example, that Foxtel had taken up the pay television rights to the 2005 Ashes cricket tour of England but no free-to-air network was planning to broadcast the event. Communications Minister Senator Helen Coonan noted that the commercial rights were still available and there was no infringement of the rules. News.com.au, 18 November 2004.

10   See Minister for Communications, 'Information Technology and the Arts', press release, 7 April 2004.

11   See I Carroll (1995) 'Pay TV and sport: will your sport miss out?', paper presented at the Sport Federation Parliament House Forum, NSW, 'Funding issues in sport', generally, and particularly at p. 17, where the example of US National Basketball Association franchise of the Phoenix Suns is related. A combination of a successful team, a sold-out arena and a lack of free-to-air television opportunities is said to have effectively doubled the size of their 20 000 seat arena for important season games.

12   P Staudohar (1989) *The sports industry and collective bargaining* (2nd edn) ILR Press, Cornell University, p. 7.

13   See chapter 7.

14   P Montgomery (1986) 'The role of government, sport, politics and the law', paper presented at the Seminar on Sports Administration, College of Law. See also Nafziger, p. 111.

15   The 1971 Rugby Union football tour of Australia by South Africa provoked violence. An unofficial visit by Australian cricketers in 1985 caused public controversy. See also chapter 4, which details the predicament of former Australian

cricket captain Kim Hughes after his participation in the rebel tour (*Hughes v Western Australian Cricket Association Inc & Ors* (1986) ATPR 40–736).

16   Department of Sport, Recreation and Tourism, *Annual Report* (1987), AGPS, Canberra, p. 13.

Chapter 3

1   Nafziger, *International Sports Law.*
2   See *Corporations Act 2001*(Cth). As to the area of unincorporated associations generally, see R Baxt, K Fletcher & S Fridman (eds) (2003) *Corporations and Associations: Cases and materials* (9th edn), Butterworths LexisNexis, Sydney.
3   See, for example, *Bradley Egg Farm v Clifford* [1943] 2 All ER 378.
4   *Leahy v A-G* [1959] 2 All ER 300.
5   *Freeman v McManus* (1958) VR 15.
6   *Carlton Cricket and Football Social Club v Joseph* (1970) VR 487.
7   The actual term of the contract (21 years) was an important factor in the court refusing to find that individuals were liable in this case.
8   *Carlton Cricket and Football Social Club v Joseph* at p. 488. See also *Amery v Fifer* [1971] NSWLR 685, where the trustees of a sporting club attempted to sue a firm of accountants for damages for breach of contract, but the contract itself was held to be defective.
9   See, for example, *Bradley Egg Farm v Clifford*; *Smith v Yarnold* [1969] 2 NSWLR 410.
10   *Peckham v Moore* (1975) 1 NSWLR 353. As to workers' compensation generally, see chapter 7.
11   For a practical example of the implications of the constitution as a contract, see the arguments in *Wilson v Hang Gliding Federation of Australia Incorporated* [1997] (Unreported, Sheller, Powell, Dunford JJA, NSWCA 15 April 1997). The appellant unsuccessfully argued that it was an implied term of the contract between the members that a disciplinary tribunal would apply the rules of natural justice, and that he was entitled to damages for breach when they did not.
12   S.140(1). See also, for example, *Associations Incorporation Act 1984* (NSW), s.11(2).
13   The establishment of other proprietary or property rights in a social organisation situation may provide a basis for relief to a club member apart from relief based on contract .
14   *Cameron v Hogan* (1934) 51 CLR 358.
15   *McKinnon v Grogan* [1974] 1 NSWLR 295; see more recently *Liddle v Central Australian Aboriginal Legal Aid Service Inc* (1999) 150 FLR 142.
16   In light of the decision in *McKinnon v Grogan*, and others in the same vein, it would seem fair to assume that the courts would be more prepared to infer such an intention now than they were when *Cameron v Hogan* was decided. The courts have always been more inclined to intervene in situations involving the unincorporated trading association. See, for example, *Harbottle Brown & Co Pty Ltd v Halstead* [1968] 3 NSWR 493.
17   *Drummoyne District Rugby Football Club Inc v New South Wales Rugby Union Ltd* [1993] (Unreported, Young J, NSWSC (Equity Division) 3 December 1993). The club succeeded on grounds of general unconscionability, his Honour citing the decision in *Waltons Stores (Interstate) Ltd v Maher* (1988) 164 CLR 387.
18   *Associations Incorporation Act 1984* (NSW); *Associations Incorporation Act 1981* (Vic); *Associations Incorporation Act 1981* (Qld); *Associations Incorporation Act 1987* (WA); *Associations Incorporation Act 1985* (SA); *Associations Incorporation Act 1964* (Tas); *Associations Incorporation Act 1990* (NT); *Associations Incorporation Act 1991* (ACT).

19   See chapter 7 on the insurance crisis and relevant amendments.
20   *Commonwealth Bank v Friedrich & Ors* (1991) ACLC 946.
21   *Daniels t/a Deloitte Haskins and Sells v AWA Ltd* (1995) 13 ACLC 614.
22   S.1317E. A penalty of up to $220 000 may be imposed, as well as orders for compensation and disqualification.
23   Schedule 3 *Corporations Act 2001* (Cth). As to the *Corporations Act* generally, see HAJ Ford et al. (2003) *Ford's Principles of Corporations Law* (11th edn) LexisNexis Butterworths, Sydney.
24   S.9.
25   S.180.(1). A statutory business judgment rule is contained in s.180(2,(3).
26   S.181.
27   S.184(1).
28   S.182, 183.
29   S.588G.
30   S.95A.
31   S.588G.
32   S.588H.
33   *Associations Incorporation Act* (NSW).
34   S.38.
35   S.37.
36   S.49AD.
37   S.3.
38   Cases involving the interpretation of the legislation of the various states are too numerous to include in this book.
39   See ASC, *National Sporting Organisations – Governance: Principles of Best Bractice* (May 2002) available from the ASC website: http://www.ausport.govau.

Chapter 4

1   See generally M Brabazon (1999) 'The legal structure of the Sydney Olympic Games', 22(3) *UNSW Law Journal* 662.
2   *Jordan Grand Prix Ltd v Vodaphone Group plc* [2003] EWHC 1956 (Comm); [2003] 2 All ER (Comm) 864.
3   The age of majority has been reduced from 21 at common law to 18 by statute in all states and the ACT. For a detailed treatment of the law of contract generally, see JW Carter (2002) *Contract Law in Australia*, Butterworths, Sydney.
4   See *2004 Olympic Team Agreement*, cl. 21 and schedule 6.
5   The rights of sportspersons in respect of their names and reputations is discussed in chapter 5.
6   [1987] AC 59.
7   See also T Buti (1999) 'AOC Athletes Agreement for Sydney 2000: The implications for the athletes', 22(3) UNSW *Law Journal* 746, although some terms have changed since that time.
8   D Healey, 'Unfairness in sporting agreements', paper presented at ANZSLA Conference, Adelaide 1996.
9   At the time of the 2004 Olympics these issues were contained in the by-law to rule 49 of the Olympic Charter. Following amendment they are now in the by-law to rule 45.
10   *Thompson v Deakin* (1952) Ch 646.
11   See M Williams (1995) 'Sport and the law in Australia 1995', paper presented at the ANZSLA Conference, Auckland, p. 7. See also *Zhu v The Treasurer of the State of New South Wales* [2004] HCA 56 (17 November 2004), which involved claims of interference with a marketing contract by SOCOG.

12   See, for example, *Performing Rights Society Ltd v Mitchell and Booker (palais de danse) Ltd* [1924] 1 KB 762; *Humberstone v Northern Timber Mills* (1949) 79 CLR 389; *Mersey Docks and Harbour Board v Coggins & Griffith (Liverpool) & Ors* [1947] AC 1.

13   For a detailed treatment of the law of employment, see JJ Macken, GJ McCarry & C Sapideen (2002) *The Law of Employment* (5th edn), Law Book Company, Sydney.

14   See *Nordenfelt v Maxim Nordenfelt Guns Ammunition Co* [1894] AC 535.

15   See B Dabscheck (1983) 'Foschini: Before and beyond – Some reflections on the relation between players and their employers', paper presented at conference, History of Sporting Traditions IV, Melbourne Cricket Ground, p. 6.

16   Dabscheck, 'Foschini', p. 25ff. See also discussion at p. 25 of *Eastham v Newcastle United* [1964] Ch. 413.

17   *Canberra Bushrangers Baseball Team Pty Limited v Earl Byrne* [1994] ACTSC 136. See also *Newport Association Football Club Ltd & Ors v Football Association of Wales Ltd* (1995) 2 All ER 87, a situation involving a dispute between the Welsh soccer authorities and several former Welsh clubs.

18   (1972) 125 CLR 353. See also *Hawick v Flegg* (1958) 75 WN (NSW) 255.

19   (1982) VR 64. Two cases where contracts were not void both involved restraints during the contract period: see *Buckenara v Hawthorn Football Club* (1988) VR 39; *Hawthorn Football Club Ltd v Harding* (1988) VR 49.

20   *Adamson v West Perth Football Club* (1979) 39 FLR 199.

21   *Foschini v VFL & South Melbourne Club Limited* [1983] (Unreported, Crockett J, VSC, 15 April 1983)

22   *Nobes v Australian Cricket Board* [1991] (Unreported, VSC, 16 December 1991)

23   B Dabschek (1995) Submission to Soccer Inquiry conducted by the Hon D Stewart.

24   *Wickham & Ors v Canberra District Junior Rugby League Inc & Ors*, 10 September 1998, ACTSC (Miles CJ).

25   *Avellino v All Australian Netball Association Ltd* [2004] SASC 56.

26   *Adamson & Ors v NSW Rugby League Limited & Ors* (1991) ATPR 41–141.

27   *Greig v Insole* [1978] 1 WLR 302.

28   *Hughes v Western Australian Cricket Association (Inc) & Ors* (1986) ATPR 40–736, p. 48, 55ff.

29   [1966] 2 QB 689.

30   [1980] (Unreported, NSWSC 30 April 1980).

31   See A Goldberg & B Ward (1980) 'Players' contracts and collective bargaining', from Seminar on Sport and Law, Monash University, Faculty of Law, Sports and Recreation Association in conjunction with the Department of Youth, Sport and Recreation.

32   Goldberg & Ward, p. 72.

33   *FCT v Maddalena* 71 ATC 4161.

34   *News Limited & Ors v Australian Rugby Football League & Ors* (1996) ATPR 41–521.

35   s.106. There is a monetary cap on the use of this provision.

36   1983 AILR 340.

37   *Daley v New South Wales Rugby League* (Industrial Court of NSW (Hungerford J) 19 September 1995). A further proceeding involving a rugby league player and the disputed inclusion in payment of a block of land occurred in *Gibbs v Gold Coast Tweed Giants Rugby League Football Club Ltd* (1993) 52 IR 469.

38   *Daley v New South Wales Rugby League* (1995) 78 IR 247.

39   *Pay & Ors v Canterbury Bankstown Rugby League Club Limited & Ors* (1995) 78 IR 247.

40   See chapter 7

41   *NSW Rugby League Ltd v Allen* (1998) 83 IR 397.

42   Standard form contracts may be subject to attack generally under provisions like the *Trade Practices Act 1974*, Part IVA (Unconscionable conduct), the mirror state *Fair Trading Act* provisions, and the *Contracts Review Act 1980* (NSW).

43   That dispute followed the setting up of a new and parallel Rugby League competition (Super League) by interests associated with media figure Rupert Murdock, and defence of the status quo by the ARL and interests associated with Kerry Packer, a rival media owner.

44   *News Limited & Ors v Australian Rugby Football League & Ors* (1996) ATPR 41–521.

45   *News Limited & Ors v South Sydney District Rugby League Football Club Limited* [2003] HCA 45 (13 August 2003). For information on the position in New Zealand see S Duggan (1999) 'Sporting Entities and Trade Practices Law: What is best and fairest?' 7 TPLJ 201.

46   See Trade Practices Commission press release, 24 March 1994. A further increase in penalties is proposed at the time of writing.

47   *Lowe v New South Wales Cricket Federation* (1994) ATPR 41–358.

48   *ACCC v Fila Sport Oceania Pty Ltd (Administrators Appointed)* (2004) ATPR 41–983. It is important to note in assessing the impact of this case that these findings were not the subject of argument before Heerey J.

49   S.47(6) & (7).

50   *Hospitality Group Pty Ltd v Australian Rugby Union Ltd* (2001) ATPR 41–831. The *Trade Practices Act* provides that certain types of behaviour which would otherwise be unlawful may be approved by the ACCC in processes known as 'authorisation' and 'notification'. The ARU notified exclusive dealing conduct in relation to exclusive licences for corporate hospitality and ticket booking arrangements with News in 2002. Proposed amendments would apply a purpose or effect test to third line forcing.

51   *Forbes v Australian Yachting Federation Inc & Ors* (1996) 131 FLR 241. See (1996) ATPR (Digest) 46–158 for a digest of the case. See D Healey (1996) 'Olympic Selection Dispute', *ANZSLA Newsletter*, vol 6 no 3 pp3–4.

52   That is, the Australian Yachting Federation, because of its conduct, was prevented from arguing that it had no responsibility for the loss suffered.

53   John Coates, 2000.

54   See, for example, September 2000: 'The legal nightmare that has been strangling Australia's Olympic selection process became farcical yesterday when the case of the warring canoeists headed for judgment for the fourth time'.

55   [2000] 50 NSWLR 236 (NSWCA).

56   TR Morling (2001) *Australian Olympic Selection Process*.

57   ANZSLA Conference, *Getting it right – guidelines for selection*, Australian Sports Commission (2002). For a detailed review of the legal issues applicable to selection see A Sullivan (2001) 'The Duties of Selectors – The Sydney 2000 experience', paper presented at the ANZSLA Conference, Perth.

Chapter 5

1   R Gray (2003) 'Sports marketing: brand athletes', *Marketing*, 27 November, p.27.

2   'DPP to decide Bulldogs' charges by week's end', *The Sun Herald*, April 25 2004, p.17.

3   When allegations of match fixing were levelled at players the International Cricket Council instituted an inquiry. See U Naidoo, 'On the Front Foot Against Corruption' (2004) 1(Feb) *I.S.L.R.* 3–8.

4   See chapter 2.
5   See P Trisley (1986) 'Corporate sponsorship legal aspects', paper presented at the Seminar on Sports Administration, College of Law.
6   See, for example, reference to the rules of the IOC in chapter 2.
7   See *Optus Vision Pty Ltd v Australian Rugby Football League Ltd & Ors* [2004] NSWCA 61 for a recent case involving a contractual dispute between a sponsor and a sport on the issue of exclusivity.
8   See AOC, 'AOC approves body suits', press release, 23 March 2004.
9   See J Magney (1994) ' Officials furious over expulsion threat', *Sydney Morning Herald,* 11 August, p 50; Q Smith (1994) 'Games ban', *Daily Telegraph Mirror,* 10 August.
10 The ASI did, however, sign a subsequent contract with Telecom. See Richardson, 'Sport's great sell-out'.
11 D Healey (1994) 'Legal issues in marketing and sponsorship', presented at 'From Centre Court to High Court', ASC Seminar, Canberra.
12 *Tobacco Advertising Prohibition Act 1992* (Cth) ss. 6, 13, 15. See also *Broadcasting Services Act 1992* (Cth), which makes the prohibition a condition of licences granted. See generally J McLachlan & P Mallam, *Media Law and Practice,* Sydney, LBC (looseleaf).
13 *Tobacco Advertising Prohibition Act* ss. 14, 19.
14 See, for example, *The Benson and Hedges Company Pty Ltd v Australian Broadcasting Tribunal* (1985) 58 ALR 675; see more recently *TCN Channel Nine Pty Ltd v Australian Broadcasting Authority* [2002] FCA 896 (re Russell Crowe smoking on 60 Minutes).
15 *Tobacco Advertising Prohibition Act* s.9.
16 *Tobacco Advertising Prohibition Act* s.10(5).
17 *Broadcasting Services Act* s.101, *Tobacco Advertising Prohibition Act* s.18.
18 Under the *Broadcasting Services Act* s.123.
19 The Commercial Television Industry Code of Practice, July 2004, para. 6.7.
20 The *Lanham Act* prohibits unauthorised use of an aspect of a person's identity in connection with goods or services where it is likely to cause confusion or mistake, or deceive as to affiliation, connection or association with the person.
21 *Midler v Ford Motor Co 849 F 2d 460* (9th Cir) 1988.
22 *Waits v Frito-Lay 978 F 2d 1093* (9th Cir) 1992.
23 *White v Samsung Electronics 971 F 2d 1395* (1991).
24 *Abdul-Jabbar v General Motors Corp 85 F 3d 407* (9th Cir) 1996. The plaintiff's former name, Lew Alcindor, was used to suggest an endorsement of cars.
25 See, for example, *Fair Trading Act 1985* (Vic.); *Fair Trading Act 1987* (NSW); *Fair Trading Act 1987* (SA); *Jurisdiction of Courts (Cross-vesting) Act 1987; Jurisdiction of Courts (Miscellaneous Amendments) Act 1987.*
26 *Hornsby Building Information Centre Pty Ltd & Anor v Sydney Building Information Centre* (1978) ATPR 40–067.
27 See, for example, *Janssen Pharmaceutical Pty Ltd v Pfizer Pty Ltd* (1986) ATPR 40–654.
28 *CRW Pty Ltd v Sneddon (1972)* 72 AR 17.
29 See *Trade Practices Act 1974* (Cth) s.4(2).
30 See *Taco Co of Australia Inc & Anor v Taco Bell Pty Ltd & Ors* (1982) ATPR 40–303, particularly pp. 43, 751–2.
31 *Parish v World Series Cricket* (1977) ATPR 40–039; 40–040.
32 *Coonan & Denlay Pty Ltd v Superstar Australia Pty Ltd* (1981) ATPR 40–231; 40–253 (appeal dismissed). See also *S & I Publishing Pty Ltd v Australian Surf Life Saver Pty Ltd* (1999) ATPR 41–667, a case involving the similar get-up of two sports magazines.

33 *Mundine v Layton Taylor Productions Pty Ltd* (1981) ATPR 40–211.

34 *Kiley v Lysfar Pty Ltd & Anor* (1985) ATPR 40–614.

35 *Wickham v Associated Pool Builders Pty Ltd & Ors* (1986) ATPR 40–741; (1988) ATPR 40–510.

36 *Global Sportsman Pty Ltd & Anor v Mirror Newspapers Ltd & Anor* (1984) ATPR 40–463.

37 *Honey v Australian Airlines Ltd & Anor* (1989) ATPR 40–961.

38 *Talmax Pty Ltd & Anor v Telstra Corporation Limited* (1996) ATPR 41–535.

39 *Campomar Sociedad Limited v Nike International Limited* (2000) 202 CLR 45.

40 *South Australian Brewing Co Pty Ltd v Carlton & United Breweries Ltd* [2001] FCA 902.

41 *Seven Network Limited & Ors v News Interactive Pty Ltd & Ors* [2004] FCA 1047.

42 *New Zealand Olympic and Commonwealth Games Association Inc v Telecom New Zealand Ltd & Anor* (1996) 35 IPR 55.

43 As to passing off generally see J McKeough et al (2004) *Intellectual Property in Australia* (4th edn) LexisNexis Butterworths, Chatswood.

44 *Irvine & Anor v Talksport Ltd* [2003] EWCA Civ 423; [2003] 1 WLR 1576.

45 E Kolivos (2004) 'Playing by the rules: brand protection legislation in sport', 16(9) *IP Bulletin* 136. The article also refers at p. 3 to the position in South Africa where the *Merchandise Marks Act 1941* was amended in 2002 to make ambush marketing a criminal offence.

46 See generally Report by the Senate Legal and Constitutional References Committee, *Cashing in on the Sydney Olympics: Protecting the Sydney Olympic Games from ambush marketing*, March 1995.

47 *Commonwealth Games Arrangements Act 2001* (Cth).

48 *Australian Grand Prix Act 1994* (Vic).

49 A Clement (2002) 'Contemporary Trademark Law and Sport', 12 *Journal of Legal Aspects of Sport* 1, p.1.

50 See D Healey & A Terry (1990) *Misleading or Deceptive Conduct*, CCH Australia, Sydney.

51 S.6.

52 *Arsenal Football Club PLC v Reed* [2003] All ER (D) 289 (May).

53 *Torpedoes Sportswear Pty Limited v Thorpedo Enterprises Pty Limited & Anor* [2003] FCA 901.

54 See *Copyright Act 1968* (Cth) ss. 32, 89–92. As to whether athletic routines are able to be copyrighted, see W Tucker Griffith (1998) 'Beyond the Perfect Score: Protecting routine-orientated athletic performance with copyright law', 30 *Conn. L. Rev.* 675.

55 *Sydney Organising Committee for the Olympic Games v Pam Clarke* [1998] 792 FCA (25 June 1998).

56 *Network Ten Pty Ltd v TCN Channel Nine Pty* Ltd [2004] HCA 14. As to issues of passing title in copyright see *Australian Olympic Committee Inc and Anor v Big Fights Inc & Ors* [1999] FCA 1042.

57 Operative June 2004.

58 See J Smith (1999) 'Its Your Move – No its not! The application of patent law to sports moves', 70 *U. Colo. L. Rev.* 1051.

59 See ABC Television *Four Corners* program, 1 December 1987. See more recently allegations arising in relation to cyclists prior to the Athens Olympics.

60 JF Fleming (1998) *The Law of Torts* (9th edn), Law Book Company, Sydney.

61 See *Defamation Act 1974* (NSW); *Wrongs Act 1958* (Vic) (Pt I); *Defamation Law of Queensland 1889, Criminal Code of Queensland*; *Wrongs Act 1936* (SA) (Pt I); *Defamation Act 1957* (Tas); *Defamation Act 1938* (NT); *Defamation*

Act 1901 (NSW) and *Defamation (Amendment) Act 1909* (NSW), relevant to the ACT. Many other provisions of state Acts will be relevant to defamation.

62 *Lange v ABC* (1997) Aust Tort Reports 81–434

63 *Chappell v Mirror Newspapers* (1984) Aust Torts Reports 80–691.The Court of Appeal (Moffit, Samuels and Priestly JJA) allowed Chappell's appeal and ordered a new trial on procedural grounds.

64 *Lloyd v David Syme and Co* [1982] (Unreported, Begg CJ, NSWSC, 18 April 1982); *David Syme and Co Ltd v Lloyd* [1984] 3 NSWLR 346; *Lloyd v David Syme and Co* (1985) 60 ALJR 10.

65 *Tolley v JS Fry and Sons Ltd* [1930] 1 KB 467.

66 *Boyd v Mirror Newspapers Ltd* [1980] 2NSWLR 449.

67 *Ettingshausen v Australian Consolidated Press* (1991) Aust Torts Reports 81–125.

68 *Harrigan v Jones* (2001) Aust Torts Reports 81–621.

69 *Hall & Ors v Gould* [2002] NSWSC 359.The judge found that several of the comments were capable of being defamatory and referred them to a jury.

Chapter 6

1 See also chapter 3.

2 As to the law of domestic tribunals generally, see JR Forbes (2002) *Justice in Tribunals*, Federation Press, Sydney.

3 See, for example, *Carter v NSW Netball Association* [2004] NSW SC 737, Palmer J, 17 August 2004

4 See, for example, *Nagle v Fielden* [1966] 2 QB 633; *Lee v Showman's Guild* [1952] 1 All ER 1175; *McInnes v Onslow-Fane* (1978) 1 WLR 1520.

5 See *McKinnon v Grogan*, discussed in chapter 1.

6 See *Thomson v Earlwood-Bardwell Park RSL* [1999] NSWSC 243 (25 March 1999) for discussion of the position where there is no issue of employment.

7 The circumstances of *Wilson v Hang Gliding Federation of Australia Incorporated* [1995], set out in this chapter, involved a finding at first instance that the tribunal had made an order outside its power in cancelling a licence (Unreported, Windeyer J, NSWSC, 22 September 1995); CA (Sheller, Powell, Dunford JJA) 15 April 1997.

8 *Australian Football League v Carlton Football Club* [1998] 2 VR 546 (Tadgell & Hayne JJA; Ashley JA dissenting).

9 See p. 47.

10 *R v Jockey Club ex parte the Aga Khan* [1993] 2 All ER 853.

11 See *Byrne v Kinematograph Renter Soc. Ltd* [1958] 1 WLR 762, referred to in *Boyd v Humphreys* [1978] (Unreported, 24 May 1978).

12 *Sweeney v Committee of South East Racing Association & Ors* (1985) FLR 191.

13 Boyd had resigned from his membership of the football club and its committee prior to the first meeting, and argued that as coach, he was not a 'member, player or official' over whom the committee had power. This argument was upheld.

14 *Boyd v Kelly & Ors* [1985] (Unreported, Needham J, NSWSC, 21 August 1985).

15 See generally *Carlton Football Club Ltd & Anor v Australian Football League & Ors* (1997) 71 ALJR 1546, where Hedigan J recognised this proposition.

16 *Enderby Town Football Club Ltd v Football Association Ltd* [1971] Ch. 591 per Denning LJ, but compare judgments of Fenton, Atkinson and Cairns LLJ in the same case.

17 See, for example, *Pett v Greyhound Racing Association Ltd* [1969] 1 QB 46; compare *McNab v Auburn Soccer Sports Club Ltd* [1975] 1 NSWLR 54; *Freedman v Petty & Ors* (1981) VR 1001; *Sweeney v Committee of South East Racing Association* (1985) FLR 191.

18   See *Hann v Swain & Ors* [1993] (Unreported, Gobbo J, VSC, 12 March 1993) referred to in G Galloway (1995) 'Judicial review: an impossible dream', paper presented at ANZSLA Conference, Auckland.

19   *Hollioake & Anor v Western Australian Cricket Association & Anor* (1994) 11 WAR 423.

20   See note 11.

21   *Nowlan v Sydney Rugby Union* [1991] (Unreported, Rolfe J, NSWSC) 27 March 1991.

22   See Gallaway, ' Judicial review'.

23   *Maloney v National Coursing Association Ltd* [1978] 1 NSWLR 161.

24   *Ainsworth v Criminal Justice Commission* (1992) 106 ALR 11. The High Court in that decision extended the categories of rights which might be protected in tribunals to legitimate expectations and commercial reputation.

25   *Australian Football League v Carlton Football Club Limited* [1998] VR 546. See generally M Kosla (2001) 'Disciplined for bringing a sport into disrepute: a framework for judicial review' 25(1) MULR 654

26   *Stollery v Greyhound Racing Control Board* (1973) 128 CLR 509.

27   *Australian Football League v Carlton Football Club Limited* [1998] 2 VR 546, referring to *Bugden v NSW Rugby League Ltd* [1985] (Unreported, Powell J, NSWSC, 22 April 1985) where the parties accepted that a standard of beyond reasonable doubt applied.

28   *Dale v NSW Trotting Club Ltd* [1978] 1 NSWLR

29   *Wilson v Hang Gliding Federation of Australia Incorporated*, NSWCA.

30   See *Calvin v Carr* [1977] 2 NSWLR 2; *Stollery v Greyhound Racing Control Board* (1972) 128 CLR 509, p. 526; confirmed in *Australian Football League v Carlton Football Club Limited* [1998] 2VR 546.

31   *Australian Football League v Carlton Football Club Limited* [1998] 2 VR 546.

32   See, for example, *Raguz v Sullivan* (2000) 50 NSWLR 237.

33   *Australian Football League v Carlton Football Club Limited*.

34   *Lee v Showman's Guild of Great Britain* [1952] 2 QB 329, p. 342 per Denning LJ.

35   This is taken from D Healey (2000) 'Sports Tribunals: A practical guide', paper presented at Sports Tribunals and Sports Administration, LAAMS Seminar, October.

Chapter 7

1   Snow skiing: *Taylor & Ors v British Columbia* (1978) DLR (3d) 82; *Gilsenan v Gunning* (1982) 137 DLR (3d) 252; *Rides Pty Ltd v Gauci* (1984) Aust Torts Reports 80–637. Water skiing: *Wyong Shire Council v Shirt* (1980) 54 ALJR 283; *Rogers v Rawlings* (1969) Qd R 262. Trampolining: *Robertson v Hobart Police Citizens Youth Club* (1984) Aust Tort Reports 80–629; *Bills v SA* (1985) Aust Torts Reports 80–703. Hockey: *Payne v Maple Leaf Gardens* (1949) 1 DLR 369; *Murray v Haringay Arena* [1951] 2 KB 529. Football: *Simms v Leigh Rugby Football Club* [1969] 2 All ER 923; *Watson v Haines*, NSWSC (1987) Aust Torts Reports 80–094 ; *Condon v Basi* [1985] 1 WLR 866; *Nowak v Waverley Municipal Council* (1984) Aust Torts Reports 80–200; *Davis v Kitching* (1986) Aust Torts Reports 80–029. Cricket: *Bolton v Stone* [1951] AC 850; *Miller v Jackson* [1977] 3 All ER 368. Swimming: *Schiller v Gregor* (1986) Aust Torts Reports 80–751. Golf: *Cleghorn v Oldham* (1927) 43 TLR 465; *Albany Golf Club Inc v Carey* (1987) Aust Torts Reports 80–139. Motor racing: *Hall v Brooklands AC* [1933] 1 KB 205. Horse riding: *Wooldridge v Sumner* (1963) 2 Q.B. 43.

2   *Financial Review*, 28 July 1995.

3   *Agar v Hyde* (2000) 201 CLR 552; see also *Cook v ACT Racing Club* [2001] ACTSC 106 in relation to the liability of a racing club for injuries to a jockey in relation to the use of a sauna.

4   At p.561.

5   'Terms of Reference: Principles-based review of the law of negligence' in Panel of Eminent Persons (2002) *Review of the Law of Negligence Final Report* at p. ix (the Ipp Report). See also Trowbridge Consulting (2002) *Public Liability Insurance: Practical proposals for reform*.

6   See, for example, JJ Spigelman (2002) 'Negligence: The last outpost of the welfare state', 76 *ALJ* 432. For an alternative point of view see H Luntz (2002) 'Reform of the Law of Negligence: Wrong questions – wrong answers', 8 *UNSW Law Journal Forum* 18.

7   See note 5 for full title.

8   Second Reading Speech to Civil Liability Amendment (Personal Responsibility) Bill.

9   *Civil Liability Act* 2002 (NSW), *Civil Liability Amendment (Personal Responsibility) Act* 2002 (NSW); *Civil Liability Act* 2003 (Qld); *Wrongs Act* 1958 (Vic); *Civil Law (Wrongs) Act* 2002 (ACT); *Civil Liability Act* 2002 (WA); *Civil Liability Act* 2002 (Tas); *Wrongs Act* 1936 (SA); *Personal Injuries (Liability and Damages) Act* 2003 (NT). Some states have enacted separate leglislation to protect volunteers.

10   *Trade Practices (Personal Injuries and Death) Act* 2004 (No 2) from July 2004; *Commonwealth Volunteers Protection Act* 2002 (Cth). In addition, options for a scheme for the catastrophically injured are being investigated by federal state and territory insurance ministers (press release, Minister for Sport, Racing and Gaming, Minister for Economic Development, Business and Tourism, 27 February 2004).

11   There is a variety of exclusions from these provisions in NSW where, for example, they do not apply to intentional acts, sexual assault, dust diseases or injuries arising from smoking or the use of tobacco products.

12   See chapter 3 for the difficulties of formulating proceedings against unincorporated associations and the position of office bearers in such organisations.

13   Fleming, *The Law of Torts*, p.114, and see Fleming as to tort law generally.

14   (1932) AC 562 per Lord Atkin at p. 580.

15   As to foreseeability, see *Overseas Tankship (UK) Ltd v Morts Dock and Engineering Co Ltd* [1961] AC 381; *Shirt v Wyong Shire Council & Ors* [1978] 1 NSWLR 631. Proximity as a concept has become less important of late; see *Jaensch v Coffey* (1984) 155 CLR 549; *Stevens v Brodribb Sawmilling Co Pty Ltd* (1986) 160 CLR 16; compare *Hill v Van Erp* (1997) 188 CLR 159; *Sullivan v Moody* (2001) 207 CLR 562.

16   *Commonwealth of Australia v Introvigne* (1982) 41 ALR 577; see also *Wyong Shire Council v Shirt* (1980) 146 CLR 40.

17   See, in a non-sporting context, *Paris v Stepney Borough Council* [1951] AC 367, where the plaintiff had only one eye, and injury to his remaining eye rendered him blind.

18   NSW s.5B(1).

19   NSW s.5B(2).

20   *Recreational Services (Limitation of Liability) Act* 2002 (SA).

21   There is no liability for inherent risks. The majority judgment in *Waverley Municipal Council v Swain* [2003] NSWCA 61 referred to the inherent risks of body surfing and compared them to risks in cases involving diving such as *Nagle v Rottnest Island Authority* (1993) 177 CLR 423. See also Barwick in *Rootes v Shelton* (1967) 116 CLR 383; *Romeo v Conservation Commission of NT* (1998)

151 ALR 263 per Kirby J at 299; *Woods v Multi Sport Holdings* (2002) 186 ALR 145 per Kirby J & Gleeson CJ; *University of Wollongong v Mitchell* [2003] NSWCA 94 per MeagherJ. It has also been suggested that the scrum injuries in *Agar v Hyde* resulted from an inherent risk. See H Opie (2001) 'The Sports Administrator's Charter: Agar v Hyde', 9 *Torts Law Journal* 131.

22 NSW s.5F. In *Prast v Town of Cottesloe* (2000) WASCA 274 Ipp J characterized the risk faced by body surfers of being hurled onto the sand as an obvious risk.

23 NSW s.5H. Queensland, South Australia, Tasmania Victoria and Western Australia all have or intend to introduce a similar provision.

24 NSW s.5G

25 See, for example, *Barnett v Chelsea and Kensington Hospital Management Committee* [1969] 1 QB 428; *March v Strahmere Pty Ltd* (1991) 171 CLR 506; *Lilley v Alpine Resorts Commission & Anor* (1998) Aust Torts Reports 81–475.

26 NSW ss. 5D, 5E.

27 See *Ruddock v Taylor* [2003] NSWCA 262, where Ipp JA discusses the NSW causation provisions.

28 *Nagle v Rottnest Island Authority;Romeo v Conservation Commission of the Northern Territory* [1998] HCA 5 (2 February 1998).

29 *Council of the Municipality of Waverley v Bloom* (Unreported, NSWCA 5 August 1999); *Mulligan v Coffs Harbour City Council* [2003] NSWSC 49 (appeal dismissed [2004] NSW CA (27 July 2004)); *Waverley Municipal Council v Swain* [2003] NSWSC 61 (appeal to the High Court and judgement reserved); *Vairey v Wyong Shire Council* [2002] NSWSC 881 (appeal allowed [2004] NSW CA 247 (27 July 2004)).

30 Many of these cases involved public authorities. Civil liability legislation affects the liability of public authorities as well as recreational activities.

31 These are the implied conditions and warranties and manufacturers' liability provisions found in Part V of the Act, which are discussed in what follows. Ss. 68 and 68A provide that these provisions cannot generally be excluded from consumer contracts. Other laws protecting against unfair contracts or other behaviour have applied where, for example, contract terms heavily favour the seller and discriminate against the ticket buyer.

32 *Lee Gowan v Graham Windsor* (DCNSW, Shillington J, 24 August 1991); *Gowan v Hardie & Anor* (CA 8 November 1991).

33 *Neil v Fallon & Ors* (1995) Aust Torts Reports 81–321. There is a similar trend to enforcement of such clauses in the US. See, for example, L Hastings (1988) 'Playing with Liability: The risk release in high risk sports', 24 *California Western Law Review* 127, p. 127.

34 NSW s.5K

35 NSW s.5M(2). Queensland, South Australia, Tasmania, Victoria and Western Ausralia have provisions limiting in some way liability arising from recreational activities.

36 NSW s.5M.

37 S.5M(9). This might be relevant to a school situation.

38 NSW s.5K.

39 NSW s.5L.

40 It has been suggested that jumping into a canal from a fence and playing indoor cricket and suffering an eye injury would fall within both categories. See M Davies & I Malkin (2003) *Torts* (4th edn) LexisNexis Butterworths, p 154.

41 See s.68B.

42 See *Civil Liability Act (NSW)* s.3B, which provides that the amendments do not generally apply to intentional acts.

43 See Fleming, *The Law of Torts*

44 *McNamara v Duncan* (1971) 26 ALR 584. See also *Smith v Emerson* (1986) Aust Torts Reports 80–022

45 *Canterbury Bankstown Rugby League Football Club Ltd v Rogers; Bugden v Rogers* (1993) Aust Torts Reports 81–246. The position in relation to these damages in NSW has been changed by the civil liability amendments.

46 *Wallace v Grinter and Melbourne Football Club Limited,* VSC No. 8348 of 1990.

47 *Rootes v Shelton* (1967) 116 CLR 383.

48 *Rootes v Shelton.*

49 *Condon v Basi* [1986] AC 453, p. 455. The County Court judge awarded almost 5000 pounds in damages and this finding was upheld on appeal. It might be thought that assault would have been a more appropriate cause of action in the circumstances.

50 *Frazer v Johnston* (1989) Aust Torts Reports 80–248.

51 *Frazer v Johnston,* p.15.

52 *Johnston v Frazer* (1990) 21 NSWLR 89.

53 *Ollier v Magnetic Island Country Club & Anor* [2004] QCA 137. The golf course was found not to be liable. This case is on appeal to the High Court.

54 *Wooldridge v Sumner* [1963] 2 QB 43.

55 RL Yasser (1985) *Torts and Sports: Legal liability in professional and amateur athletics,* Quorum Books, Connecticut, p. 46.

56 For an interesting commentary on the numerous US decisions in the area, see Yasser, *Torts and Sports,* which categorises the cases under the sport involved: baseball, ice hockey, auto racing, horse racing, golf, wrestling.

57 See T Hurst & J Knight (2003) 'Coaches liability for athletes' injuries and deaths', 13 *Seton Hall J. Sport L.* 27.

58 *Watson v Haines* (1987) Aust Torts Reports 80–094. Civil liability legislation in NSW is likely to affect the outcome of similar cases, particularly in regard to the social utility of the activity, the fact that an activity might be required and the fact that the school may be a public authority. For liability of schools in NSW, see H Harrison (2004) 'Civil Liability Act 2002 – Update: Issues for schools', paper presented at State Legal Conference, 27 August.

59 *Watson v Haines,* p. 6.

60 See *Commonwealth of Australia v Introvigne* (1982) 41 ALR 577. The non-delegable duty has been amended by some states under civil liability legislation.

61 As to the standard of care in relation to children see comments in *Agar v Hyde* (2000) 201 CLR 552.

62 *Watson v Haines.*

63 *Foscolos v Footscray Youth Club & Anor* [2002] VSC 148; (2002) Aust Tort Reports 81–658

64 It was not necessary in the case to decide the argument about whether or not the opponents had been mismatched.

65 See L Duckett (1995) 'Top gymnast sues coach', *Daily Telegraph Mirror,* 15 May, p. 1. Following complaints by other parties, an investigation of the practices of the coach and the gymnastics program at the ASC was instigated in 1995.

66 Yasser, *Torts and Sports,* cites the famous US example of gridiron player Dick Butkus of the Chicago Bears. Butkus claimed that extensive cortisone injections had irreparably damaged his knee and that he had not been told of the long term effects of the drug. Butkus was reportedly paid $600 000 in settlement of his claim in 1976.

67 See *Barker v South Australia* (1978) SASR 416; compare *Barnes v Hampshire County Council* [1969] 1 WLR 1563.

68 *Morrell v Owen & Ors* [1993] (Unreported, Mitchell J, Queens Bench Division, 14 December 1993).

69   See ASC, *Pregnancy in Sport Guidelines* (2001). The guideline was issued before the introduction of civil liability legislation.
70   Sports Medicine Australia Statement, *The Benefits and Risks of Exercise during Pregnancy,* notes that there are no reported examples of foetal injury or death in relation to trauma or contact during sporting activities, although a risk of severe blunt trauma is present in relation to some activities.
71   See chapter 10.
72   South Australia, Victoria, Queensland.
73   Other relevant issues may be occupational health and safety legislation for employees, duties owed to employees where athletes are employed, and restraint of trade.
74   In *Anderson v Mount Isa Basketball Association Inc* (1997) Aust Tort Reports 81–451 the organisation was found to be negligent in not giving a basketball referee a warning of the dangers of running backwards on the court. The magnitude of the risk was high and the expense and difficulty of giving the warning was low.
75   (2000) 173 ALR 665.
76   (1996) TLR 249. The case was decided on its particular circumstances.
77   *Woods v Multi Sport Holdings,* (2002) 186 ALR 145.
78   One was acquitted, while charges against the other were dropped when a jury could not agree on a verdict (http://news.bbc.co.uk/onthisday/hi/dates/stories/apri;/15/newsid–2491000/2491195.stm)
79   See A MacDonald (1987) 'The Bradford football fire', 137 *New Law Journal* 481.
80   As to occupiers' liability under the traditional legal approach, see for example *Indermaur v Dames* [1866] LR 1 CP 274.
81   See *Occupiers' Liability Act 1983* (Vic) (amendment to the *Wrongs Act 1958* (Vic)); *Wrongs Amendment Act 1987* (SA) (amendment to the *Civil Liability Act 1936* (SA)); *Occupiers' Liability Act 1985* (WA). The Victorian Act, for example, imposes a statutory duty of care on occupiers.
82   See *Hackshaw v Shaw* (1983–1984) 155 CLR 614; *Papantonakis v Australian Telecommunications Commission & Anor* (1984–1985) 156 CLR 7; *Australian Safeway Stores Pty Ltd v Zaluzna* (1987) 69 ALR 615.
83   *Australian Safeway Stores v Zaluzna*, p. 617, where the statement of Deane J in *Hackshaw v Shaw* pp. 662–3 was adopted.
84   *Nowak v Waverley Municipal Council* (1984) Aust Torts Reports 80–200. See also *Canterbury Municipal Council v Taylor & Ors* [2002] NSWCA 24, where the council was liable to an injured cyclist who hit and killed a touch football player on a dual use velodrome.
85   In a case involving the disaster, the plaintiffs were a woman suing on behalf of her dead husband and a minor son injured in the accident, and a policeman injured rescuing spectators. They sued the football club, the Health and Safety Executive, a body charged under the *Health and Safety at Work Act 1974* with the duty to enforce that Act, and the West Yorkshire Metropolitan County Council, who had responsibilities under the *Fire Precautions Act 1971* and the *Sports Ground Act*. The court found that both the football club and the fire authority had been negligent.
86   *Sotiropoulos v Canterbury Municipal Council* [1994] (Unreported, James J, NSWSC, Common Law Division, 12 May 1994).The liability of public authorities who are occupiers or organisers of events may be affected by recent civil liability legislation in some states.
87   [1951] AC 850.
88   A retrial was ordered on the matter in amended pleadings. *Davis v Kitching* (1986) Aust Torts Reports 80–029.

89   *Cowell v Rosehill Racecourse Co Ltd* (1937) 56 CLR 605.

90   See *Civil Liability Act* (NSW) Part 9.

91   (1993) ATR 81–246

92   *Rogers v Bugden* (1993) ATR 81–246, p. 62, 544ff. See also *Duncan by her next friend Duncan v Trustees of the Roman Catholic Church for the Archdiocese of Canberra and Goulburn* (Unreported, ACTSC, 14 October 1998, where it was found that a school could also be vicariously liable for the conduct of volunteers. See also *Civil Liability Act* (NSW) s.5Q.

93   RS Magnusson & H Opie (1994) 'HIV and hepatitis in sport: a legal framework for resolving hard cases', 20 *Monash University Law Review* 214, p. 218. The ASMF policy was updated in 1997. The NSW Privacy Committee, under its general power to report, released *Private Lives and Public Health – Privacy guidelines for HIV testing* (August 1993).

94   Magnusson & Opie, 'HIV and hepatitis in sport', p. 226.

95   The position varies from state to state. In NSW, jockeys and harness racing drivers are specifically covered by the Act, as are boxers, wrestlers and other 'entertainers' (see Schedule 2, *Accident Compensation Act 1985* (NSW)); presumably other professional sportspeople will be classified according to the nature of their actual contracts (see chapter 4). In Victoria and Queensland, a person engaged by an employer to compete in athletic activity will not fall within the Act if the person is injured competing, travelling or training in relation to an athletic contest, and is not entitled to payment other than for those activities: jockeys are deemed workers (*Accident Compensation Act 1985* (Vic) s.16; *Workers' Compensation and Rehabilitation Act 2003* (Qld)). In South Australia a worker employed solely to participate as a contestant or referee is not eligible for compensation. Exception is made, however, for some jockeys, boxers and wrestlers and for anyone who earns their entire livelihood or in excess of $25 000 per year from the activity (*Workers' Rehabilitation and Compensation Act 1986* (SA) s.58). Western Australia has provisions similar to those in force in Victoria (*Workers' Compensation and Assistance Act 1981* (WA) s.11).

96   *Sydney Morning Herald*, 2 September 1994, p. 5.

97   See, for example, *Commonwealth of Australia v TH Lyon* (1979) 24 ALR 300.

98   NSW, Victoria, South Australia, Western Australia, Tasmania.

99   See *Sporting Injuries Insurance Act 1978* (NSW), which sets up the Scheme and the Suplementary Sporting Injuries Benefits Scheme that was introduced by amendment to the main Act in 1984.

100 See *NSW Rugby League Ltd v Allen* (1998) 83 IR 397 where the issue of the scheme in the context of unfair contracts was considered – see chapter 4.

101 *Tonkin v Gunn* (1988) Aust Tort Reports 80–219.

102 See Yasser, *Torts and Sports*, p. 78ff. Yasser also cites cases involving snapping pole vault poles, malfunctioning automatic baseball pitching machines, golfing machines.

103 See Yasser, *Torts and Sports*, p. 82.

104 See *Trade Practices Act*, Part V, Div 2 and 2A.

105 See *Trade Practices Amendment (Personal Injuries and Death) Act 2004* (No.2) (Cth).

106 Schedule 3 of the *Corporate Law Economic Reform Program (Audit Reform and Corporate Disclosure) Act 2004* (Cth).

107 *See Trade Practices Act* Part V Div 1A.

108 See Gazette No. S242, 30 October 1980.

109 See Gazette No. S620, 1 December 1986; Gazette No. S221, 19 May 1986.

Chapter 8

1   R Box (2003) 'Sports insurance: how strong is your bungee cord?' paper presented at UNSW Seminar on Civil Liability, 22 September; L Morris (2003) 'Foreign insurers take risk on liability', *Sydney Morning Herald*, 18 July.

2   The Ipp Report; Standing Committee on Recreation and Sports, *Review of Austraian Sports Insurance*, prepared for the Sport and Recreation Ministers Council, March 2002; Productivity Commission Research Report, *Public Liability Claims Management*, December 2002; Ernst & Young, *Australian Sports Commission: Insurance report*, January 2003; Minister for Revenue and Assistant Treasurer Hon. Helen Coonan, *Reform of Liability Insurance Law in Australia*, February 2004.

3   In its most recent report (July 2004) the ACCC noted that most public liability insurers had observed a fall in claims frequency in their emerging claims; they expected reforms to affect public liability insurance costs in the short term; all but one expected reforms to have an impact on costs in the medium term; in the longer term there were concerns about circumvention of the reforms. See ACCC, *Public Liability and Professional Indemnity Insurance: Third monitoring report* (July 2004) at pp. xi–xii.

4   See Box, 'Sports insurance', p. 1. She notes the establishment by a co-insurance panel of the Community Care Underwriting Agency to assist not-for-profit organisations in certain states to obtain public liability insurance for activities including community events, community centres and home care. The NSW government has also provided funding to the Council of Social Services of NSW for the establishment of a bulk buying scheme for not-for-profit community organisations (Minister for Commerce, press release, 27 April 2004).

5   Box, 'Sports insurance'.

6   AS/NZS 4360: 1999.

7   AS/NZS 4360:1999 at p iii.

8   ASC, *Risk Management for the Directors and Board Members of National Sporting Organisations*, prepared for the Management Improvement Group, ASC, by Standards Australia International.

9   See ASC, *Risk Management for Directors and Board Members*, p. 36.

10   Civil liability legislation that removes liability from volunteers and places it on the organisation provides further incentive for insurance.

11   Reference should also be made to the Sporting Injuries Compensation Scheme (NSW) – see chapter 7.

12   See ASC, *Risk Management for Directors and Board Members*, p. 14.

Chapter 9

1   See chapter 1.

2   See *Criminal Code Act 1899* (Qld); *Criminal Code Act 1913* (WA); *Criminal Code Act* 1924 (Tas).

3   The whole of the law dealing with murder is contained in the codes of the states of Queensland, Tasmania and Western Australia.

4   Other countries have created offences specific to sport. In the US, for example, it has been reported that there have been imprisonments for breach of laws requiring registration as a sports agent. See R Bascuas (1996) 'Cheaters, not criminals: antitrust invalidation of statutes outlawing sports agent recruitment of student athletes', 105 *Yale Law Journal* 1603.

5   See chapter 7.

6   AP Bates et al. (1976) *The System of Criminal Law*, Butterworths, Sydney, p. 559.

7   *Stanley* (Unreported, NSWCCA, 7 April 1995) referred to in D Brown et al (2001) *Criminal Laws: Materials and commentary on criminal law and process in New South Wales,* Federation Press, Sydney, p. 849. See also D Brown & R Hogg (1997) 'Violence, masculinity and sport: governance and the 'swinging arm', 3(1) *UTS Review* 129.

8   (1995) *Daily Telegraph Mirror,* 8 March, p. 73.

9   *R v Coney* (1882) 8 QBD 534, particularly p. 549 per Stephen J.

10   *R v Donavon* [1934] 2 KB 4498.

11   *R v Bradshaw* (1878) 14 Cox CC 83; *R v Moore* (1989) 14 TLR 229.

12   *R v Billinghurst* 17 CH.D 615.

13   *Pallante v Stadiums Ltd* [1976] VR 331.

14   (Unreported, 7 April 1986); see also *Jones v Carr* (Unreported, noted in *Daily Mirror* 13 February 1989, p. 8). The defendant was reportedly put on a $25 000 good behaviour bond for assault on the field during a rugby league match.

15   *Watherston v Woolven* [1987] (Unreported, Johnston J, SASC October 21 1987) noted in *The Australian,* 9 November 1987, p. 4.

16   See Lord Justice Coke (1797) 'Institutes of the Laws of England', *3 Inst.* 47, quoted in P Gillies (1985) *Criminal Law,* Law Book Company, Sydney.

17   *R v Moore.*

18   *R v Southby* (1969) (Unreported, noted in E Grayson (1978) 'Injuries on and off the sporting field', paper presented at Conference on Sport and Law, Birmingham University.

19   *R v Bradshaw,* p. 85.

20   (1992) 142 *New Law Journal* 815.

21   *R v Coney,* per Stephen J.

22   (1985) *The National Times,* 19–25 July, p. 50.

23   See *Watherston v Woolven.*

24   See Sport and Recreation Ministers' Council (SRMC), *Strategies Endorsed by SRMC in Relation to Violence in Sport,* 30 April 1986, p. 2. See also RB Horrow (1980) *Sports Violence: The interaction between private lawmaking and the criminal law,* Carrollton Press, Arlington and Inverness.

25   The council is a body consisting of Commonwealth, state and territory ministers, and observers from New Zealand and Papua New Guinea. It was set up in 1973 to coordinate the development of sport and recreation in Australia. SRMC, *Violence in Sport: An Australian study, Summary of major issues and strategies* (December 1985), p. 1.

26   SRMC, *Violence in Sport,* p. 13.

27   The role of television in sports violence is noted in R Cashman (1986) *Some Reflections on Crowd Behaviour,* College of Law, 14 March, p. 7, where the problem of cricket advertisements said to encourage combative violence leading to a more violent atmosphere at the ground in question is discussed. Commercialism is also there targeted as a possible cause. The article attempts various explanations of the problem of crowd violence.

28   *Victims Support and Rehabilitation Act 1996* (NSW); *Victims of Crime Assistance Act 1996* (Vic); *Criminal Injuries Compensation Act 1977* (SA); *Criminal Injuries Compensation Act 1985* (WA); *Criminal Injuries Compensation Act 1976* (Tas); *Crimes Compensation Act 1982* (NT); *Criminal Injuries Compensation Ordinance 1983* (ACT).

Chapter 10

1   P Hoch (1972) *Rip Off the Big Game: The exploitation of sports by the power elite,* Anchor Books, New York, p. 147ff. The fight against the problem of racial discrimination in US sport is also outlined in chapter 9 of the book.

2   The definitions and requirements of the various laws may vary.
3   As to discrimination generally, see Austr*alian and New Zealand Equal Opportunity Law and Practice*, CCH Australia Ltd, Sydney; C Ronalds & R Pepper (2004) *Discrimination Law and Practice,* The Federation Press, Sydney.
4   See note 3.
5   *Hagan v Trustees of the Toowoomba Sports Ground Trust* [2001] FCA 123 (23 February 2001).
6   The *Racial Hatred Act 1995* (Cth) inserted a new Part IIA into the *Racial Discrimination Act 1975* (Cth).
7   A Canterbury Bulldogs player was fined $10 000 by an NRL tribunal in 1998 for racially abusing another player. See 'Ward fined $10,000 for racial abuse', *Northern Star,* 2 October 1998,t p30.
8   [2003] FMCA 81.
9   Parliament of the Commonwealth of Australia, Disability Discrimination Bill 1992, Explanatory Memorandum, p. 2.
10 'A disorder or malfunction that results in the person learning differently from a person without the disorder or malfunction; a disorder, illness or disease that affects a person's thought processes, perception of reality, emotions or judgment, or that results in disturbed behaviour and includes a disability that: presently exists; previously existed but no longer exists; may exist in the future; is imputed to a person.'
11 SC 29 May 2001.
12 [2003] FCA 10.
13 (2000) EOC 93–041.
14 [1999] VCAT 627(3 April 1999).
15 *Anti-Discrimination Act 1977* (NSW); *Equal Opportunity Act 1995* (Vic); *Equal Opportunity Act 1984* (SA); *Equal Opportunity Act 1984* (WA); *Anti-Discrimination Act 1991* (Qld); *Anti-Discrimination Act 1992* (NT); *Anti-Discrimination Act 1999* (Tas). Some state Acts deal with physical impairment; some deal also with intellectual impairment; all deal with discrimination on the ground of sexuality. To avoid constitutional problems that have arisen (see *Viskauskas & Anor v Niland* (1983) 57 ALJR 414), the Commonwealth *Racial Discrimination Act* was amended to allow Commonwealth and state Acts to operate concurrently.
16 See See *Women, Sport and the Media: A report to the federal government from the working group on women in sport* (1985) AGPS, Canberra, pp. 20, 48.
17 *Sex Discrimination Act 1984* (Cth), s.42.
18 *Waterhouse v Bell* (1991) EDC 92–376.
19 *Henderson v NBL Management Limited & Anor* (1992) EOC 92–435.
20 *Gulliver v Council of City of Sydney & Anor* (1986) EOC 92–185.
21 *The Mayor, Councillors and Citizens of the City of Moe v Pulis* (1988) EOC 92–243.
22 *Ross & Ors v University of Melbourne* (1990) EOC 92–290.
23 *City of Brunswick; re application for exemption from provisions of the Equal Opportunity Act 1984 (1992)* EOC 92–450.
24 *Corry & Ors v Keperra Country Golf Club* (1986) EOC 92–150.
25 See *Umina Beach Bowling Club Ltd v Ryan* (1984) EOC 92–110; *Tullamore Bowling and Citizens Club Ltd v Lander* (1984) EOC 92–109 (both decisions under the NSW Act).
26 *Mead v Southern Districts Football League Inc* (1992) EOC 92–247.
27 *McInnes v Confederation of Australian Motor Sport* (1990) EOC 92–286; *Keefe v McInnes* (1990) EOC 92–331; *McInnes v Confederation of Australian Motor Sport* (1991) EOC 92–343. See former *Equal Opportunity Act 1984* (Vic) s.33(1), (3).

28 *Sex Discrimination Act* (Cth), s.42(1).
29 *Taylor & Ors v Moorabin Saints Junior Football League and Football Victoria Ltd* [2004] VCAT 158.
30 *Sydney Morning Herald*, 15 April 1991, p.1.
31 *Richards v United States Tennis Association* 400 NYS (2d) 267.
32 'Sex change rules introduced', Associated Press, 18 May 2004. See generally J Pilgrim et al. (2003) 'Far from the finish line: transsexualism and athletic competition', *Fordham Intell.Prop.Media & Ent L. J.* 495.
33 *R v Harris; R v McGuinness* (1988) 17 NSWLR 158; *Corbett v Corbett* [1971] All ER 83; rulings of Social Security Appeals Tribunal; *Attorney-General (Cth) v Kevin and Jennifer* (2003) 172 FLR 300.
34 A transgender person is defined in s.38A as a person whether or not a recognised transgender person, who identifies, lives or is seeking to live as a member of the opposite sex or if of indeterminate sex, identifies as a meber of a particular sex by living as a member of that sex, and includes a reference to a person being thought of as transgender whether or not that is the case (*Anti-discrimination Act* (NSW) s.38A)
35 An inquiry by the Senate Standing Committee into Sex Discrimination proposed amending the *Sex Discrimination Act* to prohibit discrimination against transgender persons, but did not propose an exemption for sport. This recommendation was never implemented.

Chapter 11

1 *Income Tax Assessment Act 1936* (Cth); *Income Tax Assessment Act 1997* (Cth).
2 *Stone v Commissioner of Taxation* [2003] FCAFC 145 (27 June 2003).
3 See *Income Tax Assessment Act 1997* Div 6. As to the law of taxation generally, see *Australian Income Tax Guide*, CCH Australia.
4 *Stone v Commissioner of Taxation*.
5 *Kelly v FC of T*, 85 ATC 4238; see also Taxation Ruling IT 167.
6 (1991) 22 ATR 3450.
7 Taxation Ruling IT 2307.
8 See *Jarrold v Boustead* [1964] 3 All ER 76 (footballer); Case R 123, 81 ATC 4578 (runner); compare 72 ATC D38 (footballer); Taxation Ruling IT 2307.
9 See Taxation Ruling IT 2262.
10 Taxation Ruling TR 1999/17
11 *Stone v Commissioner of Taxation*. Each case will need to be considered on its own facts.
12 'The Waratahs' RUFC Ltd v FC of T 79 ATC 4337; compare Case U128, 87 ATC (ski club); *Cronulla Sutherland Leagues Club Limited v FC of T* 90 ATC 4215; *Teranora Lakes Country Club Limited v FCT* (1993) 93 ATC 4078; see also Taxation Ruling TR95/D18.
13 See *Income Tax Assessment Act 1997* (Cth) s.8-1.
14 *FC of T v Ballesty* (1977) 77 ATC 4181.
15 (1977) 77 ATC J3.
16 *Kemp v FCT* (1992) 110 ALR 375.
17 Material on deductions for particular sports may be found in *Australian Income Tax Guide*.
18 See comments made earlier and also s.160M(6).The ATO has released a draft tax ruling that specifically refers to payments of a kind mentioned in Jarrold's case as one which would be caught by the section.
19 *Fringe Benefits Tax Assessment Act* (Cth) s.136.
20 Taxation Ruling MT 2032.

Chapter 12

1   *Sydney Morning Herald*, August 31 2004.
2   See IAAF press release, 'IAAF statement on Greek athletes and coach', 22 December 2004.
3   J Magnay (2004) 'Kersten's chances raise after Dajka hits a bump', *The Age*, 29 July.
4   *The Australian*, 6 April 2002.
5   The *Australian Sports Drug Agency Act* was amended in June 2004 to comply with the WADA Code.
6   ASDA media release, 28 July 2004.
7   Official publication of the World Anti-Doping Agency, *Play True* (spring 2003).
8   *Play True*.
9   See K Knowler et al (2002) 'Implications of the World Anti-Doping Code for national anti-doping programs', paper presented at ANZSLA Conference, Wellington, October.
10   Weightlifter Caroline Pileggi failed to comply with a request for a test, and lost an appeal to the Federal Court on reinstatement to the Olympic team: *Pileggi v Australian Sports Drug Agency* [2004] FCA 955.
11   The WADC List replaced the 2003 IOC List of Prohibited Substances and Methods. Major changes were the removal of caffeine and pseudoephedrine, and the banning of cannabinoids and glucocorticosteroids (administered orally, rectally or by intravenous or intramuscular administration).
12   Situations involving athletes such as rugby player Ben Tune highlighted the need for a clear and consistent policy in relation to therapeutic use exemptions.
13   See *Australian Sports Drug Agency Act s.*15(4). For an example of an athlete seeking such a review see *Henderson and Australian Sports Drug Agency* [1999] AATA 1010 (23 December 1999).
14   *Robertson v Australian Professional Cycling Inc*, unreported, NSWSC (Waddell CJ in Equity) 10 September 1992

McInnes v Confederation of Australian Motor Sport (1990) EOC 92–286;
   (1991) EOC 92–343   **149, 150**
McInnes v Onslow-Fane [1978] 1 WLR 1520   80
McKinnon v Grogan [1974] 1 NSWLR 295   **13, 27, 80**
McNab v Auburn Soccer Sports Club [1975] 1 NSWLR 54   85
McNamara v Duncan (1971) 26 ALR 584   101
Maguire v SOCOG (2000) EOC 93–041   145
Maloney v National Coursing Association Ltd [1978] 1 NSWLR 161   87
Mead v Southern Districts Football League Inc (1992) EOC 92–247   149
Mersey Docks and Harbour Board v Coggins and Griffith (Liverpool) & Ors
   [1947] AC 1   42
Midler v Ford Motor Co 849 F 2d 460 (9th Cir) 1988   63
Miller v Jackson [1977] 3 All ER 368   91
Mitchell v Australian Football League, unreported, VCA, 12 June 1992 117
Morrell v Owen & Ors, unreported, Queens Bench Division, 14 Division 1993 108
Mulligan v Coffs Harbour City Council [2003] NSWSC 49; on appeal (2004) Aust
   Torts Reports 81–754   98
Mundine v Layton Taylor Productions Pty Ltd (1981) ATPR 40–211   66
Murray v Haringay Arena [1951] 2 KB 529   91
Nagle v Fielden [1966] 2 QB 689   **14, 47, 80**
Nagle v Rottnest Island Authority (1993) 177 CLR 423   **97, 98**
Neil v Fallon & Ors, unreported, Qld CA, 20 February 1995   98
Network Ten Pty Ltd v TCN Channel Nine Pty Ltd [2004] HCA 14   75
Newport Association Football Club Ltd & Ors v Football Association of Wales Ltd
   (1995) 2 ALL ER 287   44
New South Wales Rugby League Limited v Allen (1998) 83 IR 397   **50, 119**
*New Zealand Olympic and Commonwealth Games Association Inc v Telecom
   New Zealand Ltd & Anor* (1996) 35 IPR 55   69
News Limited v Australian Rugby League Limited (1996) ATPR 41–521   **49, 51**
News Limited & Ors v South Sydney District Rugby League Football Club Limited
   [2003] HCA 45 (13 August 2003)   **8, 51**
Nobes v Australian Cricket Board (VSC 16 December 1991)   45
Nordenfelt v Maxim Nordenfelt Guns and Ammunition Co [1894] AC 535 42
Nowlan v Sydney Rugby Union (1991)   86
Ollier v Magnetic Island Country Club & Anor [2004] QCA 137   103
Optus Vision Pty Ltd v Australian Rugby League Limited & Ors [2004] NSWCA
   61   59
Overseas Tankship (UK) Ltd v Morts Dock and Engineering Co Ltd [1961] AC
   381   95
Pallante v Stadiums Ltd [1976] VR 331   134
Papantonakis v Australian Telecommunications Commission & Anor (1984–
   1985) 156 CLR 7   112
Paris v Stepney Borough Council [1951] AC 367   96
Parish v World Series Cricket (1977) ATPR 40–039; 40–040   65
Pay & Ors v Canterbury Bankstown Rugby League Club Limited & Ors (1995) 78
   IR 247   50
Payne v Maple Leaf Gardens (1949) 1 DLR 369   91
Peckham v Moore [1975] 1 NSWLR 353   25
Performing Right Society Ltd v Mitchell and Booker (palais de danse) Ltd [1924] 1
   KB 762   42
Pett v Greyhound Racing Association Ltd [1969] 1 QB 46   85
Pileggi v Australian Sports Drug Agency [2004] FCA 955   163

Table of cases

                                                                     page
ACCC v Fila Sport Oceania Pty Ltd (Administrators Appointed)
   (2004) ATPR 41–983   52
Re Adamson: Ex parte West Australian Football Club (1979) 23
   ALR 439   **13, 45, 49**
Adamson & Ors v New South Wales Rugby League Limited & Ors
   (1991) ATPR 41–084; (1991) ATPR 41–141   45
Agar v Hyde (2000) 201 CLR 552   **91,106,110**
Ainsworth v Criminal Justice Commission (1992) 106 ALR   87
Albany Golf Club Inc v Carey (1987) Aust Torts Reports 80–139   91
Amery v Fifer [1971] NSWLR 685   24
Anderson v Mount Isa Basketball Association Inc (1997) Aust
   Torts Reports 81–451   **110, 114**
Arsenal Football Club PLC v Reed [2003] All ER (D) 28 May   74
Attorney-General v Kevin and Jennifer (2003) 172 FLR 300   151
Australian Football League v Carlton Football Club Limited
   [1998] 2 VR 546   **14, 81, 87, 88, 89**
Australian Olympic Committee Inc & Anor v Big Fights Inc & Ors
   [1999] FCA 1042   74
Australian Safeway Stores Pty Ltd v Zaluzna (1987) 69 ALR 615   112
Avellino v All Australian Netball Association Limited [2004] SASC 56 46
Barker v South Australia [1978] SASR 416   108
Barnes v Hampshire County Council [1969] 1 WLR 1563   108
Barnett v Chelsea and Kensington Hospitals Management Committee
   [1969] 1QB 428   97
Beetson & Masters v Humphreys, unreported, NSWSC 30 April 1980   48
Bills v SA (1985) Aust Torts Reports 80–703   **91,113**
Bolton v Stone [1951] AC 850   **91,113, 118**
Boyd v Humphreys, unreported, NSWSC 24 May 1978   85
Boyd v Kelly & Ors, unreported, NSWSC 21 August 1985   **83,84**
Boyd v Mirror Newspapers Ltd [1980] 2 NSWLR 449   77
Bradley Egg Farm v Clifford [1943] 2 All ER 378   **24,25**
Buckenara v Hawthorn Football Club Ltd [1988] VR 39   45
Buckley v Tutty (1972) 125 CLR 353   44
Bugden v NSW Rugby League Ltd, unreported, NSWSC 22 April 1985   89
Bugden v Rogers (1993) Aust Torts Reports 81–246   116
Byrne v Kinematograph Renter Society Ltd [1958] 1 WLR 762   82
Calvin v Carr [1977] 2 NSWLR 2   88
Cameron v Hogan (1934) 51 CLR 358   **26, 27**
Campomar Sociedad Limited v Nike International Limited (2000) 202
   CLR 45   68
Canberra Bushrangers Baseball Team Pty Limited v Earl Byrne [1994]
   ACTSC   44
*Canterbury Bankstown Rugby League Football Ltd v Rogers;
   Bugden v Rogers* (1993) Aust Torts Reports 81–246   **101,102**
Canterbury Municipal Council v Taylor & Ors [2002] NSWCA 24   112
Carlton Cricket and Social Club v Joseph [1970] VR 487   **29, 30**

Carlton Football Club Ltd & Anor v Australian Football League & Ors (1997) 71 ALJR 1546   84
Chappell v Mirror Newspapers Ltd (1984) Aust Torts Reports 80–691   77
Clarke v Dunraven [1987] AC 59   36
Cleghorn v Oldham (1927) 43 TLR 465   91
Commissioner for Fair Trading v Pashalides t/as Bodyworks Fitness Club, unreported, Crispin J, SCAC), 23 April 2004   12
Commonwealth of Australia v Introvigne (1982) 41 ALR 577   96, 106
Commonwealth of Australia v T H Lyon (1979) 24 ALR 300   118
Commonwealth Bank v Friedreich & Ors (1991) ACLC 946   30
Condon v Basi [1985] 1 WLR 866   91, 102
Cook v ACT Racing Club [2001] ACTSC 106   92
Coonan & Denlay Pty Ltd v Superstar Australia Pty Ltd (1981) ATPR 40–231; 40–253   66
Corbett v Corbett [1971] All ER 83   151
Corry & Ors v Keperra Country Golf Club (1986) EOC 92–150   148
Council of Municipality of Waverley v Bloom, unreported, NSWCA, 5 August 1999   98
Cowell v Rosehill Racecourse Co Ltd (1937) 56 CLR 605   114
Cronulla Sutherland Leagues Club Limited v FC of T 90 ATC 4215   157
CRW Pty Ltd v Seddon (1972) AR 17   64
Dale v NSW Trotting Club [1978] 1 NSWLR 551   88
Daley v New South Wales Rugby League Ltd (1995) 78 IR 247   49, 50
Daniels t/a Deloitte Haskins and Sells v AWA Ltd (1995) 13 ACLC 614   31
David Syme and Co Ltd v Lloyd [1984] 3 NSWLR 346   77
Davis v Kitching (1986) Aust Torts Reports 80–029   91, 114,
De Alwis v Hair [2003] FCA 10   144
Donoghue v Stevenson [1932] AC 562   95
Drummoyne District Rugby Football Club Inc v New South Wales Rugby Union, unreported, NSWSC, 3 December 1993   27
Duncan by her next friend Duncan v Trustees of the Roman Cathloic Church for the Archdiocese of Canberra and Goulburn, unreported, SCACT, 14 October 1998   116
Eastham v Newcastle United [1964] Ch 413   43
Enderby Town Football Club Ltd v Football Association Ltd [1969] 1 QB 46   85
Ettingshausen v Australian Consolidated Press (1991) Australian Torts Reports 81–125   77
FCT v Ballesty 77 ATC 4181   157
FCT v Maddalena 71 ATC 4161   49
Forbes v Australian Yachting Federation Inc & Ors (1996) 131 FLR 241   53
Foscolos v Footscray Youth Club & Anor [2002] Aust Torts Reports 81–658   107
Frazer v Johnston (1989) Aust Torts Reports 80–248   102
Foschini v AFL, unreported, VSC 15 April 1983   45
Freedman v Petty & Ors (1981) VR 1001   85
Freeman v McManus (1958) VR 15   24
Gardner v AANA Ltd [2003] FMCA 81   143
Gibbs v Gold Coast Tweed Giants Rugby Football Club Ltd (1993) 52 IR 469   49
Gilsenan v Gunning (1982) 137 DLR (3d) 252   91
Global Sportsman Pty Ltd v Mirror Newspapers Ltd & Anor (1984) ATPR 40–463   67
Greig v Insole [1978] 1 WLR 302   41, 46

Gulliver v Council of City of Sydney & Amor (1986) EOC 92–185
Hackshaw v Shaw (1984) 155 CLR 614
Hagan v Trustees of the Toowomba Sports Ground Trust [2001] FCA 123 (23 February 2001)
Hall v Brooklands AC [1933] 1 KB 205
Hall & Ors v Gould [2002] NSWSC 359
Hall v Victorian Amateur Football Association [1999]VCAT 627 (3 April 1999)
Hall v VFL [1982] VR 62
Harbottle Brown & Co Pty Ltd v Halstead [1968] 3 NSWLR 493
Harrigan v Jones (2001) Aust Torts Reports 81–621
Hann v Swain & Ors, unreported, Gobbo J, VSC, 12 March 1993
Hawick v Flegg (1958) 75 WN (NSW) 255
Hawthorn Football Club Ltd v Harding [1988] VR 49
Henderson v Australian Sports Drug Agency [1999] AATA1010 (23 December 1999)
Henderson v NBL Management Limited & Anor (1993) EOC 92–435
Hill v Van Erp (1997) 188 CLR 159
Hollioake & Anor v Western Australian Cricket Association & Anor (1994) 11 WAR 423
Honey v Australian Airlines Ltd & Anor (1989) ATPR 40–961
Hornsby Building Information Centre Pty Ltd & Anor v Sydney Building Information Centre Pty Ltd (1978) ATPR 40–067
Hospitality Group Pty Ltd v Australian Rugby Union (2001) ATPR 41–831
Hughes v Western Australian Cricket Association (Inc) & Ors (1986) ATPR 40–736   2
Humberstone v Northern Timber Mills (1949) 79 CLR 389
Indermaur v Dames (1866) LR 1CP 274
Irvine & Anor v Talksport Ltd [2003] EWCA Civ 423; 2003 1 WLR 1576
Jaensch v Coffey (1984) 155 CLR 549
Janssen Pharmaceutical Pty Ltd v Pfizer Pty Ltd (1986) ATPR 40–654
Jarrold v Boustead [1964] 3 All ER 76
Johnston v Frazer (1990) 21 NSWLR 89
Jordan Grand Prix Ltd v Vodaphone Group plc [2003] EWHC 1956 (Comm); [2003] 2All ER (Comm) 864   3
Kelly v FCT 85 ACT 4238
Kemp v FCT (1992) 110 ALR 375
Kiley v Lysfar Pty Ltd & Anor (1985) ATPR 40–614
Lange v ABC (1997) Aust Torts Reports 81–434
Leahy v AG [1959] 2 All ER 300
Lee Gowan v Graham Windsor, unreported, District Court (NSW) 24 August 1991; *Gowan v Hardie & Anor*, unreported, 8 November 199
Lee v Showman's Guild of Great Britain [1952] 2 QB 329   8
Liddle v Central Australian Aboriginal Legal Aid Service Inc (1999) 150 FLR 142
Lilley v Alpine Resorts Commission & Anor (1998) Aust Torts Reports 475
Lloyd v David Syme and Co, Supreme Court (NSW) 18 April 1982; (1985) 60 ALJR 10
Lowe v New South Wales Cricket Federation (1994) ATPR 41–358
March v Strahmere Pty Ltd (1991) 171 CLR 506

Prast v Town of Cottersloe (2000) WASCA 274   97
R v Billinghurst 17 CH.D 615   134
R v Bradshaw (1878) 14 Cox C C 83   134, 137
R v Coney (1882) 8 QBD 534   134, 137
R v Donavon [1934] 2 KB 498   134
R v Harris; R v McGuinness (1988) 17 NSWLR 158   151
R v Jockey Club ex parte the Aga Khan (1993) 2 All ER 853   81
R v Moore [1898] 14 TLR 229   136
Raguz v Sullivan (2000) 50 NSWLR 237   20, 55, 89
Richards v United States Tennis Association 400 NYS (2d) 267   151
Rides Pty Ltd v Gauci (1984) Aust Torts Reports 80–637   91
Robertson v Australian Professional Cycling Inc, unreported, NSWSC
    10 September 1992   173
Robertson v Hobart Police Citizens Youth Club (1984) Aust Torts Reports 80–629
    91
Rogers v Bugden (1993) ATR 81–246   101, 116
Rogers v Rawlings (1969) Qd R 262   91
Romeo v Conservation Commission of NT (1998) 151 ALR 263   97, 102
Rootes v Shelton (1967) 116 CLR 383   100, 106
Ross & Ors v University of Melbourne (1990) EOC 92–290   148
Ruddock v Taylor [2003] NSWCA 262   97
S & I Publishing Pty Ltd v Australian Surf Life Saver Pty Ltd (1999)   66
Schiller v Gregor (1986) Aust Torts Reports 80–751   91
Seven Network Limited & Ors v News Interactive Pty Ltd & Ors [2004] FCA
    1047   69
Shirt v Wyong Shire Council & Ors [1978] 1 NSWLR 631   95
Simms v Leigh Rugby Football Club [1969] 2 All ER 923   91
Smith v Emerson (1986) Aust Torts Reports 80–022   91
Smolden v Whitworth (1996) TLR 249   110
Sotiropoulos v Canterbury Municipal Council, unreported, NSWSC, Common
    Law Division, 12 May 1994   113
Smith v Yarnold [1969] 2 NSWLR 410   25
South Australian Brewing Co Pty Ltd v Carlton & United Breweries Ltd [2001]
    FCA 902   68
Stevens v Brodribb Sawmilling Co Pty Ltd (1986) 160 CLR 16   95
Stollery v Greyhound Racing Control Board (1973) 128 CLR 509   87, 88
Stone v Commissioner of Taxation [2003] FCAFC 145 (27 June 2003) **153, 154, 156**
Sulkowicz v Parramatta Football Club 1983 AILR 340   49
Sullivan v Moody (2001) 207 CLR 562   95
Sweeney v Committee of South East Racing Association & Ors (1985) FLR 19178
    82, 85
Sydney Organising Committee for the Olympic Games v Pam Clarke [1998] 792
    FCA 925 June 19980   75
Taco Co of Australia Inc & Anor v Taco Bell Pty Ltd & Ors (1982) ATPR 40–303   64
Talmax Pty Ltd & Anor v Telstra Corporation Limited (1996) ATPR 41–535   67, 70
Taylor & Ors v British Columbia (1978) DLR (3d) 82   91
Taylor & Ors v Moorabin Saints Junior Football League and Football Victoria Ltd
    [2004] VCAT 158   150
TCN Channel Nine Pty Ltd v Australian Broadcasting Authority [2002] FCA 896
    61
Teranora Lakes Country Club Limited v FCT (1993) 93 ATC 4078   157

The Benson and Hedges Company Pty Ltd v Australian Broadcasting Tribunal (1985) 58 ALR 675   **61**

Thomson v Earlwood-Bardwell Park RSL [1999] NSWSC 243 (25 March 1999)   **80**

The Mayor, Councillors and Citizens of the City of Moe v Pulis (1988) EOC 92–243   **147, 148**

'The Waratahs' RUFC Ltd v FCT 79 ATC 4337   **157**

Thompson v Deakin (1952) Ch 646   **41**

Tolley v J S Fry and Sons Ltd [1930] 1 KB 467   **77**

Tonkin v Gunn (1988) ATR 80–219   **119**

Torpedoes Sportswear Pty Limited v Thorpedo Enterprises Pty Limited & Anor [2003] FCA 901   **74**

Tullamore Bowling and Citizens Club Ltd v Lander (1984) EOC 92–110   **149**

Umina Beach Bowling Club Ltd v Ryan (1984) EOC 92–110   **149**

University of Wollongong v Mitchell [2003] NSWCA 94   **97**

Viskauskas & Anor v Niland (1983) 57 ALJR 414   **145**

Vairey v Wyong Shire Council [2002] NSWSC 881; on appeal (2004) Aust Torts Reports 81–754   **98**

Waits v Frito-Lay 978 F 2d 1093 (9th Cir) 1992   **63**

Wallace v Grinter and Melbourne Football Club Limited, VSC No 8348 of 1990   **102**

Waltons Stores (Interstate) Ltd v Maher (1988) 164 CLR 387   **27**

Waterhouse v Bell (1991) EOC 92–376   **146, 147**

Watherston v Woolven, unreported, Supreme Court (SA) 9 November 1987   **135, 138**

Watson v Haines (1987) Aust Torts Reports 80–094   **91, 105**

Waverley Municipal Council v Swain [2003] NSWCA 61   **97, 98**

White v Samsung Electronics 971 F 2d 1395(1992)   **63**

Wickham v Associated Pool Builders & Ors (1986) ATPR 40–741; (1988) ATPR 40–865   **66**

Wickham & Ors v Canberra District Junior Rugby League Inc & Ors, unreported, Supreme Court of ACT, 10 September 1998   **45**

Wilson v Hang Gliding Federation of Australia Inc, unreported, NSWCA, 15 April 1997   **26, 81, 88**

Woods v Multi Sport Holdings (2002) 186 ALR 14   **97, 111**

Wooldridge v Sumner [1963] 2 QB 43   **91, 104**

Wyong Shire Council v Shirt (1980) 146 CLR 40   **91, 96**

Wyong Shire Council v Vairey (2004) Aust Torts Reports 81–754   **101**

Zhu v The Treasurer of the State of New South Wales [2004] HCA 56 (17 November 2004)   **42**

Table of statutes

page

Accident Compensation Act 1985 (NSW)   117
Accident Compensation Act 1985 (Vic)   117
Anti-Discrimination Act 1977 (NSW)   109, 145, 148, 151
Anti-Discrimination Act 1991 (Qld)   109, 145
Anti-Discrimination Act 1992 (NT)   109, 145
Anti-Discrimination Act 1999 (Tas)   109, 145
Associations Incorporation Act 1964 (Tas)   29
Associations Incorporation Act 1981 (Qld)   29
Associations Incorporation Act 1981 (Vic)   29
Associations Incorporation Act 1984 (NSW)   11, 26, 29, 32, 33
Associations Incorporation Act 1985 (SA)   29,33
Associations Incorporation Act 1987 (WA)   29,33
Associations Incorporation Act 1990 (NT)   29
Associations Incorporation Act 1991 (ACT)   33
Australian Grand Prix Act 1994 (Vic)   73
Australian Sports Drug Agency Act 1991 (Cth)   162, 166
Broadcasting Services Act 1992 (Cth)   17, 61, 62
Civil Law (Wrongs) Act 2002 (ACT)   93
Civil Liability Act 2002 (NSW)   93, 96, 97, 99, 100, 115
Civil Liability Act 2002 (Tas)   93
Civil Liability Act 2002 (WA)   93
Civil Liability Act 2003 (Qld)   93
Civil Liability Amendment (Personal Responsibility) Act 2003 (NSW)   93
Commonwealth Games Arrangements Act 2001 (Cth)   73
Contracts Review Act 1980 (NSW)   50
Copyright Act 1968 (Cth)   74, 75
Corporate Law Economic Reform Program (Audit Reform and Corporate Disclosure) Act 2004 (Cth)   120
Corporations Act 2001 (Cth)   22, 26, 28, 29, 30, 31, 32, 124
Crimes Act (Cth)   133
Crimes Act 1900 (NSW)   133
Criminal Code Act 1899 (Qld)   133
Criminal Code Act 1913 (WA)   133
Criminal Code Act 1924 (Tas)   133
Criminal Injuries Compensation Act 1976 (Tas)   139
Criminal Injuries Compensation Act 1985 (WA)   139
Crimes Compensation Act 1982 (NT)   139
Criminal Injuries Compensation Ordinance 1983 (ACT)   139
Defamation Act 1901 (NSW)   76
Defamation Act 1938 (NT)   76

Defamation Act 1957 (Tas) 76
Defamation Act 1974 (NSW) 76
Defamation (Amendment) Act 1909 (NSW) 76
Defamation Law of Queensland (1889) 76
Designs Act 2003 (Cth) 75
Disability Discrimination Act 1992 144, 145
Equal Opportunity Act 1984 (SA) 109, 145
Equal Opportunity Act 1984 (WA) 109, 145
Equal Opportunity Act 1995 (Vic) 109, 145, 149
Fair Trading Act (various states) 54, 65
Fair Trading Act 1992 (ACT) 12
Fair Trading Act (NZ) 69
Fringe Benefits Tax Assessment Act (Cth) 158
Income Tax Assessment Act 1936 (Cth) 153
Income Tax Assessment Act 1997 (Cth) 153, 157, 158
Industrial Relations Act 1996 (NSW) 49, 50
Lanham Act (US) 63
Merchandise Marks Act 1941 (South Africa) 73
Minors (Property & Contracts) Act 1970 (NSW) 37, 38
Occupiers' Liability Act 1983 (amendment to the *Wrongs Act 1958* (Vic)) 112
Occupiers' Liability Act 1985 (WA) 112
Olympic Insignia Protection Act 1987 (Cth) 72
Patents Act 1991 (Cth) 75
Personal Injuries (Liability and Damages) Act 2003 (NT) 93
Racial Discrimination Act 1975 (Cth) 142, 143, 147
Sale of Goods Act (various states)
Recreational Services (Limitation of Liability) Act 2002 (SA) 96
Sex Discrimination Act 1984 (Cth) 109, 143, 146, 150
Sporting Injuries Insurance Act 1978 (NSW) 50, 92, 118, 119
Sydney 2000 Games (indicia and Images) Protection Act 1996 (Cth) 72
Tobacco Advertising Prohibition Act 1992 (Cth) 61
Trade Marks Act 1995 (Cth) 73, 74
Trade Practices Act 1974 (Cth) 8, 47, 50, 51, 52, 53, 64, 65, 66, 67, 68, 69, 70, 77, 93, 98, 100, 120
Trade Practices Amendment (Personal Injuries and Death) Act 2004 (No 2) (Cth) 93
Victims of Crime Assistance Act 1996 (Vic) 139
Victims Support and Rehabilitation Act 1996 (NSW) 139
Workers Compensation Act (NSW) 25
Workers' Compensation Act 1916 (Qld) 117, 118
Workers' Compensation and Assistance Act 1981 (WA) 117, 118
Workers' Rehabilitation and Compensation Act 1986 (SA) 117, 118
Workplace Relations Act 1996 (Cth) 43
Wrongs Act 1936 (SA) Pt 1 76, 93, 117, 118
Wrongs Act (Vic) Pt 1 93
Wrongs Amendment Act 1987 (amendment to the *Wrongs Act 1936* (SA)) 93

Index

administrative law 9
advertising
    endorsements 4, 56
    marketing advantage 61
    use of sportspeople 62
AIS *see* Australian Institute of Sport
alcohol
    advertising 61
amateur sport
    amateur/professional distinction 3
    financial support 5, 6
ambush marketing 70
anti-doping
    ASDA 162
    athletics 160
    Australian Sports Drug Agency 162
    breach of policy 165
    Copenhagen Conference 162
    drug use 161
    EPO 162
    failure to provide a sample 166
    hearing 165
    natural justice 167
    notification 166
    Olympics 160
    penalty 167
    prohibitions 163
    refusal 166
    regulation 161
    restraint of trade 167
    testing 162, 165, 166
    the problem 160
    WADA Code 162, 167
    whereabouts information 167
anti-siphoning list 17
ANZSLA *see* Australia and New Zealand
  Sports Law Association
AOC *see* Australian Olympic Committee
appeals 9
application of law 1
ASC *see* Australian Sports Commission
ASDA *see* Australian Sports Drug Agency
assault 100, 101
    Australian football 101, 102
    collisions 101
    consent 101, 134
    foul play 101
    implied consent 101
    inherent risks in sport 97
    karate 100
    netball 100
    penalties during game 101
    rugby league 101, 102
    rugby union 134
    rules of sport 101
    tennis 101
    tort 100

associations 29
    incorporation legislation 29, 32, 33
athletes agreement 8
audi alterem partem *see* natural justice
Australia and New Zealand Sports Law
  Association 109
Australian Institute of Sport 19
Australian/New Zealand Standard on Risk
  Management 123
Australian Olympic Committee 12, 54, 55,
  71, 163
Australian Sports Commission 19, 123, 163
Australian Sports Drug Agency 162, 164,
  165, 166, 167,168
Australian Sports Medicine Federation 117

balance of probability 7, 140
basketball 30
beyond reasonable doubt 7, 132
bicycles 127
binding precedent 17
boxing match 14, 17, 119, 124
boycotts 20
Bradford fire 113

CAS *see* Court of Arbitration for Sport
cautionary signs 121
child protection 1
children 108
children's flotation devices 120
civil law 7
civil liability laws 1, 8, 121, 122
club constitutions 11
club rules 11
coaches and managers
    liability for injury 105
    liability for spectators 108
codes 12
    Commercial Television Industry 62
    Ethical Behaviour By-Law 17
    IOC Code of Ethics 17
    mandatory 17
    voluntary 17
Commercial Television Industry Code of
  Practice 62
commercialism
    and sport 18
common law 6
Community Justice Centres 11
compensation legislation
    workers' compensation 117
    Sporting Injuries Insurance Scheme 117
competition laws 50
competition rules 8
conflict resolution 60
constitutions and rules
    contents 28
    contracts 26

criticism 47
enforcement 24
exclusionary practices 47
intention 14, 27, 28,
member complaints 26
non-contractual rights 28
reasonable restraint 43
restrictions on comment 47
rights and liabilities 25
zoning and transfer restrictions 44
contact sports 100
contract of employment 42
vicarious liability of employer 116
tests 42
contracts 8, 48–65
acceptance 36
capacity 37
certainty 36
conditions 36
consideration 36
constitutions and rules 25
damages 41
definition 35
doping, *see* anti-doping
employment 42
exclusivity 51
Host City contract 35
illegal agreements 38
independent contractors 42
inducing breach 41
intention 37
management 39
minors 37
monopoly restrictions 46
offer 36
oral 35
Olympic Team Agreement 38, 40
parties 35, 38
remedies 38
representation 36
restraint of trade 43
sponsorship 40
standard form 50
statement of intent 36
terms 36
unfair 49
vicarious liability 116
written 35
control test 42
control and ownership 8
conventions 3
copyright 74
corporate governance 33
corporate sponsors 15
Corporations Act 28
directors and officers 31
insolvent trading 32
officer 44
Court of Arbitration for Sport 9
Ad Hoc Division 10
Code of Sports Related Arbitration 9
doping 160, 167
exclusive jurisdiction 10
powers 9
Sydney 16
criminal law 7, 9, 133
criminal liability 132
accessory 137

assault 133
Australian football 134
compensation 139
consent 134
contact sport 139
court intervention 135
crowd violence 139
deliberate conduct 136
intention 133
manslaughter 135
murder 135
negligence 137
no Australia-wide law 133
policy issues 137
public interest 137
rough play 134
rugby league 136
rugby union 134
soccer 136
sporting crowd 139
sports rage 139
standard of proof 132
state laws 133
unlawful killing 136
violence 138
criminal negligence 137

defamation 75
cricket 77
golf 77
no uniform law 76
rugby league football 85
defective equipment 120
directors and officers
associations law 32
common law 30, 31
confidential information 31, 32, 33
duties of 30
good faith 31, 32, 33
insolevent trading 32, 33
Corporations Act 31
disabled athletes 9, 108
disciplinary proceedings *see* domestic tribunals
discrimination 9
basketball 147
clubs 148
conciliation 143
court 143
cricket 144
definition 141
direct 141
disability 144
disciplinary proceedings 149
employment 146
facilities 147
federal laws 143
gender identity 151
golf 144, 149
HIV 144, 145
horse racing 146
Human Rights and Equal Opportunity Commission 143
indirect 142
laws 109, 142
licensing 149
marital status 143
motor sport 149

netball 143
penalty 149
pregnancy 143
racial 142, 147
registered clubs 148
school sport 150
services 148
sex 143
single sex sport 150
SOCOG 145
sporting clubs 148
state laws 145
transgender athletes 151
UN Convention on Elimination of All
  Forms of Discrimination against
  Women 143
use of facilities 147
weight room 148
women's night 147
women's sport 145
dispute resolution 10
domestic tribunals 15
  Court of Arbitration for Sport 79
  court intervention 81, 89
  disciplinary proceedings 79, 81
  discrimination 149
  disqualification 89
  erroneous decisions 88
  good faith 86
  jurisdiction 88
  legal intervention 80
  natural justice 81, 82
  notification 83
  penalty 86
  practicalities 90
  procedural fairness 82
  prejudicial conduct 87
  proper hearing 83
  proper penalty 86
  right to legal representation 84
  trotting 88
  ultra vires 81
  unbiased judges 86
dispute resolution 10, 11
drugs see anti-doping
duty of care 95
duties of directors 31

eligible amateur 3
employee 42
employment
  common law rights and obligations 42
  contract 8
  restraint of trade 43
endorsement 62, 63
exclusion clauses 98, 99
exclusion of liability 96, 98, 99
exclusionary provisions 51
exclusive dealing 51

fair play 5
fair trading laws 120
faulty equipment 119
  football helmets 119
  golf practice kit 120
  implied terms 120
  merchantable quality 120
federal system 6

flotation devices 11
formulation of proceedings 25

good Samaritans 115
government
  financial support 5
  guidance 15
  role in sport 19
Grand Prix symbols 73
guarantee
  company limited by 29

hepatitis 117
HIH 122
Hillsborough Stadium 111
HIV 117
HREOC see Human Rights and Equal
  Opportunity Commission
Human Rights and Equal Opportunity
  Commission 144

inconsistent laws 6
incorporation 8, 28
  associations incorporation legislation
    29
  Corporations Act 29
independent contractors 42
injuries and compensation 91–121
  assault 100, 103
  breach of duty 103
  causes 91
  changes to law 92
  children 108
  coaches 105, 107
  contact sports 101
  court view of sport 92
  cricket 91
  crowd control 115
  crowd violence 108
  dangerous techniques 107
  Department of Education 105
  differing state laws 93
  disabled athletes 108
  dissemination of information 105
  drugs 108
  encouraging aggression 108
  exclusion of liability 98, 99
  fans 114
  fault 91
  faulty equipment 120, 121
  football 91
  golf 91
  government view 93
  gymnastics 109
  hockey 91
  infectious diseases 116
  insurance crisis 93, 122
  involvement of law 99
  Ipp Report 93, 94
  horse racing 102
  horse riding 91
  manager 105
  motor racing 91
  negligence 102
  obligations of participants 102
  occupiers' liability 112
  organisers 110, 111
  over-zealous fans 114

participants 102, 119
participants' duty of care 102
penalties 102
pregnant athletes 109
referees 110
removing injured players 107
schools 105
signs 121
snow skiing 91
spectators 108, 111
sporting bodies 110
Sporting Injuries Compensation
    Scheme 126
standard of care 106
strangers 108, 113
summary of changes 100
swimming 91
torts 92
trampolining 91
volunteers 115
vicarious liability 115
water skiing 102
who gets sued 94
insurance 122–131
    admissions 130
    alternative arrangements 131
    association liability 129
    broker 130
    claims made' policies 133
    coaches 128
    defamation 128
    directors and officers 129
    'events occurring' policies 128
    excess 126
    gaps 130
    general rules 130
    legal expense 129
    limits 126, 130
    notification 130
    participants 127
    player accident 127
    premium 126
    product liability 127
    professional indemnity 128
    property 129
    public liability 126
    workers compensation 129
insolvency
    personal liability 32,33
intellectual property 8, 73
    copyright 74
    patents 75
    registered designs 75
    trade marks 73
International Federations 9
International Olympic Committee 3, 9,
    161, 162
IOC *see* International Olympic Committee

judiciary tribunals *see* domestic tribunals

law
    civil 7
    common 7
    Commonwealth 6, 7
    criminal 7
    definition 6
    how is it made? 6

remedies 7
state 6,7
statute 7
view of sport 6
legal nature of organisation 8
legal personality
    problem 23
liability of committee 24, 25

manager 105
manslaughter 135
master/servant relationship 42
minors 37
misleading or deceptive conduct 64, 74
    athletics 67
    Australian football 68
    boxing match 66
    civil liability 75
    cricket 65, 67
    swimming 66, 67
    tennis 66
    website 69
    Olympic rings 69
misleading representations 64
    criminal liability 65
misuse of market power 51
monopoly restrictions 59
motor cycle helmets 120
murder 135

nationalism 20
natural justice 9
    audi alterem partem 83
    Australian football 81
    additional charges 83
    charge under particular rule 83
    good faith 86
    knowledge of charges 83
    legal representation 84
    nature of accusation 83
    notification of hearing 83
    opportunity to attend hearing 83
    proper hearing 85
    proper notice of hearing 83
    right to be heard 83
    rugby league 83, 85
    rugby union 86
    unbiased judges 86
negligence 91
    categories of risk 96
    causation 97
    civil liability summary 100
    coach 107
    code for high risk activities 96
    dangerous recreations activity 99
    definition 94
    duty of care 95
    duty to warn 97
    foreseeability 95
    foul play 103
    golf 103
    inherent risks 97
    obvious risk 97
    occupier's liability 112
    participants 102
    professionals 97
    proximity 95
    reasonable person 96

risk and duty 99
  standard of care 106
  waivers and exclusions 98, 99
  water skiing 102
non-contractual rights
  protection of 28

Olympic Charter 5, 9, 20, 40, 41, 161
Olympic Insignia Protection Act 72
Olympic symbols 72, 73
Olympics
  ancient Greece 4
  Athens 16, 17 160
  Barcelona 21
  Beijing 16
  Berlin 20
  Calgary 20
  disqualification 3
  'eligible amateur' 3
  eligibility code 5
  eligibility rules 5
  Greece 3
  Moscow 21
  Salt Lake City 16
  Sarajevo 4
  Seoul 4, 162
  Stockholm 3
  sports 20
  Sydney 1, 2, 15, 55, 160
  Turin 16
  TV rights 16, 17
organisation
  levels 27
organisers
  control of spectators 111

participants
  assault 103
  liability of 102
  injury to spectators 105
  negligence 102
passing off 69, 70
pay TV *see* subscription television
player drafts 46
political boycotts 21
politics 20
pregnancy
  discrimination 143
  negligence 109
price fixing 51
privacy 1
product liability 120, 127
product safety standards 120
professional sport
  theatrical spectacle 12
protection of non-contractual rights 41
public opinion 8
public school system 3

racial discrimination 142
racial vilification 142
registered designs 75
representations 36
reputation
  protection of 56
remedies 7
reputation 8
resale price maintenance 51

restraint of trade 43
  prima facie void 43
  reasonable restraint 43, 45
right of personality 63
right to work 47
risk assessment 130
risk management 129
  business 124
  dangerous conditions 125
  experience 125
  group workshops 125
  monitoring and review 125
  records 125
  risk assessment 125
  risk reduction 130
  risk standards 123
  risk treatment 125
role of government
  Australian Sports Commission 19, 21
  budgets 19
  Department of Sport, Recreation and
    Tourism 19, 21
rules and conventions 11
rules of game 8

sale of goods laws 120
selection 9
  AOC policy 55
  appeals 55
  CAS 55
  disputes 55
  guidelines 55
  jurisdiction 55
sex discrimination 153
sex testing 160
skin cancer 124
SOCOG 74
sponsorship 4, 8, 56
  alcohol 61
  conflicts 8, 59, 60
  contracts 58
  legal view 12
  misleading conduct 64–69
  professional 14
  reputation 56
  rights and obligations 58
  types 57
  tobacco 61
  use of name 62
  use of products 62
sport
  athletics 20, 67, 153, 154, 156, 164
  Australian football 9, 13, 14, 29, 30,
    45, 49, 68, 81, 84, 89, 91, 102, 117,
    134, 135, 138, 149, 150
  baseball 3, 44
  basketball 20, 147
  bowls 149
  car racing 70, 80, 91, 104, 114
  cricket 3, 18, 20, 41, 46, 47, 66, 77, 85,
    91, 113, 118, 144
  croquet 119
  cycling 161, 167
  court intervention 21
  definition 2
  diving 20
  golf 91, 104, 141, 144, 148

greyhound racing 85, 87, 88
gymnastics 20
hang gliding 26, 81, 88, 119
hockey 20, 91, 134
horse racing 14, 47, 80, 92, 102, 103, 104, 146, 147
ice hockey 91
indoor cricket 97, 111
judo 20, 55, 89
kick boxing 147
lawn bowls 119
netball 20, 46, 143
parachuting 98, 119
rowing 20
rugby league 25, 27, 44, 45, 48, 49, 50, 77, 78, 83, 84, 85, 89, 101, 102, 105, 116, 134
rugby union 20, 27, 44, 52, 86, 91, 106, 110, 134, 157, 158
scuba diving 119
show jumping 91, 104
skiing 91, 97
soccer 20, 43, 74, 85, 113, 134
squash 20
surfing 20, 67, 70, 91, 97, 98, 101, 105, 141
tennis 20, 42, 101, 115, 141, 143, 151
touch 134
trotting 85, 88
water polo 20, 134
water skiing 91, 95, 100, 106
weightlifting 163
wrestling 107
yachting 53, 54
sporting club
    nature of 23
Sporting Injuries Compensation Scheme 118
sporting organisations
    advice 5, 6
    constitutions and rules 22
    fundraising 5
    grassroots sport 5
    incorporation 23
    legal nature of 22
    legal personality 23
    non-profit 23
    paid employees 23
    profit motive 23
    rules 36
    social 34
    subscription television 17
    unincorporated voluntary associations 22-34
sporting tribunals *see* domestic tribunals
sports law 4
'sportsmanship' 18, 77
standard form contracts 50
standard of proof 7
state law
    inconsistency with federal law 7
statute law 6
subscription television 1, 21
    anti-siphoning 17
    delisting of events 17
    effect on sport 17
suppression of criticism 47, 48

taxation 152–159
    allowances 154
    appearance fees 153
    averaging 158
    athletics 153, 156
    capital gains 158
    commission 155
    deductions 157
    exempt income 156
    fitness training 157
    fringe benefits 158
    grants 153, 154
    income 153
    income outside Australia 156
    legal expenses 158
    match fees 155
    prizes 155
    provisional 158
    salaries 154
    signing on fees 154
    sponsorship fees 155
    sporting awards 154
    travel 155
    transfer fees 155
    trust funds 156
    wages 154
    windfalls 163
tobacco and alcohol advertising 61
tort 7
    assault 100
    negligence 94
trade marks 73
Trade Practices Act 50, 64
transgender athletes 9
tribunals *see* domestic tribunals
two tier system 5

unincorporated voluntary associations 23
    committee members 25
    enforcement of rights 25
    formulation of proceedings 25
    group intention 25
    leases 24
    liability 24
    nature of 23
    ownership of property 24
unfair contracts 49
unsafe goods 120
use of name 5

vicarious liability 116
violence in sport 138
volunteers 5, 105, 115

WADA Code *see* World Anti-Doping Agency Code
workers compensation laws 117
World Anti-Doping Code (WADA Code) 9, 40, 162
    implementation 163
    medical use 164
    penalties 164
    prohibited conduct 163
    prohibited list 164
World Series Cricket 65

zoning and transfer restrictions 44